ADHD: Children Who Challenge

Take care of yourself.
It is a long Journey!.
Robert W. Atwood

ADHD: Children Who Challenge

A Survival Manual
for parents, educators, and other professionals

Robert W. Atwood, Ph. D.
Catherine Pugsley Getty, M.S.
Ruth Wohlwend-Lloyd, M.S.

iUniverse, Inc.
New York   Bloomington   Shanghai

ADHD: Children Who Challenge
A Survival Manual for parents, educators, and other professionals

Copyright © 2008 by Robert W. Atwood

iUniverse books may be ordered through booksellers or by contacting:

iUniverse
1663 Liberty Drive
Bloomington, IN 47403
www.iuniverse.com
1-800-Authors (1-800-288-4677)

Because of the dynamic nature of the Internet, any Web addresses or links contained in this book may have changed since publication and may no longer be valid.

The information, ideas, and suggestions in this book are not intended as a substitute for professional advice. Before following any suggestions contained in this book, you should consult your personal physician or mental health professional. Neither the author nor the publisher shall be liable or responsible for any loss or damage allegedly arising as a consequence of your use or application of any information or suggestions in this book.

ISBN: 978-0-595-47665-7 (pbk)
ISBN: 978-0-595-91930-7 (ebk)

Printed in the United States of America

Contents

Acknowledgments

We especially thank the children with ADHD, their families, and educators for allowing us to be a part of their lives over the past thirty-five years.

We are also grateful to our extended team members: Laura, Casey, Tom, Rachel, and Riley, who practiced patience and encouraged our persistent efforts. Special thanks to team members no longer with us: Mae and Doc.

Robyn Pugsley Arredondo, Dianne Heckman, Cari Bickley, Trudy Weston, and Tom Lloyd provided valuable editorial feedback.

We would like to acknowledge Dr. Russell Barkley's pioneering work, it influenced our philosophy on diagnosis and treatment of ADHD.

Preface

As a young man, I was fascinated with chemistry and biology; with this interest, I was steered toward dentistry. A year later, the draft called, and I went off to Germany to become a dental assistant. Trying to allay soldiers' fear of dentists became one of my consuming interests. The detail work of fixing teeth, however, was far from a good fit.

One night, a soldier slipped out of the hospital ward and found his way to my living quarters in the dental clinic. He was so afraid of being hurt that his entire body shook. I was able to calm his fears with some "unlearned skill," and he was able to return to the hospital. My future profession was chosen. I would become a psychologist and help those who suffer from pain and anxiety. I felt very equipped to help others because of the practical knowledge learned as a farm boy and the extensive theoretical education learned in graduate school. Surprise—I needed to learn a great deal more from the people who came to me for help. I learned to listen more carefully, be less judgmental, prioritize, and simplify everything. What my clients taught me helped shape my love of this important work.

Crying mothers, children failing at school, and exhausted teachers visited my office desperate for assistance. I was hooked—my quest to understand attention deficit hyperactivity disorder (ADHD) and to be helpful permeated the rest of my professional career.

When my co-authors—Catherine and Ruth—started working with me in private practice, our discussions frequently centered on the question "how did you know to do that?" Their questions helped me clarify and organize the strategies I had developed for helping people dealing with ADHD. Their encouragement to write this information down, so that others could benefit from my knowledge and experience, led to writing this book. Thank you!

It is our hope that this book is helpful to you—the reader—by bringing confidence, success, and joy into your life. Be persistent, be patient, and pace yourself for the long-term. It takes more than luck, but good luck anyway.

Introduction and Overview of Children Who Challenge

You probably chose this book because you interact with a challenging child. Quite possibly, you are the parent of a child described as "extremely busy, very energetic, impulsive" or as a "daydreamer and space cadet." You suspect something is wrong, or perhaps your child has been diagnosed with ADHD. Locking yourself in the bathroom to get a break is not working anymore. Maybe you are a teacher and feel that if you have to repeat your instructions *one more time*, you will run screaming from the room pulling your hair out. You want to survive and you want the child to thrive. Where are the answers? This book provides that training!

Children with ADHD "push your buttons," leaving you feeling overwhelmed, frustrated, and inadequate. But, just when you feel like running away or giving up, the child comes to you in tears and asks, "Why does no one like me?" or "Why am I always in trouble?" You quickly realize the child is hurting and needs help. This rollercoaster of emotions is an exhausting ride for parents and teachers.

It has been Dr. Atwood's privilege to counsel families and consult with educators and medical personnel who work with challenging children. He began working with children and their families in 1967 at a mental health center. Dr. Atwood encountered many challenging children and their families desperately seeking help. The heartrending depth of their frustration, sadness, and confusion led to Dr. Atwood's desire to throw the families a lifeline—and so began his extensive quest to learn more about ADHD.

At the time, limited research on ADHD existed, making it difficult to diagnose and treat. Dr. Atwood observed through interactions with families and schools that the most frequent strategy was to use punishment in an attempt to control challenging behavior. Children were frequently spanked, sent to their room for long periods of time, or sent to the principal's office. Far from being effective, this punitive approach actually escalated the child's problem behavior. Additionally, the punitive approach decreased the child's self-confidence and increased adult frustration, therefore creating an adversarial relationship between the child and adult. No one won!

Dr. Atwood subsequently formed a support group to provide education about ADHD and much-needed emotional support for the parents. Parents rapidly learned that others were experiencing similar feelings. The parents' interactions helped allay their intense feelings of hopelessness and guilt, as did Dr. Atwood's assurance that they did nothing to *cause* their child to have ADHD. He introduced effective and positive behavioral techniques for dealing with challenging behavior, developed through his interactions with the children and their families. The information and support decreased their frustration, feelings of inadequacy, and their negative attitude toward the child. It soon became apparent that in order to be the most effective, there needed to be a consistent application of treatment methods by parents, educators, physicians, and mental health professionals (MHPs). He made regular visits to schools to involve educators in treatment, then physicians for medical management. The concept of a treatment team naturally evolved with the desire to minimize the children's failures and maximize their successes.

A lifetime of studying, treating families, reviewing research, teaching, and training professionals has fueled a passion for educating others about ADHD. Throughout his career, Dr Atwood addressed and educated adults on the same basic questions regarding ADHD, including: "How do I know if this child has ADHD?" "How can I best help him or her?" and "Will they grow out of it?" The frustration and confusion regarding the diagnosis and treatment of ADHD is understandable, given the deluge of conflicting and inaccurate information on the Internet, in magazines, and on TV shows. Too often, the information is superficial and of little help to the people in the trenches. Inaccurate and superficial information also increases the likelihood of misdiagnosis, over-diagnosis, and ineffective treatment. It is virtually impossible for the layperson to determine which theories and approaches are based on good science.

In this book, we explore theories of causation and treatments and explain which theories and treatments are well-researched and effective. Also provided are useful guidelines to evaluate current and new information about ADHD.

This book is written in a unique format, specifically designed to assist parents, mental health professionals, educators, and physicians in cooperative team efforts. In a multidisciplinary team approach, it is essential that each team member understand the other members' perspectives and roles. Too often, the parents want someone to *fix* the child or the teacher expects the parents or the mental health professional to take sole responsibility for modifying the child's behavior. Although these feelings are understandable, the most effective approach to help children with ADHD is for everyone involved to work as a team. A multidisciplinary team approach requires a *shared* responsibility and uses a consistent treatment strategy. The team approach also reduces the physical and emotional exhaustion of each individual.

This book is divided into three major sections: understanding, diagnosing, and treating these children who challenge. A comprehensive and accurate *understanding* of ADHD requires education about the diagnostic criteria, causative factors, and the debunking of negative stereotypes. *Diagnosing* ADHD necessitates a complete evaluation requiring the participation of the child, the family, the educators, and the medical and mental health professionals. A complete evaluation precedes an accurate diagnosis and is the foundation in formulating treatment plans. *Treating* a child with ADHD starts with selecting appropriate multidisciplinary team members, clarifying roles, and learning to implement the key treatment principles. We discuss when and how to use different types of treatment, including medical, behavioral, and structural interventions. There is a quick reference section outlining the dynamics and interventions for common and enduring problems associated with ADHD. These interventions have been tried and proven to be successful. Also, we discuss the development and use of individualized treatment plans utilizing the child's unique and specific information. And we provide tips for parents and educators to help promote their emotional and physical well-being while dealing with this long-term disorder. Three longitudinal case studies describe the treatment challenges and successes from childhood into adulthood to further educate and encourage.

While some chapters focus more intently on parents, educators, mental health professionals, or physicians' issues, all chapters are valuable and the entire team should read them. Reading the book in its entirety promotes better communication for effective teamwork and creates increased opportunity for success. We include note pages after each section to record important thoughts and questions. Reading and understanding this book takes effort. You will be rewarded! Do not be discouraged if all your attempts do not parallel the ideal strategies presented in the book. Keep reaching—this is important life work. Celebrate each success. A child can be saved!

Part One

Understanding

1

What Is ADHD Really?

ADHD is the diagnosis given to a child who exhibits a number of characteristics that have a powerful and negative impact on a child's life. Over the past fifty years, the name of the diagnosis has changed many times to reflect the popular theories of the time. ADHD was initially diagnosed as "minimal brain damage" in-line with the theory that mild brain damage—holes in the brain—caused the problem behavior. When this theory could not be supported, the term eventually was changed to attention deficit hyperactivity disorder (ADHD). The theory underlying ADHD assumes the hallmark characteristic is the inability to focus and/or sustain attention and that it stems from a brain dysfunction or malfunction of the chemistry of the brain. It is likely that ADHD will again change names to reflect any one of the advancing theories, including brain dysfunction that limits the child's ability to "self-talk" and/or brain dysfunction that restricts the child's ability to be motivated. Despite the differing theories underlying the diagnosis, the identified problem behaviors have remained remarkably consistent.

In the last fifteen years of literature, the name attention deficit disorder (ADD) and ADD/ADHD appear as interchangeable with ADHD, which can be confusing. Therefore, we have chosen to use ADHD, which is the most recent diagnostic name.

The criteria used by MHPs and physicians to reach a clinical diagnosis of ADHD are set forth in the *Diagnostic and Statistical Manual of Mental Disorders-IV-TR* (DSM-IV-TR, 2000). The DSM-IV-TR identifies three types of ADHD: Attention-Deficit/Hyperactivity Disorder, Combined Type; Attention-Deficit/Hyperactivity Disorder, Inattentive Type; and Attention-Deficit/Hyperactivity Disorder, Predominantly Hyperactive/Impulsive Type.

> The three types of ADHD have four criteria in common*:
>
> 1. Hyperactive-impulsive or inattentive symptoms that cause impairment present before age seven
> 2. Impairment from problem behaviors present in two or more settings (e.g., school, work, and home)
> 3. Clear evidence of clinically significant impairment in social, academic, or occupational functioning
> 4. The problem behavior is not due to other disorders

Source: DSM-IV-TR

The three types of ADHD are further differentiated by the following specific criteria.

Type 1: Attention-Deficit/Hyperactivity Disorder, Combined Type

Six (or more) of the following symptoms of inattention and six (or more) of the following symptoms of *hyperactivity-impulsivity* have persisted for at least six months to a degree that is maladaptive and inconsistent with developmental level.

> ### *Hyperactivity*
> 1. Often fidgets with hands or feet or squirms in seat
> 2. Often leaves seat in classroom or in other situations in which remaining seated is expected
> 3. Often runs about or climbs excessively in situations in which it is inappropriate (in adolescents or adults, may be limited to subjective feeling of restlessness)
> 4. Often has difficulty playing or engaging in leisure activities quietly
> 5. Is often "on the go" or often acts as if "driven by a motor"
> 6. Often talks excessively

> ### *Impulsivity*
> 7. Often blurts out answers before questions have been completed
> 8. Often has difficulty waiting for a turn
> 9. Often interrupts or intrudes on others (e.g., butts into conversations or games)

Source: DSM-IV-TR

Type 2: Attention-Deficit/Hyperactivity Disorder, Inattentive Type

Six (or more) of the following symptoms of *inattention* have persisted for at least six months to a degree that is maladaptive and inconsistent with developmental level.

> ### *Inattention**
> 1. Often fails to give close attention to details or makes careless mistakes in schoolwork, work, or other activities
> 2. Often has difficulty sustaining attention in tasks or play activities
> 3. Often does not seem to listen when spoken to directly
> 4. Often does not follow-through on instructions and fails to finish schoolwork, chores, or duties in workplace (not due to oppositional behavior or failure to understand instructions)
> 5. Often have difficulty organizing tasks and activities
> 6. Often avoids, dislikes, or is reluctant to engage in tasks that require sustained mental effort (such as schoolwork or homework)
> 7. Often loses things necessary for tasks or activities (e.g., toys, school assignments, pencils, books, or tools)
> 8. Is often easily distracted by extraneous stimuli
> 9. Is often forgetful in daily activities

Source: DSM-IV-TR

Type 3: Attention-Deficit/Hyperactivity Disorder, Predominantly Hyperactive/Impulsive Type

Six (or more) of the following symptoms of *hyperactivity-impulsivity* have persisted for at least six months to a degree that is maladaptive and inconsistent with developmental level.

Hyperactivity*

1. Often fidgets with hands or feet or squirms in seat
2. Often leaves seat in classroom or in other situations in which remaining seated is expected
3. Often runs about or climbs excessively in situations in which it is inappropriate (in adolescents or adults, may be limited to subjective feeling of restlessness)
4. Often has difficulty playing or engaging in leisure activities quietly
5. Is often "on the go" or often acts as if "driven by a motor"
6. Often talks excessively

Impulsivity

7. Often blurts out answers before questions have been completed
8. Often has difficulty waiting for a turn
9. Often interrupts or intrudes on others (e.g., butts into conversations or games)

---

*Source: DSM-IV-TR

The DSM IV-TR is a psychological diagnostic tool used as a reference for mental health professionals and can be difficult to understand. We have listed characteristics that are present in most children diagnosed with ADHD as reported by parents, teachers, and other children. Many children exhibit *some* of the characteristics listed below; however, to receive a diagnosis, the characteristics are present from an early age and have a negative impact on more than one area of the child's life.

- Impulsive
- Inattentive
- Easily bored
- Noncompliant
- Restless
- Academic underachievement
- Immaturity
- Self-centered
- Does not anticipate consequences
- Seeks immediate rewards
- Rapidly changing and overly strong emotional reactions
- Poor frustration tolerance
- Difficulty remembering rules and frequently breaking them
- Difficulty making plans and executing those plans
- Talking over others
- Frequently changing physical positions
- Inaccurate school work

- Incomplete school work
- Difficulty maintaining friendships
- Physical punishment seems ineffective.
- Engaging in dangerous activities
- Difficulty inhibiting responses

- Socially outgoing
- Adventuresome
- Mechanically inclined
- Artistic
- Creative
- Less fearful

The diagnosis and treatment of ADHD is complicated, and the unique circumstances of each child must be considered. For instance, two seven-year-old boys diagnosed with ADHD might appear quite different from each other. One of the boys may be highly intelligent and an excellent reader who completes his schoolwork without significant effort but is constantly bothering other students. The other boy may be of average intelligence, have difficulty reading, and may seem to be daydreaming all the time and seldom complete his schoolwork. The first boy described has Type 1-Predominately Hyperactive, and the second boy has Type 2-Inattentive. Because children with ADHD can appear quite different due to individual differences, the diagnosis by some may be challenged as inaccurate. This perceived inaccuracy has lead to skepticism about ADHD. If individual differences are not taken into consideration, then under-diagnosis, misdiagnosis, and over-diagnosis occurs. Individual differences include such things as age, severity of the disorder, intellectual ability, gender, and physical challenges or disorders. Physically and mentally, a three-year-old child presents a different picture than a seventeen-year-old. Appropriate assistance for these children requires an understanding of the group characteristics and individual differences. For example, Type 1 and 3 benefit more from medical interventions, and Type 2 benefits most from behavioral interventions that focus on finding and increasing the use of incentives. *All three types of ADHD can benefit from multiple interventions; therefore, the specific type of ADHD will not be regularly specified unless it is relevant for treatment.*

What ADHD Is Not

Some children receive an inaccurate diagnosis because a few other mental disorders share similar characteristics with ADHD. In order to accurately make a diagnosis of ADHD or another mental disorder or to determine if they coexist, it is necessary to identify and evaluate the characteristics that the disorders do not share. ADHD is most commonly confused with the following mental disorders: depression, bipolar disorder, anxiety disorders, pervasive developmental disorders, fetal alcohol syndrome, and mental retardation. The similarities and differences are described to assist in making an accurate diagnosis.

An individual with ADHD or depression can appear similar in two major ways: suicidal statements and periods of sadness. The differences are that the sad periods are transitory in children with ADHD; whereas, the sad periods of depression are lasting and pervasive. For example, a child with ADHD is told he cannot go outside to play. He cries and expresses sadness for twenty minutes or until distracted. If a child has depression, the expressions of sadness would last longer and generally, using distraction would be ineffective in changing his mood. The second major difference is the context of the suicidal statements. When a child with ADHD expresses suicidal statements, he often receives a "payoff," e.g., avoidance of completing an unpleasant task or getting special attention. A child experiencing depression makes suicidal statements that usually do not appear to receive a "payoff." Two examples of a child with ADHD receiving payoffs after expressing suicidal statements are described. A child is asked to clean the bedroom. He throws himself onto the bed and declares he might as well be dead. The parent then allows the child to escape from bedroom cleaning. In the second example, a teacher firmly asks the child to complete an assignment. The child responds, "You hate me and I might as well just kill myself." The teacher spends the next fifteen minutes giving the child individual attention. In both examples, the child receives a payoff for making the suicidal statements. The frequency of these statements will often increase as payoffs increase.

Individuals with ADHD or bipolar disorder are similar in their expression of dramatic mood swings, however different in their manifestation. The mood of a child with ADHD can vary from euphoria to tears in just a few minutes. An individual with the bipolar disorder expresses the same mood, either euphoria or depression, for days and weeks at a time. The length of the euphoric or sad and depressed mood is the key to separating the two disorders.

Anxiety disorders can manifest by decreased ability to concentrate and restlessness, which are some of the characteristics of ADHD. Children with ADHD are more impulsive and outgoing, whereas a child with an anxiety disorder is constricted and fearful. Also, children with anxiety express many feelings of worry, which is not typical of children with ADHD. If children with anxiety disorders are treated with an anti-anxiety medication like Buspar™, the inability to concentrate and restlessness will usually disappear.

Children with pervasive developmental disorders or ADHD have three similar characteristics. They are hyperactive, non-responsive to verbal requests, and have attention problems. There is a difference in the expression of hyperactivity. A child with ADHD frequently changes activities. A child with pervasive developmental disorder engages in repetitive and ritualistic activities. A child with ADHD is often unresponsive to verbal requests because he does not want to interrupt their current activity, whereas a child with pervasive developmental disorder is unresponsive to requests because he does not understand the language being used. A child with ADHD has short attention-span difficulties. A child with pervasive developmental disorder has difficulty paying attention or differentiating what social cues are important.

Individuals with fetal alcohol syndrome (FAS) or ADHD share all of the main behavioral characteristics. Separating the two disorders can be extremely difficult when dealing with the milder forms of FAS. Severe forms of FAS in individuals can be differentiated from ADHD on lowered intellectual functioning and physical anomalies. The intellectual functioning will be significantly lower than the rest of the family. The physical anomalies are: almond-shaped eyes with a wider distance than average between the eyes; a reduction in the size of the indentation between the upper lip and the base of the nose; and thin lips are frequently part of the pattern. In less severe cases, the physical characteristics may be less dramatic. In these less severe cases, a history of the mother's drinking habits during the pregnancy is the most reliable information to help separate the two disorders. In many cases, it will be almost impossible to differentiate between FAS in its mild form and ADHD.

Individuals with mental retardation or ADHD share some behavioral characteristics. However, if the child scores in the mental-retardation range on an individual IQ test, he or she is excluded from being given the diagnosis of ADHD.

Other Related Mental Disorders

Some experts believe that oppositional-defiant disorder, conduct disorder, and antisocial personality disorder as defined by the DSM IV-TR are more extreme manifestations or severe forms of mistreated ADHD. Others believe that they are separate disorders. In fact, many individuals who have been diagnosed with oppositional-defiant disorder, conduct disorder, or antisocial personality disorder were observed to have ADHD characteristics as young children. If children diagnosed with ADHD have severe problems with authority figures, social customs, and law-breaking, then they have an increased likelihood of being additionally diagnosed with oppositional-defiant disorder. They also have an increased probability of an additional diagnosis of conduct disorder in adolescence and increased likelihood of being diagnosed as antisocial personality disorder in adulthood. Typically, for these three related disorders, society intervenes by gradually increasing levels of punishment. The result is usually more anger and acting-out by the individual. Whether or not these are different disorders or manifestations of the same disorder, the treatment philosophy and many of the interventions described in this book are effective in treating these disorders.

2

Significant People in the Lives of Children with ADHD

Every child lives within a dynamic mini-culture that consists of parents, authority figures, school personnel, and peers. The significant people within this mini-culture have the greatest impact on challenging children's *self-confidence* and *success*. Our approach to effective diagnosis and treatment requires eliciting the help of all of the significant people in the challenging child's life.

Acquiring an understanding and appreciation for the individual roles, different interaction patterns, and feelings of those regularly involved with the challenging child reduces negative judgments and stereotyping. Thus, positive interactions and empathy among team members is increased when understanding is enlarged.

Parents

Parents of children with ADHD have been stereotyped in negative terms. The most common stereotype is that the parents are incompetent or bad. Despite this stereotype, we have come to understand that parents that have challenging children are as varied as their children. They range from those who are almost totally incompetent to those who have been successful with other children and have excellent coping and problem-solving skills. Some parents are well-educated, motivated, and well-adjusted. They have read several books and taken classes on parenting but are still having difficulty. In between those two extremes are parents with all kinds of unique experiences and life circumstances.

A common emotional theme is that they usually feel guilty and discouraged about their inability to manage a child. It is extremely easy to feel guilty and incompetent when you are an adult and still cannot manage the behavior of a forty-five pound five-year-old. Parent's feelings of guilt and inadequacy lead to feelings of frustration and anger toward the child. As frustration feelings escalate, parents sometimes report their anger as "out of control."

All parents seem to have built into their psyche the notion of wanting or expecting a "perfect child." With these children, there is anything but a perfect relationship, so the parents must grieve the loss of a dream of "the perfect child."

Having a challenging child in the home increases the chances of broken spousal relationships. Frequently, parents do not have adequate rest or time away from this child. Parents will be required to make extra effort with some of these challenging children even into their advanced adulthood.

The increasingly embarrassing behavior of the child with ADHD and the parents' inability to manage the child often limits their social interactions with friends and relatives. They start staying home or avoiding contact in social situations that trigger increased problems with the child. The limited social contact only tends to reinforce the negative thoughts about themselves and their children.

Public misbehavior by the child especially reinforces the decision to stay home. A common scenario that results in parents feeling frustrated and angry can be seen almost daily in the grocery store. The child pulls her favorite temper tantrums at the check-stand (screaming, kicking, and lying on the floor) because the parent will not let her have double bubble gum. The people waiting in the checkout line of the store give the parent negative looks or make comments suggesting they are totally incompetent.

Siblings

The siblings often feel neglected and unloved because the child with ADHD takes so much time and attention from the parents. They frequently find that when they are in trouble, it is easy to divert the parent's focus from themselves by taunting the challenging child into naughty behavior. This scapegoat technique is a way of escaping responsibility for their own behavior but creates more problems for the child with ADHD. Another problem can occur when siblings observe how much attention the child with ADHD gets by behaving in a negative way; this encourages them to also seek attention with negative behavior. The parents will often then focus more on the compliant children when they behave in a noncompliant manner. As the child with ADHD becomes more difficult to cope with, often the siblings stay away from home, quit bringing friends home, and become busy outside the home so they will not have to cope with this sibling.

The more compliant siblings are embarrassed, angry, and ashamed of their sibling's disruptive behaviors. Sometimes they feel like they have to be perfect to make up for their sibling. Often they choose not to bring up their own concerns and needs because they think this would be just another burden to place on the parents.

Grandparents

Some grandparents have excellent parenting skills and are willing to be of assistance. Others feel their parenting days are over and do not want to share responsibility for a challenging child. Others have health problems that make it difficult for them to be of long-term assistance. These children are typically much better when they are on a one-to-one basis with an adult and do not have to compete for attention. Frequently, grandparents provide this attention, and initially, the children behave in an acceptable manner. Grandparents frequently see the child in a situation that brings out the best in the child, and the grandparents may begin to be judgmental and negative with the parents, saying things like, "What's the matter with you? He's okay with me. If you parented like I did, there wouldn't be any problems." With more complex and frequent contact, the "honeymoon" is over for the grandparents and their judgmental feelings decrease.

Teachers

Teachers, just as parents and children with ADHD, have commonalties and unique characteristics. Most teachers are responsible, concerned individuals who desire the children under their tutelage to grow and to develop.

Some are at the end of their career, while others are in their first year of teaching. Many are relaxed with a laissez-faire approach and difficult to provoke. Certain others are perfectionists with high and rigid standards. Some have a happy, content home life; some are going through personal trauma. All of these characteristics and circumstances are important to consider as we work with children with ADHD. They often wonder why this child does not respond to their methods that have worked with many other children. They think, "I have tried all the best things I know. I have worked hard, and nothing seems to work." The sense of loss of control can sometimes be overwhelming.

Teachers frequently feel strong frustration toward children with ADHD because they require tremendous amounts of energy and time. Challenging children regularly test rules and teachers' authority. On some occasions, a teacher may get three or four of these children in one classroom. This may lead to a sense of loss of control in the classroom and feelings of inadequacy by the teacher. The fatigue and burnout rate among teachers as they work with these children is high. Some teachers are better at finding ways to rest, recuperate, and re-energize themselves. A teacher with low self-esteem will find extra difficulty in dealing with these challenging children. If teachers derive too much of their self-esteem from teaching, then failures at teaching may have a profound impact on them.

When the teacher is most frustrated, he or she frequently wonders, "What is the matter with the parents?" The teacher may develop a negative attitude toward the parents, even though sometimes, they have limited information about them. The negative attitude toward the parents is not helpful and in fact is detrimental in effectively working together.

Other Students

The students in the classroom often feel confused about why their classmates with ADHD are repeatedly disruptive. They wonder why they won't just stop it and behave. Some students experience feelings of anger and frustration. The students' overwhelming feelings of frustration can result from their belongings and personal space being disregarded or violated. On other occasions, they are distressed because their classroom learning time is being used to cope with problem behaviors. Students express their frustration with phrases like, "I'm tired of this kid in our classroom getting all the attention. Why can't he go to a different classroom? He is always bugging us on purpose." The students may cope by blaming, avoiding, or scapegoating their classmate with ADHD.

A few students feel sad for their classmate and do not think they are treated fairly and try to protect and befriend the "underdog." Some students feel anxious because of the turmoil and negative emotions that permeate the classroom and tend to withdraw or try to be helpful.

A common dynamic occurs when some students learn they can get the teacher off task by provoking the child with ADHD. The student may use this tactic to get even with his or her classmate or get out of completing schoolwork.

Principals

The major role of a principal is to keep the school running smoothly with as little disruption as possible. This responsibility is often accomplished by setting up a system of rules. The rules are usually set up by using stepwise interventions: if there is one infraction, a punishment follows; if the infraction is repeated, the punishment gets more severe; if it is repeated again, it gets even more severe. Some children respond well to this model, but it is typically counterproductive with the challenging child. Remember that punishment often is ineffective with these children. The principal's level of frustration increases when this system fails to bring about the desired results. The principal also tends to have more interactions with the parents of these children. If the principal develops a stereotype of "bad parents create bad children," that attitude will be conveyed to the parents, either directly or indirectly. The principal then loses the parent's cooperation, and an effective intervention program cannot be implemented. A final problem a principal will have is simply, "I don't know what to do," and there is a searching for some legitimate answers to the question of, "What do I do next? We have tried everything that we normally do—nothing is working."

Authority Figures

Many other people in authority positions, e.g., the police and storeowners, also interact with children with ADHD. These authority groups often have difficulty with these children because of rule violations and lack of respectful behavior. Power struggles are inevitable with authoritarian figures. When rule violations repeatedly occur, these adults feel angry and, again, often respond with punishment and rejection. It is desirable to educate and select carefully the people who are going to be in authority positions with the child.

Neighbors

Neighbors with limited information have a tendency to be judgmental toward the child and parents. Some of the negative thoughts of neighbors are, "How can you have a child like that?" and "Why don't you make him mind?" At times neighbors say, "Keep that child away from my place!" Other neighbors who have more information and understanding think, "How can I be helpful?" or "I feel so sorry for the children and parents." Neighbors with empathy and understanding can be valuable allies for the family.

3

Causation

What causes children to become like this? Whose fault is it? Am I to blame? Am I doing something wrong? Parents and teachers often feel unnecessarily guilty and responsible for a challenging child. Those involved with a challenging child desperately want explanations about what causes ADHD. Parents may tend to accept popular theories that are unsupported by "good science" because, understandably, they desire a fix or cure for their child. Media testimonials for popular theories are frequently used to promote causes and treatments for ADHD. Testimonials are appealing to desperate people because of their emotional and hopeful presentation. Can we trust testimonials? No! What we can trust is the causative theories that have been well researched.

After a mother heard a testimonial on a talk show that sugar causes ADHD behavior, she reorganized her family's eating habits for six months. This sounded like an easy task, but she found that more than 75 percent of the food she purchased contained sugar. Feeling punished and angry with the change, the family sabotaged her efforts. The challenging child was having a Twinkie exchange at school lunchtime, and the other family members were hiding assorted goodies around the house, which were usually discovered by the challenging child. The parent felt undermined and unappreciated. She initially thought the "removal" of the sugar from the diet was making a difference. However, after six months, she started doubting its effectiveness.

A teacher, hearing the testimonial about sugar, led a drive to rid schools in the district of candy machines. A great deal of time and effort was expended. The most significant change in the school was a lack of money for the band uniforms.

The parent and teacher had admirable intentions, but they did not have the skill to evaluate the theory and treatment using good science. Good science can determine if there was a change in the children's behavior and if it was due to the removal of sugar from their diet.

New and clear-cut answers for causation develop gradually with good science. Read reviews of the scientific research on ADHD by experts; these articles can provide a great deal of useful information. While discerning whether good science has been accomplished in the search for causation of ADHD, use these guidelines.

- Testimonials are a beginning point in deciding what to investigate. Someone thought that they saw a connection and inferred causation. They are not scientific explanations because they have not been scientifically researched.
- Many studies, done over many years by different scientists obtaining consistent results, are required to understand causal relationships.
- Studies need to be done by individuals without a conflict of interest.
- Individuals who understand research principles will rarely tell you that they have the only answer about the causation of human behavior.
- Be skeptical of a professional who tells you the cause of ADHD is just one factor and they can fix it in a short time. Their research is probably limited and biased.
- Studies evaluating the cause of ADHD should always use a control group (e.g., children without ADHD) for comparison purposes.

An extensive review of good scientific research indicates there are some factors that exaggerate the behavioral problems, some causative factors, and some factors that have been eliminated as causative agents. Recent explanations (along with a few oldies) about causation of ADHD are discussed.

Heredity

Research data supports the idea that many of these children (more than 55 percent) have problems because of a hereditary component. Of this group of children, their biological parents and other family members may demonstrate similar characteristics, e.g., impulsivity, addictive behaviors, and a greater desire for immediate gratification. Many research studies completed in the past twenty-five years using different approaches have consistently shown a heredity connection. Children born to parents having ADHD have an increased incidence of ADHD, even when adopted early in life by parents without ADHD characteristics. The genes responsible for passing on the characteristics of ADHD are being studied. The genes of current interest are DAT1 and D4RD.[1]

Problem Brain Functions and Structure

Since the 1980s, ADHD research with the brain has focused on blood flow, metabolism, wave patterns, and structure. As new methods of scanning the brain have developed, research continues to find new associations between ADHD and the brain.

Recent research data reveals a significantly lower blood-flow rate in the frontal lobes of children who have ADHD. This finding might explain their difficulty with planning and execution of plans, because that is one of the functions of the frontal lobes. In addition, two other areas of the brain, the caudate nucleus and the limbic system, showed lower levels of blood-flow rate. These two areas are involved in memory, emotions, motivation, and inhibiting behavior, which are all problem areas for individuals with ADHD.[2]

Metabolism in the brain can now be studied using a new technique called positron emission tomography (PET) scan. Radioactive glucose (sugar) is injected into the blood stream and then pictures are taken of the brain using the PET scan. One study with adults and adolescents having ADHD found lower levels of metabolic activity in the frontal lobes than in the brains of those in the control group.[3]

Brain-wave patterns have been studied for many years using the electroencephalograph or EEG. Studies have provided data indicating there is less electrical activity in the frontal lobes of children with ADHD.[4]

Recent studies have found differences in the structure of the brain using magnetic resonance imagining (MRI). It was found that the right side of the caudate nucleus was larger than the left in children diagnosed with ADHD. This is the opposite of what is seen in children without ADHD. Other studies have found the cerebellum, the right frontal area, and the corpus callosum was smaller in children with ADHD as compared to a control group.[5]

Traumatic injury to the frontal lobes of the brain frequently produces ADHD-like behavior. Car accidents have been a major source of these injuries. Infectious diseases of the brain can also produce damage to the brain and the result is a change of behavior.[6]

In the past twenty years, scientists have been trying to understand how the brain works chemically. A group of chemicals called neurotransmitters continue to be investigated. Dopamine, a neurotransmitter, has been of interest in explaining the behavior of the children with ADHD. It has been theorized[7] that this neurotransmitter is out of balance in the limbic system. Research continues on dopamine, but no systematic conclusions have been reached.

The collective data just reviewed indicates that brain functioning and structure are different in the individual with ADHD. The data allows us to infer that brain function and structure are somehow involved in producing ADHD behavior.

Delayed Brain Development

In November 2007, the National Institute of Mental Health funded a study that was widely publicized in the media regarding delayed brain development in children with ADHD. This study used imaging technology to investigate the development of the child's cortex. The cortex is the part of the brain which helps regulate attention, planning, and judgment. According to the study, the cortex of children with ADHD was about three years behind in normal development as compared to other children. The study revealed that the cortex continues to develop in children and on average, in children with ADHD, thickening of the cortex appeared to peak at age 10.5, compared with age 7.5 in children without the disorder. The study supports a biological cause for ADHD. However, if delayed cortex development were the major cause of ADHD, it follows that when the cortex normalized, the child's behavioral problems would also normalize. Although the research suggests that most children with ADHD improve with age, and some children even grow out of the disorder, approximately two-thirds of children with ADHD have symptoms into adulthood. This suggests that the developmental delay in the cortex may be only one of the causes of ADHD.[8]

Lead and Mercury Poisoning

Lead, mercury, and other heavy metals, if ingested on a regular basis even in small amounts, can accumulate in the central nervous system or the brain. The heavy metals are extremely slow to leave the brain. As the accumulation of heavy metals increases, mild forms of brain dysfunction start developing which interfere with the child's intellectual capability and normal development. The first three years of development seem especially important. If heavy metals are ingested during the first three years, then the child is more likely to sustain damage to the brain. Some children who have been poisoned by heavy metals, especially lead, develop ADHD. Many children have been impacted by lead or other heavy metals.[9]

The lead often comes from paint, old toys, and sometimes in mining or industrial areas where the metals are deposited in the soils. Cities where old smelters have been located can have high levels of lead which fell from the smokestacks, contaminating the surrounding soil. Programs have been developed to find contaminated soil with high lead content and replace it with fresh uncontaminated soil.[10]

Mercury also damages the central nervous system with the severity of damage varying with the exposure. One[11] of the most common sources of mercury poisoning is from eating significant amounts of contaminated fish.

If a child lives in an old home or building painted before 1975, testing for lead would be advisable. If the child lives in a mining area, or lives downstream from mines or smelters, talk with a doctor regarding concerns about heavy-metal contamination.

Underweight Babies

Babies whose birth weight is significantly below normal levels are at high risk for many physical and psychological disorders, including becoming children who have ADHD. We know certain behaviors by the mother during pregnancy can impact birth weight. Poor nutrition, smoking, alcohol use, and very young motherhood are factors that contribute to babies being born underweight. Mothers who smoke during pregnancy or who expose their child to secondhand smoke during their early years of development have children who are at extra risk for the development of ADHD-like behavior. Likewise, if the mother drinks alcohol during pregnancy, the child is at higher risk of developing ADHD-like behavior.[12]

We do not at this point understand what happens within the child to make him or her more ADHD-prone, but we think the brain development could somehow be delayed or damaged.

Ineffective Parenting

No compelling evidence exists that proves ineffective parenting causes ADHD. However, ineffective parenting can increase the extent of the behavioral problems. Not having effective skills, parents, often without knowing it, make the problems of their children worse. One ineffective parenting response is "just this once." The parents make rules but do not consistently enforce them, so the child becomes confused about the parents' expectations. Consequently, the child grows up without a clear idea of expectations for appropriate behavior. Children with ADHD already have difficulty knowing and following rules; therefore, inconsistent parenting compounds the problem. A second ineffective parenting response is "anything you want." These parents basically put no limitations on their children's behavior; they allow them complete freedom. Because the child grows up not knowing boundaries, it is difficult, if not impossible, for him to learn appropriate behavior, and he will often expect immediate gratification. Children with ADHD already have difficulty with delaying gratification; consequently, their problem behaviors are magnified. A third ineffective parenting response is "my way or else." These parents frequently respond with physical and psychological punishment. This kind of parenting increases the child's anger and resentment, leading to more "acting-out" behavior—which is already a problem for children with ADHD.[13]

Some parents typically have effective parenting skills; however, life circumstances, e.g., many children, learning disabilities, divorce, death, and limited resources, can leave them overwhelmed and exhausted, affecting their parental responses. Anytime parents are overwhelmed or exhausted, it is easier to display ineffective parenting responses, which increases problem behaviors for the child with ADHD. It is difficult for the adults to help a problem child when the family is having a hard time just existing.

Ineffective Teaching

Just as some parents behave in ways that probably exaggerate the behaviors of children with ADHD, some teachers also can exaggerate these problem behaviors. The teachers who are most problematic tend to have teaching styles which are unorganized, inconsistent, or very negative. Over-controlling or rejecting styles also exacerbate non-compliant behavior from challenging children. Again, this ineffective teaching does not account for the origin of the child's non-compliant behavior, which is usually present long before they come to school. But it certainly can exaggerate and increase the number and severity of negative behaviors.

Food Additives and Allergies

A popular notion over the past twenty years has been that food additives or an allergic reaction to food additives has been responsible for ADHD-like behavior problems; however, research indicates that *none* of the additives studied so far, e.g., red dye, have a significant causative impact on the behavior of children.[14] Children with ADHD are generally less tolerant of discomfort and more easily irritated by inconvenience, so having an allergy which causes physical discomfort tends to aggravate the acting-out behaviors. Many other chemicals and compounds which have not been studied could be presenting problems, but we will not know until effective research has been completed.

Sugar

Approximately fifteen years ago, sugar was suggested as the cause of problem behavior in children.[15] Rapidly metabolized, sugar was thought to give children excessive energy, perhaps causing hyperactivity by impacting the child's chemistry in an adverse manner. The sugar hypothesis also fit into the spirit of the times, which espoused a focus on good nutrition, especially emphasizing reduced sugar intake. Sugar as a causative agent of problem behavior became so popular that thousands of children were placed on "sugar-free" diets. Parents immediately learned that preparing a sugar-free diet is difficult and children find methods of getting sweets. They would trade a good sandwich for cookies at school or get sweets at a neighbor's house. Researchers gradually collected information that did not support sugar as the problem. Eventually, the National Institute of Mental Health designed some definitive studies showing sugar has little or no impact on children's problem behavior.[16] Many people still have strong beliefs in the sugar hypotheses despite clear evidence that it is not a factor.

Stress or Shock to the Pregnant Mother

Interest in the intrauterine environment and its influence in the developing fetus has encouraged speculation that shock and stress during the pregnancy might have negatively impacted the child's brain development. It has been theorized that stress and shock in the first and final trimesters of a child's fetal development changes the blood chemistry of the mother and child.[17] Although an interesting idea, we have little research information supporting this theory. This is a topic for continuing research.

Ionization of Air

Some people report feeling less depressed in environments containing a higher percentage of negative ions.[18] Negative ions are in higher concentration in moist, clear air. In contrast, air that is dirty and dry has low concentrations of negative ions. Smoking, for example, lowers the level of negative ions in the room where the person is smoking. Equipment that increases negative ions is currently being marketed to improve the behavior of children with ADHD. Sufficient research studying the impact of negative ions on their behavior has not been conducted.

Fluorescent Lights

The impact of light on human behavior is an idea that has been around for a long time. Today, low light levels are thought to impact the development of depression in the winter. It has been theorized that light could impact children's behavior.[19] Children spend a majority of their day in classrooms with fluorescent lighting. It was theorized that fluorescent lights with their unnatural light spectrum and pulsating electrical current could alter the function of some children's brains. The alterations in their brain functioning could help create a challenging child. Again, good research did not support this interesting theoretical idea.

Cultural Causation

It is important to also look at larger cultural issues. The impact of socialization and cultural influences is difficult to evaluate. Does our general culture promote impulsiveness, self-centeredness, and a lack of concern for the welfare of others? If it does, then as a culture, we promote the problematic behaviors we are discussing in our children. If structure and consistency promote positive behaviors, does the increasing disorganization of families encourage behavioral problems? Some experts clearly believe the Western culture, at the least, exacerbates ADHD behavior. If this belief has merit, and there is supportive evidence, then cultural changes are important. However, recent demographic data finds a similar percentage of ADHD in such divergent countries as Japan, China, Sweden, and the United States.[20] This evidence suggests that a specific culture does not cause ADHD. The evidence that a specific cultural influence could exacerbate the problems of someone who already has ADHD is a strong possibility.

Conclusions

Our belief, supported by good scientific research, is that ADHD behavior is caused by several factors or a combination of factors. There is clear evidence that heredity and problems with brain structure and function are major factors in causing ADHD. It is our hope that having a better understanding of causation leads to fewer guilt feelings by parents. It should also reduce the tendency to blame someone for the child's problem behavior.

We also have concluded that several or a combination of factors can exacerbate the symptoms of ADHD. Knowledge about causation and exacerbating factors help direct diagnosis and treatment.

Notes

Part Two

Diagnosing

4

A Complete Evaluation

A mental health professional—psychologist or counselor—or physician with specialized training regarding ADHD reaches a formal diagnosis of ADHD only after performing a complete evaluation. Detailed information obtained from mental health professionals, educators, physicians, and parents is critical to a complete evaluation. This section outlines the methods used to collect information about the child, demonstrates how to analyze the child's strengths and deficits, and shows how to evaluate the child's surrounding social systems. The roles of the mental health professional, educational staff, physicians, and parents are explained.

Good referral sources for experienced professionals are school personnel and other parents who have children with ADHD. It is important for each parent to independently research the professional's credentials and choose someone who is supportive, non-judgmental, and truly listens to your concerns.

Coordinator of the Evaluation

Because it is necessary to collect evaluative information from multiple sources, it is convenient to select a coordinator. Having the mental health professional serve as the coordinator best facilitates the collection of information. Mental health professionals are trained observers of behavior. They will determine the consistency of behaviors displayed in several environments. Problem behaviors sometimes present uniquely in different environments; therefore, it is important to closely observe the interactions and dynamics between the child, parents, and educators.

5

Psychological Evaluation

During the initial visit to a mental health professional, parents typically express strong negative feelings about their parenting abilities and their child's behaviors. The MHP listens and reassures the parents that their feelings are understandable and typical for anyone dealing with a challenging child. Important goals for the mental health professional are to communicate *hope* and build an alliance with the parent. The parent is reassured that *if* the child has ADHD, there are helpful treatments, and that the parents are not the cause of the ADHD. The mental health professional demonstrates expertise and verbalizes repeatedly that ADHD is usually a long-term disorder and offers long-term assistance.

Initial Sessions

The order of the initial session(s) will vary depending on the MHP's preference for either obtaining pertinent *historical information* or *behavioral observations*. In the Appendix, we have provided a *Structured Interview Questionnaire* for the mental health professional to assist in gathering information.

The MHP sends the following questionnaires, found in the Appendix, to the child's primary parent and asks the primary parent to be responsible for distributing and collecting the questionnaires. The structure of the child's family will dictate how many questionnaires are necessary to send, e.g., father, mother, and significant others all would fill out their own forms. (Ideally, allow enough time for the completion and return of questionnaires to the mental health professional *before* the initial meeting.)

- Parents' Questionnaire
- Parents' Stress Indicator Scale Questionnaire
- Educators' Questionnaire
- Educator's Style Questionnaire
- Common/Enduring Challenging Situations Questionnaires (Parents' and Educators')
- Positive Information Questionnaires (Parents' and Educators')
- Educational Performance Questionnaire

If the child is seriously hyperactive, the initial session should not be more than one hour. Two parents and the child should attend the first session. Having two adults present allows for flexibility; one adult can take the child for a walk if necessary. Another appointment can be scheduled without the child if the child is too disruptive, e.g., walls vibrating and paint peeling. Parents having uninterrupted time will give more accurate information and express their feelings, desires, and fears more completely.

Pertinent Historical Information

Ascertain when the child's behavior became a problem; establish whether there were any precipitating events, prior diagnoses, psychological tests or treatments utilized. It is important to investigate family history to determine whether there is a pattern of ADHD behaviors exhibited by siblings and/or other family members. Split households require extra time for evaluation and consideration of potential animosities.

Review with all the parents information obtained from the following: *Parents' Questionnaire, Parents' Stress Indicator Scale Questionnaire, Common/Enduring Challenging Situations Questionnaire (Parents'), Positive Information Questionnaire (Parents')*. Ask the parents to provide additional information when discrepancies appear in questionnaire responses. For example, a mother rated a child's behaviors as a severe problem, while the father did not identify any behavior problems. Upon further questioning, it was discovered that the father was a long-haul truck driver spending three hours a week at home.

Evaluation of the parenting style has to be done in a careful manner because parents frequently feel judged and devalued. Determine what parenting techniques or strategies have been successful and which ones have not. Parenting styles can be broken down into three general categories.[21] The authoritarian style demands obedience and does not listen to input from the child. The authoritative style is listening to the child and allowing some choices, but the parent has definite rules consistently followed. The final style is called laissez-faire. There are few stated rules and the child is allowed too many decisions with little structure from the adult.

The mental health professional should ask questions which identify in the challenging child any core characteristics described in the beginning of the book, e.g., a short attention span. Specific information needs to be obtained about situations that are typically difficult for children having ADHD. Parents often report increased difficulties in restaurants, at the store, during church services, while they are on the phone, or when visitors are in the home.

Inappropriate behaviors can be beyond challenging in the grocery store, which is a stimulating and tempting place with multiple "unstated rules." An example of a probable scenario in the grocery store makes it clear how difficult it can be for the child and the parent. In the cereal aisle, the child grabs three boxes while knocking four others on the floor, the whole time making wild and excited whooping noises. Other shoppers in the aisle are giving the parent and child disapproving looks, and the embarrassed parent attempts to return the cereal boxes to the shelf. Meanwhile, the child is throwing a tantrum on the floor, yelling, "You're a horrible, mean, stupid parent!" The humiliated parent pulls the child off the floor. The child quickly grabs the cart and starts racing down the aisle, pretending he is in the Indy 500, until he knocks down an entire display of canned goods. The exasperated parent yanks the child out from under the rubble and proceeds to offer quick apologetic remarks before running out of the store, vowing never to shop there again. When they arrive at the car, the parent realizes Grandma, who was shopping with them, has disappeared. A few minutes later, she exits the store with her sunglasses on and a scarf over her head, and she is looking down at the ground while taking the long way to the car. This is not necessarily an exaggerated dramatization. Unfortunately, for some parents, scenes like this happen far too often. Taking the time to elicit stories like the one just described is critical in completing a thorough evaluation.

Behavioral Observations

Behavioral observations are an integral component of the initial interview process. MHPs should pay attention to their own feelings while making behavioral observations. It is important to observe any attempts in the office by the challenging child to get attention by exhibiting behaviors which are likely to produce negative feelings in others. It may appear that the child is purposefully disrespectful or intrusive of personal space and belongings. Watch for violations of what would be considered normal, appropriate boundaries for the child's age group. The child may pick-up equipment, turn it on, get items from your desk, or play with items normally restricted from child touching. Other behaviors include intrusive, interrupting behavior during conversations between the adults.

We will give an example of a typical first office visit scenario with a younger, more severe challenging child. The challenging child and parents walk into the waiting area, and the child spots the candy jar immediately and has grabbed two handfuls before the parents have even sat down. Next, the child sees the dried flower arrangement in the corner and proceeds with sticky hands to break pieces off. At this point, one of the parents, embarrassed, grabs the child by the arm and begins to speak with a tight jaw. The child reacts by throwing himself on the floor.

Take notice at this time of the parent's attempts to gain control. The child usually will continue inappropriate behaviors in the office. Observe how their behavior changes when limits are set. For example, we happen to have "diagnostic" instruments in our offices. A large green houseplant with many leaves is located in the corner of the room. Younger children almost always want to touch it after their uncertainty about the new environment subsides. They touch it gently at first and sometimes pull off a leaf and look at it. The challenging child will pull off the leaf and look at the evaluator. If given a negative or disapproving response, he or she will pull off several more leaves.

If the child is not demonstrating any problem behavior, stimulate the child in order to see how quickly he can regain control of his behavior. Getting them involved in physical activity is one way of stimulating them. A competitive activity is especially effective. For example, the evaluator asks the child to try to grab a coin from the palm of their hand. The evaluator tells the child he can keep the coin if he can successfully grab the coin three times in a row. The evaluator lets the child get the coin and then says it is his turn and attempts to win it back. A child with ADHD will become very distressed if he loses the coin. After losing the coin, ask the child to sit quietly. Observe the child's emotional control; a child with ADHD has great difficulty in regaining control after becoming distressed.

Another way to stimulate the child is to perform a "soft" neurological exam, explained in the Psychological Testing section under Motor Coordination exam. We would often start out the evaluation with the "soft" neurological exam to build rapport with an older child.

Because there is a lot to accomplish in the initial session, other evaluation sessions may be necessary. It is of utmost importance that the initial contact is positive. The parents should leave the office feeling listened to, valued, and hopeful about assistance.

Psychological Testing

Psychological testing is an essential part of any evaluation if the child is thought to have ADHD. Ideally, psychological testing should be a part of every evaluation because of the objective information it provides, and in a structured situation, it allows the tester to make systematic observations of behavior. The objective information and the systematic observations make the diagnosis of ADHD more reliable and valid. If the child is diagnosed with ADHD, a further benefit from the testing is that much of the information obtained from the testing can be used to help formulate an effective treatment program.

A qualified psychologist should administer the tests described, because they must be administered, scored, and interpreted correctly for challenging children. Child psychologists and school psychologists are usually the best qualified.

Numerous psychological tests designed to test strengths, deficits, abilities, and emotional states have been developed. Psychologists often have their favorites—ones that are most familiar to them. We focus on a few psychological tests that help illuminate the core characteristics of ADHD and coexisting conditions.

Five types of tests: *ability, perceptual, attention, coordination,* and *emotional state,* are useful when evaluating challenging children.

IQ and Abilities Tests

Abilities tests measure many of the skills necessary for success in school and some characteristics of ADHD. These tests follow a standardized format. Standardized means each child is given the test in the same predetermined manner. Testing in this standardized manner helps predict how a "typical" child might function in a "typical" classroom as compared to peers. Modifying the standardized testing format is sometimes required with special populations of children. Giving blind or deaf children the tests in the usual manner would not result in valid results. Children with ADHD are another example of a special population of children that require special modifications in testing procedure.

Some of the traditional intelligence quotient (IQ) tests, such as the Wechsler Intelligence Scale for Children (WISC IV) and the Stanford-Binet, are the oldest and most widely administered ability tests. The newer ability tests include the Woodcock Johnson III, the Differential Ability Scale, and the Children's Memory Scale. Usually only one of these tests will be given because they measure very similar things and the format of the testing situations are alike.

The WISC IV is chosen to demonstrate modified administration procedures and interpretation for challenging children. The modified instructions can be generalized to other ability tests.

Wechsler Intelligence Scale for Children (WISC IV)

Children with ADHD, as a group, tend to have slightly lower overall IQ test scores, but there is a considerable range from high to low scores. An overall score below seventy on the WISC IV usually indicates that the diagnosis of ADHD should not be made. The child's problems are probably due to lowered abilities, not ADHD. However, it is important that the low score is valid and not due to an overriding deficit in attention or motivation.

To determine if a lower score is a skill deficit and/or an attention or motivational deficit, we suggest modifying testing administration procedures. After initially testing using the standardized method, re-administer some of the sub-scales with the lowest scores. Offer rewards for higher performance on the selected subscales. For example, a ten-year-old boy scored at the 30th percentile on the pic-ture-completion test of the WISC IV. This scale measures the ability to identify missing parts of a picture—a difficult task for children with attention problems, as it requires careful scanning of details. On the re-administration, the examiner placed a quarter on the table and stated, "If you score high, you get to keep the quarter!" The child scored at the 70th percentile the second time, clearly dem-onstrating that he had good skills but was not attending to the task or was not properly motivated. Another ten year-old-boy scored at the 40th percentile on the picture completion test. On the re-administration, he was unable to improve his score, although he was clearly motivated by the money. This boy clearly had a skill deficit.

Modification in the administration procedures is necessary when the child gives obvious cues indicating potential attention and motivational issues. Some of the most frequent cues are comments like, "Are we about done?" or "Is it time to go home?" which demonstrate problems with motivation. Some will give answers that show lack of effort to provide an accurate answer. Getting out of the difficult work situation seems to be one of the child's goals. If the child appears to be giv-ing up, then the testing situation needs to be modified by stopping the testing and scheduling another session or by providing some incentives or rewards for sustained effort.

The WISC IV consists of a number of subscales that measure a variety of abili-ties and knowledge. One of the subscales is called *freedom from distractibility*. This subscale identifies problems with the ability to sustain attention.

Responses to questions on some of the subtests can be indicators of a high level of impulsiveness. For an example: "If you see a purse on the sidewalk, what should you do?" Impulsive answer: "Keep it?" If the examiner then asks, "What would your mother say to do?" If the child then responds with, "Find the owner and give it back?" then there is a clear indication that the first response was an impulsive one and not a lack of understanding.

IQ and Abilities Tests

WISC IV	Typical ADHD Results*
Processing speed	Scores indicate more difficulty
Freedom from distraction	Scores indicate more difficulty
Gross and fine-motor coordination	More difficulties than average
Ability to attend	Lower than average score
Ability to pay attention to details	Lower than average score
Coding	Lower than average score
Digit span (working memory)	Lower than average score
Ability to follow directions	Lower than average
Ability to persist after failure	Lower than average

Children's Memory Scale	Typical ADHD Results*
Attention/concentration	Lower than average score
Working memory	10-12% show an impairment

Woodcock Johnson III	Typical ADHD Results*
Working memory	Lower than average score
Broad attention	Lower than average score
Executive processes	Lower than average score
Planning	Lower than average score

Differential Ability Scale	Typical ADHD Results*
Separation of ADHD and Learning Disabilities	Better than most tests

Some children with ADHD will not have these typical test scores.

Perceptual Motor Tests and Exams

The Bender-Gestalt test can be used to evaluate perceptual motor problems and an opportunity to observe many other behaviors indicating ADHD. It is easy and inexpensive to administer. This test consists of a series of geometric figures, which progressively become more difficult to replicate. One figure is contained on each card. The child is told to copy each of nine figures on a standard white sheet of paper. The figure is shown for fifteen seconds and removed. If the child has difficulty replicating the simple forms, then perceptual motor problems might be present. Select some of the poorly copied figures and re-administer offering a known effective reward. Observe the changes or lack of changes to get a better idea whether the major deficit is with attention, motivation, or perceptual motor skills.

If the child has trouble on the simple forms, it could also be a short-term memory problem. To check out memory problems, leave the card in full view of the child and ask them to copy. If the figures are replicated easily, then a short-term or working-memory problem is likely.

Observe the child's planning ability while taking the test. The test instructions require copying nine figures on a standard-sized piece of paper. A child with good planning skills will place them in rows trying to anticipate and plan the use of space. Children with ADHD tend to approach the use of space in an unsystematic manner. For example, they may use the entire space for just two of the figures. They may then distort the size and shape of the other figures to make them fit on the paper.

Bender-Gestalt Test	Typical ADHD Results*
Short-term memory	Lower than average
Perceptual skills	Lower than average
Ability to attend	Lower than average
Ability to pay attention to details	Lower than average
Perceptual organizational skills	Lower than average
Ability to follow directions	Lower than average
Gross and fine-motor coordination skills	More difficulties than average

Some children with ADHD will not have these typical test scores.

Motor Coordination Exam

An initial screening of motor coordination is sometimes called a "soft" neurological exam. The exam can be accomplished in the office without special equipment and is inexpensive in time and money. As a screening device, it provides enough information to indicate whether further medical evaluation is appropriate. A physical therapist, neuropsychologist, or a neurologist can do a more thorough evaluation if indicated. This exam also provides an excellent opportunity to make behavioral observations unrelated to motor problems.

Begin the exam by telling the child, "We are going to have some fun." This exam can also be used in the initial interview as a method of stimulating the child to look for ADHD-like behavior.

Task 1:

Initially *demonstrate* and then ask them to perform this task. "I'm going to touch the *tip* of my nose with the *tip* of my finger. Watch me. I'm going to close my eyes while I'm doing this task." Then say, "Now close your eyes and touch the *tip* of your nose with the *tip* of your finger. Use your *right* hand."

Observe the following:

1. Was the correct hand used?
2. Did they cheat by peeking?
3. Was there any difficulty finding their nose?
4. Did they place the tip of the finger on the tip of their nose or middle of their finger across the middle of their nose?

If they were unsuccessful, try again. Repeat the instructions a second time. Observe again. Then have the child do the same task with the left hand using verbal instructions without demonstration. Observe the same four basic performance areas.

Task 2:

Do not demonstrate this task; just give them verbal instructions. "I want you to hop in place on your left foot with your eyes closed and I want you to stay inside this area when you hop." Show them a clearly marked one-square-foot area. Repeat the instructions for the right foot. Stay close to the children while they perform this task, as some may fall and hurt themselves without your assistance.

Observe the following:

1. Can they hop?
2. Was the correct foot used?
3. Were they able to stay close to the one-square-foot area?
4. Did they cheat by opening their eyes?

Continue with similar tasks until there is a clear idea of any and all limitations. Children with ADHD typically have difficulty accurately following these instructions. Determine whether the inability to follow the instructions is due to actual lack of coordination or lack of attention. Request the child repeat the failed tasks, with emphasis on the missed direction. For example, please touch the *tip* of your finger to the *tip* of your nose. The general coordination problems and perceptual motor-skill deficits should become apparent if present.

If general coordination problems are apparent, then refer to a specialist for a more complete evaluation. A problem of coordination might implicate some form of brain injury and would indicate the need for an extensive history of possible events that could have produced a brain injury. A neuropsychological exam and/or a brain-scanning technique such as the CAT, MRI, or PET scan are designed to evaluate brain injury and its impact on functioning.

Motor Coordination Exam	Typical ADHD Results*
Memory short-term (working memory)	Lower than average
Perceptual motor skills, gross and fine	More difficulties than average
Ability to attend	Lower than average
Ability to pay attention to details	Lower than average
Ability to follow directions	Lower than average
Cheating	Higher than average

Some children with ADHD will not have these typical test scores.

Attention-Testing Devices

Some electronic devices, The Gordon Diagnostic System and the TOVA, have been developed to assess attention problems. These devices measure errors on boring and repetitive tasks, which are especially difficult for children with attention problems. The Gordon device requires the child to push a key each time an error appears in a series of letters. A similar evaluation system uses a computer to accomplish an evaluation of attention problems and is called the TOVA. It can be used on most computers with the software that has been developed. These two systems have norms for each age group.

Attention-Testing Devices	Typical ADHD Results*
Ability to attend to repetitive tasks	Lower than average
Ability to follow directions	Lower than average
Error rate	Higher than average
Inhibition of responses	Lower than average

Some children with ADHD will not have these typical test scores.

Emotional-State Tests

The Beck Depression Inventory for adolescents is easy to administer and economical. It consists of a number of statements that are typically made by individuals who are depressed, and the individuals taking the inventory are asked to agree or disagree with these statements. The inventory was originally designed for adults, but an adolescent form has been developed. It is useful in assessing the level of depression the person is experiencing.

Emotional-State Tests	Typical ADHD Results*
Beck's Depression Inventory for Adolescence	Higher score

Some children with ADHD will not have these typical test scores.

Summarizing the Results of Psychological Tests

If the child has ADHD, a consistent pattern of testing results and behavioral observations are apparent. The pattern is as follows:

- Higher levels of attention problems
- Slower processing speed
- Difficulty following directions
- Higher levels of distractibility
- Lower levels of persistence
- More problems with fine and gross motor coordination
- Lower levels of short-term or working memory
- Higher levels of impulsiveness
- Lower levels of planning ability
- Higher error rates
- Higher cheating levels
- Higher levels of depression in adolescents
- Lower levels of ability to inhibit responses

A child with ADHD will not have all of these characteristics but will have enough to qualify for a diagnosis of ADHD. Before a diagnosis is made, however, the information from school, home, and a physician need to be collected, evaluated, and interpreted.

6

Medical Evaluation

A physician may receive a referral from a mental health professional or parent to perform a medical evaluation on a child exhibiting challenging behaviors. The origins of the child's challenging behavior can be medical, psychological in nature, or a combination of the two. When an MHP makes the referral, the psychological history is exchanged to avoid unnecessary duplication and to facilitate discovering the origins of the challenging behavior. If the physician is the first professional to examine the child, they will first evaluate for medical problems along with gathering some psychological information. As medical origins are ruled out, more extensive psychological data is collected. Either the physician collects additional information through behavioral observations, gathering a history and utilizing the ADHD questionnaires found in the Appendix, or makes a referral to an MHP specializing in children with behavioral problems.

Some common medical or physical issues that cause, exacerbate, or mimic ADHD are described in this chapter, as well as some complicating psychological concerns. The physician will decide what medical tests and treatments are necessary.

Metabolic Problems

A hyperactive thyroid can produce some ADHD-like symptoms. They include: inability to pay attention, higher levels of activity than normal, abrupt mood changes, and inability to follow through on plans they have made. A blood test to determine the levels of thyroxin will differentiate these behaviors from those caused by ADHD.

Diabetes is a childhood disease that has the potential of producing ADHD-like behavior. When there is a blood-sugar imbalance, the following behaviors can occur: short attention span, noncompliant behavior, dramatic mood swings, aggressiveness, and hyperactivity. An appropriate blood-testing program will determine if diabetes is present or if the insulin levels are not being controlled properly.

39

Neurological Disorders

Petit mal seizures in young children are difficult to detect for several reasons. The seizures last only a few seconds, and the only outward sign might be a staring into space and fluttering eyelids. Some children have many seizures an hour and may appear inattentive and unmotivated like a child with Inattentive ADHD when, in fact, they are confused because they have lost a few seconds of consciousness with each seizure. An EEG will help make a determination about the presence of seizures, and careful observation of the child can also be very useful in diagnosis. The seizures can most often be treated with medication.

If the seizures have an early onset, the children are not able to verbalize that anything unusual is happening to them. One twelve-year-old child seen in our office for an ADHD evaluation was diagnosed instead with early-onset petit mal seizures. This child was so accustomed to having seizures that he was unaware of any problems.

Neurological damage can also occur from ingesting heavy metals, sustaining a brain trauma, or a high fever can produce ADHD-like behavior. If children have lived in situations where heavy metals are common, then a blood test is indicated. Physicians should question the parents carefully about incidents of brain trauma and high fevers. Information about whether the brain trauma resulted in unconsciousness and for how long should be sought. Brain scans can help determine the level and location of some brain damage.

Tourette's is a neurological disorder that can exacerbate the problems of children with ADHD. Fifty percent of the children diagnosed with Tourette's also have ADHD. Tourette's disorder is a tic disorder that involves involuntary movement of muscle groups of the face and upper torso. In some individuals, there is also a vocal tic, where sounds or words are stated in a rather explosive manner and may include obscenities. The tics happen more frequently under stress.

A complicating factor for children with ADHD and Tourette's is that the stimulant drug treatment for ADHD may increase the severity and frequency of the motor tics. The physician's observations in the office and questioning the parent about the tics should be sufficient to diagnose Tourette's.

Medications and Substance Abuse

Prescription drugs, as well as nonprescription drugs, may magnify the problem behaviors of children with ADHD. A careful questioning about usage of prescription drugs and nonprescription drugs is necessary and their impact on the child. There are too many prescription drugs to list all of those that could be problematic, so we will mention only a few. Phenobarbital produces increased hyperactivity and impulsiveness in some children with ADHD, rather than sedating them. Some asthma medications produce ADHD-like behavior.

It is especially important to question a child who is over ten about nonprescription drugs. When obtaining this information, ask directly and without a judgmental tone which drugs are preferred and their impact. Ask directly and without judgment, and children with ADHD will more freely give information about their drug use and abuse. Alcohol is the drug of choice for individuals with ADHD and increases the problems of impulsiveness and aggression.

Sometimes long-term drug abuse can mimic ADHD. One fifteen-year-old boy had been smoking marijuana regularly from age eight. Each time he had a strong feeling, he would "smoke it away." Forced to give up his drug while in treatment, he acted like an impulsive child. He did not have ADHD; he simply had not learned to deal with his feelings. In a few months, he learned to better deal with his feelings.

If the physician thinks the child is abusing, then a referral can be made to an agency that specializes in that problem.

Immune System

Demographic data indicates that children with ADHD have higher rates of allergies and asthma than average.[22] Many children with ADHD do not cope well with situations that they find irritating. They become more difficult to be around when irritants are present. Allergies and asthma are sources of irritation. It would be important to ascertain the severity of allergy and asthma problems and provide treatment that minimizes their impact on the child.

Sensory Problems

Children that are challenging may have uncorrected poor vision and/or undiagnosed hearing deficits, which can result in the child exhibiting ADHD-like behavior. If children cannot see or hear adequately, they may be inattentive and appear uninterested in schoolwork. They may also become very frustrated because they misunderstand and fail at tasks. Frustrated because they misunderstand and fail at tasks, they express themselves with anger and acting out. A simple hearing or vision test can rule out the more serious sensory problems.

A seven-year-old boy was kicked out of several classrooms because of his severe acting-out problems. He was thought to be ADHD. In reality, he was totally deaf and constantly frustrated. The hearing problem could not be changed, but when teaching became visual in nature, his ADHD-like behavior disappeared.

Sleep Deprivation

Sleep deprivation can cause and magnify behavioral problems. Impulsivity and negative attention-getting behaviors increase dramatically when children with ADHD become fatigued. Asking the parent specific questions about bedtime behavior and the amount of time the child is sleeping each night will often clarify the problem. If there is a problem in getting more sleep, it can be often solved with behavioral techniques.

Enuresis

Bedwetting is a common problem among young children, especially boys. The physician will probably not need to ask about this problem because it is high on most parents' priority list. Approximately 30 percent of children with ADHD have nocturnal enuresis, a problem controlling urine at night.[23] Most of the time, there is no physical problem with the urinary system that requires medical intervention. A good medical exam will determine if a medical intervention is necessary.

Enuresis can create anger and frustration for parents and create negative family dynamics. A parent may only view the child's bedwetting as laziness or defiance. When parents are negative and emotional with a child that has ADHD, it usually is more difficult to manage.

Physical and Sexual Abuse

Children who have ADHD are at a higher risk for physical and sexual abuse.[24] They are more likely to be physically abused because they are more frustrating for adults to manage and because there is an increased probability that one of the parents is also ADHD and therefore impulsive. Care needs to be taken about labeling the adult as abusive, however, because these children have more accidents than other children and appear more frequently in emergency rooms. They have little fear and do not plan safe ways of playing; therefore, they hurt themselves frequently. If the child has ADHD, asking him directly about bruises will often produce direct and honest responses about how he got them. For example, "You have lots of bruises! How did you get that biggest one?"

We are not certain why they have a higher rate of being sexually abused, but it could be because they are more adventuresome and tend to pay less attention to social rules.

Understanding the dynamics of abuse can help separate children who are acting out because of being abused and children who have ADHD. If the physician suspects the child is being abused, then a referral can be made to an agency that specializes in that problem.[25]

7

Educational Evaluation

An educational evaluation requires the coordinator to assess the child's academic performance, social behavior, and the school's philosophy regarding challenging behavior. Specifically, the coordinator evaluates the child's challenging behavior to determine why, when, and where it occurs. The evaluation process utilizes questionnaires, direct observation, and educational testing. Questionnaires found in the Appendix were expressly developed for evaluating ADHD in the educational setting. These questionnaires gather information from the teacher's perspective about the child's problem and positive behaviors, along with pinpointing when and where these behaviors occur. The child's teacher(s) also complete another questionnaire designed to collect information regarding the child's classroom learning environment. Academic completion and accuracy rates in specific subjects are gathered by a questionnaire. Collecting observational data about the school philosophy, teaching style, and the child's behavior in the school environment is described. Educational testing may be necessary to determine if the child is having academic problems because of learning disabilities, knowledge deficits and/or skills. This information collected from the educational evaluation helps determine if the child has ADHD or other learning disabilities and if the school environment is attenuating or exacerbating the challenging behaviors.

Initial Conference with School Personnel

The parent and the evaluation coordinator request a meeting with school personnel (teacher, administrator, school psychologist, and special-education director) to discuss the challenging child after questionnaires and school records have been obtained. The coordinator's goals for this meeting are to build rapport for teamwork by listening to their concerns and any ongoing attempts to remediate the challenging behavior and also to review questionnaire data, school records, and discuss any discrepancies between home and school evaluative information. The coordinator explains the process of the ongoing evaluation and the necessity of classroom observation. A classroom observation time is agreed upon.

The initial meeting also provides an opportunity to understand the school's philosophy regarding challenging children. The philosophy of the school toward challenging behavior is extremely important to determine, because *not* all schools fit the definition of a beneficial environment. In a school meeting with teachers, counselors, and the principal, their philosophy is often easy to observe. A philosophy which suggests that the challenging child must learn to fit into the existing structure of the school system may be stated very openly by the staff. If the philosophy is "we don't need to change," even though the child is having failure experiences, then in this early stage of evaluation, the question of whether the child needs to be moved to another school should be discussed with the parents.

School Observations

Objective observations as a diagnostic tool provide factual statements rather than subjective interpretations about the child's behavior, teaching style, and school environment and philosophy. The observational data obtained either corroborates previously collected subjective information or helps clarify any incongruent information between home and school. Objective observations also provide more concrete information about why, when, and where challenging behaviors occur.

In order to obtain objective behavioral observations which are representative of the usual dynamics, certain steps need to be taken. First, the teacher informs the children that an observer is coming to visit and will not be talking with them. Second, the observer quietly enters the area and avoids eye contact with the children and teacher. Without eye contact, the children and teacher rapidly forget about a new presence. Third, the observer takes a position where the child and teacher can be easily observed. Fourth, the observer prepares in advance a checklist to systematically collect information about the environment, child, and peer and teacher interactions.

School Observational Checklist

Observation of the child

- Count the number of times directions are followed after one request.___
- Count the number of positive___ and negative___ peer interactions.
- Count the number of talk-outs when hand-raising is the rule.___
- Count the number of times the child requests help.___
- Count the number of in-class assignments completed.___

Observation of the teacher

- Does the teacher have an organized and systematic educational program? Y__N__
- Percentage of classroom time in action learning. Low___ Medium___ High___
- Does the teacher consistently give precise one- or two-step instructions? Y__N__
- Count the number of verbal or nonverbal incentives given to the child.___
- Count the number of punishments or negative statements said to the child.___
- Count the number of times the child gets attention for negative behavior.___
- Count the number of times the child gets attention for positive behavior.___

Observation of classroom structure

- How many children are in the classroom? ___
- How many disruptive children are in the classroom? ___
- How many aides or helpers are in the classroom? ___
- Is the aide's or helper's behavior consistent with the teacher's style? Y___N___
- How many classroom disruptions are there from outside influences? ___
- How is the physical space of the classroom organized? Draw a picture.

After reviewing the observational information, ask the following questions. The answers to these questions assist in making an accurate diagnosis and provide valuable information for future interventions.

1. Does the information support a diagnosis of ADHD?
2. Are discrepancies between home and school reports better understood?
3. Is the teaching style exacerbating or attenuating challenging behavior?
4. Is the physical environment exacerbating or attenuating challenging behavior?
5. Are peer interactions exacerbating or attenuating challenging behavior?

Observation One

During one observation period, it became apparent that the teacher was organized and effectively used action learning. Most amazing was the number of positive statements she made to the students individually and as groups. There had been confusion about a diagnosis because the teacher reported few problems and the parents reported many. During a three-hour observation period, the teacher made seventy positive statements to the entire class. Because the children were so engaged in learning activities and positively rewarded, there were no problem behaviors present. At one point, the children spontaneously let out a cheer of enthusiasm. What a wonderful teacher; we wanted to clone her! This teacher was so effective that she attenuated many of the problems associated with ADHD.

Observation Two

Another teacher was observed for an equal period of time and only negative statements were made to the challenging child. When the observation was brought to her attention in a very gentle fashion, she asked for assistance in making appropriate changes. A later observation confirmed that she had changed her teaching approach.

Observation Three

Observation of a third teacher produced disturbing information. This teacher was disorganized and unaware of her behavior's impact on the children. Children were rewarded for not following rules and frequently punished if they did follow the rules. For example, the teacher gave the instruction: "Clean up around your desk and then raise your hand. I will then let you be first in line to go out to play." Half the class jumped to their feet and rushed to be first in line without any cleaning up around their desks. She allowed them to leave first, and the students who followed the instructions were last to leave. Almost the entire class appeared to have ADHD. The teacher was training them to behave in an ADHD style. Her observations of appropriate or inappropriate behavior were not reliable. A suggestion was given to immediately remove the child from the classroom. She was terminated from her employment before the end of her contract year.

Academic Performance

The challenging behavior of some children may arise or be exacerbated by a deficit in academic skills. Review skill test(s), the Educational Performance Questionnaire, classroom work, and teacher observations to help determine if the challenging behavior is caused by ADHD, by academic skill deficits, or whether both are present. Many children with ADHD have deficits in the skills necessary for academic achievement because of the disabilities inherent in ADHD. Additionally, approximately 30 percent of children with ADHD also have a coexisting learning disorder[26], which further impairs their ability to learn math and/or language skills. The school psychologist can help separate out the influences of ADHD skill deficits and/or learning disabilities by individually re-testing with incentives for performance, and also by giving specific learning disorder test(s) in the subject areas where the child is struggling. When the child's test scores significantly improve, a diagnosis of ADHD is supported. However, if with re-testing there is no or little improvement, consider other causes such as a learning disability. Further testing to delineate learning disorders is advisable.

Summary

A complete educational evaluation helps in determining the presence of ADHD, the appropriateness of the school, teacher effectiveness, and if any learning disabilities are present. In the process of completing an educational evaluation, a clear understanding of the child's academic needs is developed. The coordinator of the evaluation process facilitates building a bridge between home and school whether or not the child has ADHD.

8

Family Evaluation

The mental health specialist will probably be in the best position to evaluate the family and have ongoing interaction to obtain further clarifying information. The family-evaluation section addresses several areas of familial information that assist in making an accurate diagnosis.

Genetic History

It is clear genetics play a role in the development of ADHD; therefore, the family history assists in making the diagnosis. The families of children with ADHD are more likely to have a history of certain disorders. The most frequently found are ADHD, antisocial, histrionic, borderline, and mood disorders. These psychiatric disorders are described in the *Diagnostic and Statistical Manual of Mental Disorders*. Some of the characteristics that these disorders have in common are impulsivity and dramatic mood fluctuations.

Children who are diagnosed with ADHD frequently have a biological father who has ADHD. It has often not been diagnosed formally in the fathers, but a few questions can help determine if the father has some of the characteristics. The following questions will help ascertain if the biological father has/had ADHD behaviors: How did his mother describe her ability to manage him? How did he perform in school? How did the school grades compare to estimated ability? What was the number of times he got detention at school? Did he drop out of high school? Was he sexually precocious? Has he had difficulty staying employed? Has he had difficulty maintaining intimate relationships? Has he had difficulty with law-enforcement agencies? Does he now seem self-centered and impulsive? Does he seem to be a responsible adult? The father is probably a genetic carrier of ADHD if there is a similar profile to that of a child with ADHD. Similar questions can be asked about the mother or other relatives who might also be genetic carriers. If the child is adopted, statistical information indicates a much higher frequency of ADHD present in the child.

Parents' Stressors

It is important to determine if ongoing stressors or traumatic events occurring in the family are triggering ADHD-like behavior in the child. The Parents' Stress Indicator Questionnaire, found in the Appendix, addresses numerous stressful life experiences. Elaboration of responses might be helpful to completely understand the circumstances and the direct effects on the child.

Some stressors alone and some in combination can make the child appear to have ADHD. Careful consideration of the child's subculture also needs to be examined before making a diagnosis. For example, a child living with a single parent in a crime-ridden neighborhood with few financial and familial resources may seem to have ADHD, when he may simply be responding to his environment.

After some traumatic events, a child may temporarily present ADHD-like behaviors. For example, a first-grade boy was referred for evaluation by his schoolteacher. The teacher reported the boy had unfinished work and a defiant attitude. His mother reported he was uncooperative and had frequent outbursts of anger. These problems started eighteen months earlier, after a marital separation. Prior to the marital separation, there were no serious behavioral problems. The boy was extremely close to his father but had no further contact with him after the separation. After the mother remarried, the boy no longer presented serious behavioral problems. Again, history allows the separation of behavior triggered by trauma and ADHD. ADHD is a stable set of behaviors over an extended period of time and it is not a problem precipitated by stress.

Parenting Style

Today, the literature[27] contains descriptions of three parenting styles: authoritarian, authoritative, and laissez-faire (permissive). Authoritarian tends to be negative in nature, with inflexible rules and few rewards or compromises. Authoritative has clear rules with clear consequences and discussions that allow some input from the child. Laissez-faire is a parenting style that gives the child a lot of freedom to choose. The rules are not clearly specified and the child often helps make the rules. The authoritarian and the laissez-faire styles make problems more severe if the child has ADHD, and the authoritative style tends to attenuate the problems.

To determine the dominant parenting style of the parents, ask the following question: "What rules do you have in your house, and how are they enforced?" Ask them to give a description of a situation that is difficult for them to handle with the child and how they resolved the situation. A good example of a difficult time for many of the parents revolves around getting ready for bed. The individuals who use an authoritarian style report that many rules and punishment will be the dominant method of dealing with infractions. The laissez-faire approach will have few rules and use an unsystematic approach to consequences. Parents using the authoritative style have a limited number of rules and will use reward to get compliance more frequently.

Obtaining information regarding the frequency of punishment used by parents further assists in determining the parenting style. If there are two primary parents, ask them to keep a record of each other's use of punishment. Explain to the parents the difference between direct punishment and indirect punishment and ask them to keep a count of their use with the child. Direct punishment is something like spanking, taking away privileges, and having their child do an unpleasant task. Indirect punishments are usually inferred by the statements we make to the child that are demeaning. A few examples are: "Why can't you be like your sister?" (Inferred, "you dummy"); "Why can't you listen?" (Inferred, "you dummy"); or "Can't you ever get it right?" (Inferred, "you dummy"). Sometimes parents have stopped keeping tally after two days because they were so upset about the negative messages they were sending to the child. Others have shed tears when they realized the extent of their negativity toward the child. The more severe the ADHD, the more negative messages a child is likely to receive from the parents. Having a clear picture of the frequency of punishment will be important as interventions are developed.

Sibling Dynamics

Family dynamics can exacerbate or attenuate ADHD. Certain sibling interactions' patterns can increase the severity of ADHD. These styles are a part of the Structured Interview Questionnaire. The five negative styles are the following: scapegoating/blaming; protective/caretaking; confrontational/combative; acquiescent/give-in; and avoidant/ignoring. An example of scapegoating is when Harry's brother, John, provokes Harry, who then loses his temper and gets punished. An example of an avoidant style is when a brother spends increasingly longer periods of time away from home, in another room, or outdoors and is not available during the times the sibling acts out behaviorally. An example of an acquiescent interaction style is when the child with ADHD is told he cannot have the squirt gun that belongs to his brother. He throws the "super-duper scream, yell, and kick tantrum," and the brother agrees to give him the gun to end the tantrum. There is also a sixth style that is helpful and constructive. It is described as supportive/encouraging. The sibling makes positive statements to the challenging sibling when there is appropriate behavior. To observe the sibling interaction styles in the office, play a game with the sibling that focuses on losing and winning. In other words, introduce some competition between siblings. Based on your observations and parent reports, determine the dominant style of each sibling.

Sometimes the information obtained in the office is not congruent with the information given by verbal reports from parents. A large discrepancy may require a home visit to understand more fully the family dynamics. A home visit can help further clarify the parenting style, the sibling interaction styles, and the stresses found in the home environment.

While collecting familial information, it is convenient to ask and observe the following areas, which help develop treatment interventions.

Intellectual Functioning

Like the children that are of concern, the parents vary in intellectual ability and in addition may vary greatly in ability to understand remediation instructions regarding the child. It is useful to know their level of education and performance level in school. If the parent is poorly educated, has low verbal abilities and lowered intellectual functioning, then the method of training and expectations of professionals need to be modified.

Self-Confidence

If the parent has low self-esteem, helping them feel successful with the child might be the most significant intervention. Negative responses occur more frequently in homes where the parents do not have a positive image of themselves. It is difficult for a parent to positively reinforce an ADHD child if they are unable to positively reinforce themselves. Evaluating their self-confidence is possible during an interview. A person with low self-esteem will usually ask for more reassurance and will make more self-deprecating statements.

Economic Resources

Assessing financial resources will help determine the degree to which money will be a factor in selecting treatment options.

If the parents have sound economic resources, they may be able to purchase all kinds of assistance and positive reinforcements, e.g., babysitters, sports, video games, special outings, and cars. A single parent with a low income will need help to find rewards and assistance that are less expensive.

Support System

A support system is a network of family and/or friends who are willing to support and hopefully assist the parents in parenting the child with ADHD. Ideally, they should be willing at times to babysit, be a sounding board, and offer encouragement and nurturing.

Self-Care

Determine if the major caregivers for the child are using stress-reducing techniques such as, but not limited to, the following: regular physical activity, meditation, relaxation, spiritual connections, healthy diet, and adequate sleep.

9

Diagnostic Summary

The purpose of the evaluation is to make an accurate diagnosis. The evaluation also provides valuable information for developing and implementing a treatment plan.

To make a formal diagnosis of ADHD, all the following areas need to be reviewed:

- Does the child fit the diagnostic criteria in the DSM IV-TR for ADHD?
- Is there a family pattern of ADHD—for example, from the biological parents and aunts and uncles of the child?
- Does the information from school and home questionnaires reflect a similar pattern of ADHD behaviors?
- Are ADHD problem behaviors less apparent when the child is in a one-to-one relationship with an adult?
- During first grade, were significantly more problems reported?
- Do parents, teachers, and peers report disliking the child?
- Are there reports of frequent violations of the psychological and physical boundaries of others?
- Do the parents report that the child requires more energy to manage than other children?
- Do teachers report the child requires more energy to manage than other children?
- Is the child easier to manage when organized action-learning strategies are used?
- Is the child emotionally more like a child half their chronological age?
- Are ADHD behaviors more pronounced in unstructured situations?

Based on this summary of information from observations, questionnaires, history of the child and family, medical examinations, and test results, it is possible to diagnose a specific type of ADHD and severity level (mild, moderate, or severe). Coexisting disorders and exacerbating conditions can also be specified.

Notes

Part Three

Treatment

10

Overview of Treatment

Finally, following all of the information gathering and a diagnosis, this section provides information about how a multidisciplinary team makes treatment plans which foster constructive changes for a child with ADHD. It would be fantastic if we had the knowledge to cure children with ADHD. However, at this point in time, the best anyone can do is to help them be more successful. The majority of these children continue to exhibit ADHD characteristics into adulthood, although with less severity. Treatment interventions do not cure, but many children with ADHD lead very successful adult lives due to early and ongoing appropriate interventions. Think of this as a long-term adventure where pacing, patience, and persistence pay off.

The evaluation process provides information that lays the framework for treatment since a more comprehensive understanding of the child and their environment was acquired. The Treatment Assessment Summary Questionnaire, found in the Appendix, is designed to help organize this information. The information gathered during the evaluation guides the development of the individualized treatment plan and should include the following data:

- Intellectual, social, and academic skills of the child
- Completion rates of school work
- Severity and type of ADHD
- Major contact people for the child
- Family dynamics and resources
- School dynamics and resources
- Situations in which the child has the most difficulty
- Situations in which the child has the most success
- Information about complicating medical conditions
- Information about complicating learning disorders

A multidisciplinary treatment team is formed, which helps communicate new information that updates the Treatment Assessment Summary Questionnaire as circumstances change for the child. The updated information allows the team to develop relevant interventions in multiple areas of the child's life (home, school, and neighborhood). The child's chance of being successful increases academically and socially when there is a consistent approach across situations and people. A multidisciplinary team also increases objectivity and creativity through group problem-solving, which increases the development of proactive interventions. Additionally, the team members provide an ongoing source of significant emotional support for each other.

The MHP teaches the team several principles to remember when developing any treatment interventions. The team learns the importance of being proactive and to utilize depersonalization skills and formulate appropriate behavioral expectations. These principles, when applied, ensure realistic treatment goals and successful interventions.

The team needs to have a similar understanding of the child, the impact of ADHD, and the types of possible and multiple interventions. A treatment plan can only be as good as the team's knowledge, skills, and motivation. The team members will be able to create a treatment plan when they understand the general principles and rationale underlying the different types and combinations of interventions (medical, structural, behavioral). The MHP is the primary team member that facilitates and educates other team members about this information and the overall treatment philosophy. It is imperative that the MHP establish an environment which promotes trust, openness, and caring. This non-judgmental and supportive environment also encourages team members to take risks as they attempt challenging or new interventions.

To further educate the team members about how to apply potential interventions, a section on common and enduring problems associated with ADHD is highlighted to provide quick reference to assist teams struggling with these challenging areas. An additional section illustrates case studies with individuals from childhood into adulthood, which provides a long-term vision to guide team efforts.

A section is devoted to self-care for those involved with a child having ADHD. Good self-care is essential to sustain the long-term effort. The emotional impact of guilt, grief, frustration, and exhaustion must be offset with good self-care.

It is important to read the entire treatment section before developing an individualized treatment plan. Reading the entire section provides a comprehensive understanding about the best place to start intervening, how much to take on, and how to implement a realistic treatment plan. A page for notes is at the end of this section to write questions or ideas about treatment, which can be discussed with team members.

11

Multidisciplinary Treatment Team

Organizing a multidisciplinary treatment team, who formulates and implements the treatment plans, is the initial step of treatment. This may seem daunting and overwhelming, so this process is described in detail. The parent is responsible for initiating treatment for their child and choosing which professional(s) will be on the treatment team. How are team members chosen? How does the team function? What are the goals, roles, and expectations of the team members?

A few clinics around the country specialize in treating ADHD using a multidisciplinary treatment team and treatment principles consistent with our approach. These clinics have mental health professionals, teachers, consulting physicians, parents, and children working together at the same location. This arrangement is advantageous as it easily allows for regular communication between all the professional staff and parents. Clinic staff members teach behavioral management interventions to the parents and teachers. The behavioral training stresses the importance of consistency when behavioral interventions are implemented. These clinics also conduct ongoing research to evaluate the effectiveness of their interventions. Research can determine if there is an ADHD treatment clinic in close proximity. It would be important to verify that the particular clinic follows similar treatment principles. An organization named Children and Adults with Attention Deficit Hyperactivity Disorder (CHADD) is a good place to start.

If an ADHD treatment clinic is not an option, it is still possible to build a multidisciplinary treatment team resembling a clinic's team. The team-building process begins with the parent's choice of a mental health professional specializing in ADHD. The evaluating mental health professional is usually the best choice. Using this person is helpful because they already have substantial information about the child, school, and home life. If a different mental health professional is chosen, then it is imperative they be given all of the evaluation information. If parents are unable to visit a mental health professional due to cost or unavailability, a team can still be formed. The parent can seek information about which school counselor or school psychologist has good skills to assist with a team and invite them join the team. The parent can be more assertive with staff at the physician's office by asking for more assistance. The team may be more loosely connected than is ideal, but this arrangement is better than no team.

Initially, parent(s) and the mental health professional make up the treatment team. The parents and the mental health professional together evaluate the school, teachers, and physician for effectiveness and appropriateness. The evaluation information provides guidance about further invitations onto the team. For example, if the evaluation has provided data indicating that the current teacher is not an appropriate choice for the child, then asking them to be a part of the team would be counterproductive. In this case, the parent and mental health professional can work together to select a new teacher for the child. Once a physician is chosen, the parent contacts them to determine their willingness to participate on a treatment team. The physician usually agrees to regular visits with the parent and telephone contact with the rest of the team members.

The parent, who has had previous contact with the teacher, is in the best position to invite the teacher(s) onto the team. If the child has multiple teachers, include the teacher(s) most interested in helping the child. Ultimately, the team may consist of aides, siblings, neighbors, school psychologists, counselors, principals, grandparents, and others on an "as-needed basis". Too large of a team, however, can become unmanageable.

Roles of Team Members

The multidisciplinary team collaborates best if roles and objectives are clearly defined and communicated. The team generally meets at the school or the mental health professional's office. If the team cannot meet physically together, communication by phone, mail, or e-mail is acceptable.

The mental health professional roles are facilitator, mediator, and educator. The mental health professional facilitates the team meetings by organizing the agenda, keeping the team focused, and mediating any team conflict. The mental health professional develops and keeps team cohesion by providing emotional support and encouragement, specifically through the use of verbal incentives. In the role of facilitator, the mental health professional also helps initiate and revise the treatment plan. The mental health professional acts as a mediator with authority figures outside of the treatment team, such as the police and firemen. In the role of educator, the mental health professional teaches the team about ADHD and the ongoing impact of the disorder. If there is not a common understanding of the impact of negative interpersonal interactions, it is almost impossible to develop an appropriate and positive treatment plan. Also, a lack of understanding can produce inconsistency and miscommunication within the treatment team. The mental health professional describes and demonstrates various treatment options, the need for proactive treatment interventions, and appropriate use of behavioral techniques.

The parents' primary role is to advocate for the child. They act as the major communications people, setting up a communication system between home and school that occurs daily or weekly. The parent supervises the administration of medication and observation of medicine's impact. Parents provide feedback to the team about the child's behavior and the effect (success or failure) of the treatment intervention. In order to maintain effective team participation, parents have to practice good self-care.

The child, as a part of the team, should have some understanding of the disorder and his or her role in treatment. The MHP educates the child, which helps prevent using the disorder as an escape from personal responsibility. We suggest an explanation that is simple and offers assistance to the child but still gives them responsibility to change their behavior. For example:

> "Have you noticed it is hard for you to … (choose a task that is frustrating for the child, e.g., sitting still, homework)? You have a special brain that works differently than most other children, and it is called ADHD. The front part of your brain (point to the forehead) works at a slower speed. The way your brain works makes some tasks easier for you to do and it makes some other tasks more difficult. You will have to work harder on the difficult tasks, and we will help you learn new ways to do them. Sometimes, we use a medicine that speeds up this part of your brain and makes things get easier for you. Between your hard work and ours, you will do better."

The child is encouraged to ask questions about the disorder and treatment interventions. She can provide the team with valuable information about which incentives motivate her. The older the child, the more she will be able to constructively participate in treatment.

The primary role of teachers and their aides is to provide a structured action-orientated learning environment. They also help develop and implement behavioral interventions for problem behaviors and provide feedback to the physician and parents. Teachers and aides will have to practice good self-care to maintain effective team participation.

The physician's role is to collaborate with the team members and provide education about medical interventions. They also provide information regarding any medical conditions which might complicate other treatment interventions. The physician collaborates with team members about medication management and sets up a medication intervention feedback system. For example, if the physician changes the medication, letting other team members know can make them feel included and increases the probability that they will give feedback about the impact of the medication change. The physician can also offer support and encouragement to the parents' efforts.

Siblings on the team provide valuable information. They have a child's point of view of what is happening in the family that is different than the adults'. Siblings have access to information, especially when parents are not present, and offer unique insights into the family dynamics. They can also provide information about what incentives are most effective.

All team members can play a role in assessing needs and looking for additional resources for home and school. They may be able to identify financial, emotional, educational, and health resources that provide additional and flexible treatment options. Some team members may have specific knowledge of how to recruit and maintain extra help for school and home by recruiting volunteer aides or volunteer childcare workers. Some potential sources for volunteer help are listed below.

- College students majoring in a human service field
- Senior citizens
- High school students seeking volunteer hours
- "Natural helper" programs (students who help their peers)

As new individuals are invited onto the team, their roles need to be discussed and clarified. Some individuals are sensitive to the intrusion of anyone into their professional territory and those sensitivities will have to be considered as plans and role expectations are developed. Keeping regular communication will help limit problems. If team members give each other regular positive feedback about their involvement, then the team stays positive and cohesive. Team-building needs to be an ongoing process.

Understanding and Utilizing the Principles of Depersonalization, Appropriate Behavioral Expectations, and Proactive Strategies

The ability to depersonalize, having appropriate behavioral expectations, and being proactive are fundamental to developing and implementing a treatment plan. In order for the team to objectively develop appropriate behavioral expectations, it is necessary to learn depersonalization skills which help ameliorate the strong emotions elicited by the child's problem behavior. The overwhelming feelings of frustration, guilt, and anger are normal and typical for anyone involved with a child having ADHD. It takes significant, ongoing effort to reduce the negative emotions directed toward the child. Reducing the negative feelings through depersonalization will allow us to make more thoughtful and productive responses. Focusing on determining the child's intentions ("He just wants to push my buttons!") does not allow depersonalization and tends to make the relationship adversarial. If the parents or teachers attach negative intentions to the child's behavior, then objectivity is lost and interventions are now driven by strong negative feelings. If reactions to the child are strong negative feelings or behaviors, then the child's ability to have destructive power is strengthened, leading to a fiery power struggle.

Depersonalization is not occurring if one is constantly verbalizing or thinking about the child with words like lazy, mean, and stupid. A child with ADHD has never been and will never be motivated by calling them lazy, mean, or stupid. Using or thinking these words suggests the child's misbehavior is being viewed as intentional. If the adult does not depersonalize their negative feelings and responses toward the child, then the child's problem behaviors will increase. The negative feelings and responses of the child and adults intensify and the negative cycle continues.

To increase the team member's ability to depersonalize, those interacting with the child must learn to become aware of and modify their self-talk about the child and also practice effective self-care. The most important self-talk change is to eliminate the idea of "intentionality" of misbehavior, e.g., "You lost your homework on purpose." Trying to determine which misbehavior is a reflection of the disability and which is intentional is futile and impedes appropriate interventions. Besides being an impossible task, it usually turns into a negative cycle. To help reduce the impulse of blaming, repeat the self-talk phrase: "The child's behavior is a product of a disability; it is not intentional," and then the negative feelings toward the child will dissipate. Self-talk needs to be positive, frequent, and forgiving toward yourself and the child. The other method to help reduce strong negative feelings is to practice effective self-care. Practicing good self-care focuses on monitoring **S**elf-confidence, **O**omph, and **S**upport (S-O-S). A later chapter is dedicated on how to practice good self-care for those sending an S-O-S "I need help" message.

Keys to Depersonalization

- Emotional reactivity produces negativity—*act, don't react.*
- Monitor self-talk and replace negative with positive.
- Focus on behavior, not perceived intentions.
- Good self-care empowers emotional control.

After learning how to depersonalize your feelings about the child's behavior, then appropriate behavioral expectations can be generated for treatment. Formulating appropriate behavioral expectations ensures realistic treatment goals and successful interventions. For example, a child who has dyslexia, lives with a single parent, and attends a school where the teacher is rotated monthly would have a different set of expectations than a child who has many resources available. Creating appropriate behavioral expectations for the child, family, school, and team is continually reevaluated as circumstances change.

The team uses four specific guidelines when formulating appropriate behavioral expectations. First, start the process by dividing the child's chronological age in half to reflect their emotional maturity age (adjusted age). For example, a twelve-year-old child with ADHD would need some of the age-appropriate behavioral expectations for a *typical* six-year-old. *Second,* this "adjusted age" can be increased or decreased depending on the severity of the ADHD, other complicating disorders, and intelligence. *Third,* the child's ability to think abstractly indicates his capacity to follow instructions which contain abstract words. If there is a problem with the ability to abstract, they will perform at a lower developmental age. A case in point: the child is told to "be kind." "Being kind" is an abstract concept with complex behavioral expectations. If the child has difficulty understanding abstract concepts, then the instructions should be more concrete and stated in behavioral terms, for example, telling a child, "It would 'be kind' if you let your friend take a turn with the toy."

Fourth, this "adjusted age" is modified according to the ability to remain focused on a task when receiving delayed incentives (delayed gratification). This ability typically increases as a function of maturation. Parents and teachers are often confused about the child's ability to remain focused on a task because in one situation, an hour of focus may be sustained, whereas in a second situation, the child stops focusing after five minutes. This inconsistent information about the child's ability to focus makes determining appropriate behavioral expectations difficult. The child's ability to stay focused is affected by both the task and the incentive offered. The child's ability to stay focused can only be accurately determined if both the task and the incentive are evaluated. For example, a child waits in line for ten minutes without misbehaving to earn the incentive of getting to be the team captain at recess. If this same child is asked to wait ten minutes in the lunch line, where the incentive is food and they are not hungry, misbehavior is likely to occur. The task of waiting in line is the same, but the incentives are very different, which means the expectations will have to be different.

The ability to delay gratification can be tested for specific situations. It is crucial to experiment using an already proven incentive to determine whether the requests are reasonable. For example, if a six-year-old child can work quietly at their desk for fifteen minutes before immediately getting a hot fudge sundae, then there is a reasonable estimate of her ability to wait in *similar* situations. The key is to not generalize to situations that are not similar in nature; for instance, waiting in line for fifteen minutes for a turn to kick a soccer ball (a less desirable incentive) is not a similar situation.

These four guidelines are continually reviewed when developing new appropriate behavioral expectations. Failure for the team and child is guaranteed when these guidelines are not considered.

After age-appropriate behavioral expectations are established using these guidelines, it is often difficult to consistently apply them in treatment plans. Parents and teachers understandably start to question and/or forget the established behavioral expectations because they feel the child is intentionally under-performing or maliciously disregarding instructions. For example, many parents say, "But my six-year-old can play Nintendo for hours, so he has the ability to focus for a long time." However, adults may not realize playing Nintendo provides structure, continual stimulation and has built in consistent, gratifying incentives, which are necessary to motivate a child with ADHD to sustain focus. As another example, parents say, "But my child *will decide* not to do his homework, have a fit and tear up his work, even though we promised him his favorite candy bar as soon as he was done." If the parents perceive the child's actions as intentional rather than an unsuccessful intervention, then the negative cycle returns.

Appropriate Behavioral Expectations
- Emotional maturity and chronological age are different
- Adjusted age expectations are impacted by:
  - Severity of disorder
  - Intellectual ability
  - Other complications (learning disorders)
  - Ability to abstract
  - Ability to sustain focus and delay gratification
- Test ability in specific situations to delay gratification with proven incentives and only generalize to similar situations

---

Developing appropriate behavioral expectations and using depersonalization skills allows the team to create proactive strategies that anticipate and prevent problem behaviors and/or decrease automatic negative responses. Proactive interventions are more successful because they include plans or strategies to deal with strong emotional responses in both the child and the adult. The greater the severity of the ADHD, the more important the need is for proactive strategies.

Proactive Strategies
- Train yourself to anticipate challenges and develop strategies:
  - For new and future situations
  - For reoccurring situations
- Know your limits—have realistic expectations about your ability to implement a plan.
- Utilize the team.

Examples of Proactive Interventions

- A junior-high student with severe ADHD is given permission to leave the classroom five minutes early to avoid all the confusion and potential negative interactions in the hallway. He is also rewarded for getting to the next class on time. This simple proactive intervention dramatically reduces misbehavior.
- A six-year-old girl with a moderate form of ADHD is physically aggressive. The mother has protected the one-year-old sister by keeping them physically separated when she is busy.

12

Medical Treatment Interventions

Medical treatment involves much more than just giving a child a dose of medication. Everyone involved in the lives of children with ADHD needs education about when, why, and how to properly use medication and what positive changes can be expected. This section provides medical education and describes the roles played by team members regarding medical interventions.

Using Medication

A decision to use medication for ADHD in addition to other types of interventions should always be seriously considered and based primarily on the benefits to the child by well-informed parents. The parents' decision to use medication can be extremely difficult because they are exposed to conflicting information and/or emotionally loaded statements about medication (e.g., "You're a bad parent taking the easy way out," or "Medication is masking the problem."). The physician and MHP can help the parent make a more objective and informed decision about the use of medication.

The decision to use medication ought to be based on specific information about the child, the environment, and the interactive dynamics. This pertinent information is obtained from evaluations of the home and school environment, the severity of the disorder(s), and possible complications due to other medical conditions. There are an infinite number of possible scenarios for a child; therefore, examples of general situations and the interactive dynamics are described. If a child has a mild form of ADHD, an environment at home and school which is minimally competitive and complex and filled with action activities, structure, and frequent rewards, the need for medication is reduced. Behavioral management techniques may be all that is required in this situation. However, if the child's school situation is very negative with a teacher not open or willing to using behavioral techniques and there are no other educational options, then medicating at school would be advisable. If the school provides a positive environment for a child with mild ADHD but the home environment is chaotic and complex with minimal available resources, then medicating the child at home but not at school would be beneficial. If the child has a moderate to severe level of ADHD, then the medication along with behavioral and structural techniques should be used at home and school. Some children are so difficult that working with them without medication is counterproductive.

If a parent is reluctant to use medication as an intervention when it has been professionally advised after a *careful* evaluation, then the physician needs to listen carefully to the parents' concerns and explore the source of their resistance. Often the parents' reluctance comes from misinformation, which commonly comes from untrue or exaggerated stories about the danger and damage of medications. Most misinformation is about stimulants, the most frequently used type of ADHD medication. Where and why the misinformation developed is difficult to ascertain. At one point in recent history, Congress even formally investigated these rumors of injury by stimulant medication. The investigation concluded that stimulants which have been studied and used for more than fifty years are safe and effective for children with ADHD when used appropriately.[28]

Common Myths

Myth: Stimulant medication will stunt the growth of the child.

Fact: Ample evidence has been collected to verify that receiving stimulant medication lowers the level of growth hormones while the drug is in the bloodstream. When the medication is out of the system, the child's system compensates with more growth hormone. The child receives enough growth hormone over his developmental life to reach his normal height.

Myth: Stimulant medication will increase chances of drug addiction.

Fact: Children with ADHD that are *not* treated with stimulant medication are 50 percent more likely to have addiction problems than children who are treated with stimulants.

Myth: Stimulant medications make zombies out of children.

Fact: Children that are medicated for ADHD by stimulants often talk less, sit more, and listen better. The child is changed and, when compared to previous behavior, may seem like a zombie but is now more like the average child.

Myth: Stimulants are just a plot for mind control.

Fact: Children with ADHD and medicated with stimulants are better able to think about what they are doing and are less likely to be talked into inappropriate behavior by others.

Myth: Caffeine is an effective treatment for ADHD.

Fact: Research clearly indicates that caffeine is not an effective treatment for children with ADHD.

---

29 30 31 32 33

Choosing a Medication

Stimulant medication is the medication of choice for children with ADHD because of its effectiveness. The research is clear; stimulant medication benefits approximately 70 to 90 percent of these challenging children by normalizing brain activity. The stimulant increases the brain's effectiveness and thus these children's effectiveness. Their attention span lengthens, their ability to follow directions increases, and their ability to remember rules improves. They stay on task longer at home and school. With less impulsivity, increased empathy, and more appropriate levels of guilt, their ability to sustain relationships improves.[34]

The stimulant medications frequently prescribed are: Ritalin™, Concerta™, Cylert™, Dexadrine™, Adderall™, Vyvanse™, and their generic counterparts.

> *Ritalin* (methylphenidate) comes in several forms: a short-acting pill, the sustained-release pill form, and a sustained-release patch. It has been used for many years, and the research about its effectiveness is extensive.
>
> *Concerta* (methylphenidate) comes in an extended-release form that initially releases about one-third of the medication and then the remaining is gradually released over the next ten hours, for a total of twelve hours.
>
> *Cylert* (pemoline) has the positive characteristic of only one pill a day and is effective for some children who do not respond positively to Ritalin. It does have additional side effects, which require that the child needs to be monitored more frequently by blood tests, which require additional time, effort, and money. Cylert is also different than sustained-release Ritalin in one important way. Cylert takes longer to reach therapeutic dosage in the bloodstream, but the level is sustained over a longer period of time once at a therapeutic level. Do not expect to see changes in behavior for several days after the medication has been started.
>
> *Dexadrine* (d-amphetamine) is a medication that has been used for more than forty years and has the same benefits as other stimulants. It also has similar side effects and is not very expensive in the generic form. After thirty minutes, it is in the bloodstream in therapeutic amounts and leaves the system rapidly. There is also extensive research about its effectiveness.
>
> *Adderall* (d-amphetamine and l-amphetamine) is a stimulant medication that became available in the late 1990s. It is a combination of stimulants and produces positive changes in children with ADHD similar to other stimulant medications. It also has similar side effects. It is produced in both the immediate-release form and the sustained-release form. The sustained-release form is used most frequently in children. It has become very popular since 1998 and now is one of the most frequently prescribed

medications for ADHD. The research on this medication is more limited because of its recent development.

Vyvanse (lisdexamfetamine dimesylate) was developed by Shire Pharmaceutical Company. It is a stimulant medication that was recently approved for use with children who have ADHD. It is a long-acting medication similar to Adderall XR. It is marketed in 30mg, 50mg, and 70mg capsules taken once a day. There is limited research about its effectiveness when compared to other stimulants because of the recent entrance into the market.

The process of selecting which stimulant medication to use can be confusing. Deciding whether to use the short-acting or sustained-release form presents additional challenges. All of the stimulants can produce significant improvement for children. Often the choice is decided by cost or by which medication is advertised most effectively and which one the physician has the most experience using. In some instances, a decision is partially based on external factors at home or school.

If a particular stimulant does not benefit a child, usually another is tried before a decision is made not to use them. In some children, a particular stimulant seems to gradually lose its effectiveness over long periods of time, and a different one is prescribed. Below is a list of advantages and disadvantages of using the short-acting or sustained-release form of stimulats.

Short-Acting

Advantages

- A child's behavior can show dramatic improvements within 30 minutes, and in a crisis situation, that is very reassuring.
- The medication has less impact on eating behavior if given after mealtime.
- The medication produces maximum assistance during school hours.
- The rapid modification of behavior helps convince resistant parents of the effectiveness of medication.
- There is more time when the child does not have medication in the bloodstream.

Disadvantages

- The problem of delivering a noon pill
- Some children experience wide mood swings.

Sustained-Release

Advantages

- Avoid the complication of the noon pill.
- Fewer complications with mood swings

Disadvantages

- Less potent dose during school time
- Less dramatic and immediate change in behavior

Side Effects of Stimulant Medication

What about some of the fears regarding side effects? The most common side effect of stimulants is the loss of appetite. They were used extensively in the 1950s for weight loss in adults. Many children do experience this side effect; this does not mean they stop eating.

In some of these children, weight loss is not a significant problem, because they have extra pounds. Other children are such skinny little characters that if they lose weight, we are fearful they will be blown away by the wind. Weight loss in this underweight group of children can be frightening to parents. This weight loss fear can be addressed in several ways. The evening meal should be eaten after 6:00 PM, when there is less medication in the bloodstream. Feed them breakfast before they take their pill. A parent can also elect to not use the pill on weekends and/or reduce the pill usage in the summer on days that are low in stimulation or stress. Their appetite returns rapidly after the medication wears off. Keeping weight records once a week is a reasonable thing to do if there are fears about weight loss.

The child's decreased appetite can present an additional difficulty for a parent who obtains considerable satisfaction nurturing their child with food. A parent may feel that with this child, the only thing they are doing right is to feed them, and now that dynamic has changed. How could they feel good about the use of medication if they lose the most successful interaction they have with this child? The professional ought to discuss with them their feelings and reassure them there will be ample other roles to play, which will increase medication use compliance.

A very small percentage of children will get clinically depressed from taking stimulants. This, however, is usually a short-lived side effect and should wear off in a couple of weeks. If the depression does not moderate, a change in medication(s) is advisable.

Difficulty getting to sleep is a side effect that occurs in some children who are taking stimulants. If the child has this problem, it can be addressed in several ways. Lowering the dosage frequently works. Giving the child short-acting stimulants that will be out of the system before the child is ready for bed is another choice, or sustained-release stimulants can be given earlier in the day so there is less in the bloodstream at bedtime. Utilizing a "quiet get ready for bed program" helps the child be more prepared for sleep.

Headaches are a common side effect, and if they are mild, they often decrease within two weeks. If the headache is severe, then it is reasonable to either try a decreased dosage or terminate use of the medication.

Gastrointestinal problems are experienced by a small number of children and may decrease after two weeks. If the problems are severe, then reducing medication levels or terminating their use is appropriate. Like other medications used by physicians, there is a long list of rare and possible side effects. If there is concern on the part of the parents, they should consult the child's physician.

Determining the Appropriate Dosage

Several factors—weight of the child, child's reactivity to medication, behavioral observations, and treatment goals—help determine the dosage of stimulant medication. If there is no known reactivity to medications, the most common method to decide the starting dosage for stimulant medication is based on the weight of the child. It is advisable to start at the lowest recommended dosage for that weight range. After two weeks on the medication, collect systematic and accurate behavioral observations to decide if the medication and dosage is effective. Educating parents and teachers how to make accurate observations is important. The questionnaires in the Appendix, which were used in the original evaluation, can be administered again. The new set of evaluations can be compared to those given during the initial evaluation to determine if behavioral change occurred. Interpreting and evaluating any discrepancies between home and school provides crucial information. For example, some parents have reported no improvement at home and the teacher reports a dramatic change. After further investigation, it became clear that the medication was out of the child's system during the most stressful times at home. In this situation, giving the child a short-acting version when they get home from school might be appropriate. Other discrepancies can occur in questionnaires when the observer has prejudices about using medication. Also, the observer may have poor observation skills (e.g., overloaded teacher, parent with ADHD). Asking others regularly involved with the child to fill out questionnaires may provide new insights.

Asking the child about the dosage effectiveness may not produce accurate or helpful information, because self-observation skills are limited. The most common responses to the question are "I guess so" or "I don't think so." Children can start to understand if the medication is helpful when asked direct and concrete questions like, "How many times have you been in timeout this past week since taking the medication?" This concrete feedback also helps reduce resistance to taking medication.

If the dosage is not effective within two weeks, move to a higher dose and observe again. The treatment goals also impact dosage. If the priority is to impact social problems versus academic performance, it generally takes a higher dosage. One of the most common errors in dosage is giving such a small dosage that the drug is ineffective. Physicians that have little experience with ADHD and who are fearful about giving stimulant medications to children most commonly make this error. Periodic increases in dosage may be required as the child grows larger.

Medication Regime

When medication is given in the morning before school, it is helpful to establish a consistent routine. Do not leave it up to the child to be self-monitoring. If the child is reluctant to take the medication, it may be necessary to use rewards to assure compliance.

In some cases, the home environment of these children is so disorganized that the parents cannot regularly give the child the morning pill. A possible solution to this dilemma is to get written permission from the parents to have the medication sent to the school nurse from the pharmacy and then all medication can be administered at school on weekdays.

When it is decided to use the short-acting form of stimulants, the noon pill presents some problems. A clear policy regarding medication administration needs to be established. It is important to have built-in reminders for the staff to facilitate successful medication management.

If the child is asked to manage their own pill at noon, they frequently forget. In some school districts if a child is to take prescription medicine while at school, the office must know about it and be in charge. The child might need to get out of class and go to the office, usually during his lunch or recess.

Children, if they have to wait at the office, can find this very frustrating. As a child's medication regime is developed, consider that they may feel singled out, embarrassed, or "different" by this pill-taking. Make the pill-taking as inconspicuous as possible. A method of making the pill-taking inconspicuous is to give them a regular excuse to get their pill that makes them feel important, such as delivering the attendance sheet to the office. Another possibility could be assigning the child to be in charge of the classroom's playground equipment. For example, a child might be in charge of the tetherball, which is kept (for this purpose) in the school office. Each day, the child needs to go get the tetherball, take the medicine, then take the ball out to the playground and attach it to the pole.

Many school nurses are only at elementary schools one day a week. Often, it is the office secretary or some other assigned person who is in charge of dispensing medication. Make it a point to send the secretary, principal, or nurse little gifts to thank them for helping out with medication, etc. Let them know that their efforts are appreciated and that we know they are going above and beyond in an effort to help a child.

Using sustained-release medication is a method of avoiding the noon pill problem if the medication works as effectively for the child as short-acting medication.

In some cases, both the short-acting medication and the sustained-release medication are losing their effectiveness around 4-5:00 PM. If the home has a very stressful interaction pattern about that time of day, then giving a small dose of short-acting medication could be helpful if it does not dramatically increase sleep problems.

Other Medications

A new non-stimulant medication for ADHD that is gaining popularity reached the pharmacies in January 2003. It is called Strattera™ (atomoxetine HCL) and is produced by Eli Lilly Company. One dose is given early in the morning and an additional dose is given in the late afternoon if needed. The dosage strengths are 10, 18, 25, 40, and 60mg. The clinical evidence from several studies indicate Strattera is much better in modifying behavior than placebo, but data comparing it to stimulants is not available. Less research has been completed about the long-term consequences of taking the drug because of its more recent development. The side effects are similar to those of stimulants. It is not a controlled medication, so the physician and parents are less burdened by control substance issues. In 2005, the FDA required an additional warning about Strattera. This warning was required because of a small increase of suicidal thoughts reported for children and adolescents. More information is available on the Eli Lilly Web site.

Antidepressants are a second type of medication that has been successfully used with children with ADHD. When given to children with ADHD, they produce some of the same results as stimulants, but the positive changes in the child's behavior are not as great. Because stimulants produce greater positive behavioral change, they are still the medication of choice for most of these children. However, there are a percentage of children (10-30 percent) who do not respond to stimulants.[35] Furthermore, some children have other medical conditions, like depression, that benefit from the use of antidepressants. Recently, there has been some discussion about increased suicide risk for children taking antidepressants, which needs to be discussed with parents. Children having seizures or tics would also be possible candidates for antidepressant medications. Tics are frequently exacerbated by stimulants and if tics appear or increase, then lowering the dosage of the stimulant or switching to an antidepressant may be necessary.

Children may not be able to take stimulant medication because of severe side effects. Increased variability in moods as the stimulant wears off can create behavioral management difficulties for parents and teachers, and these mood swings can be decreased with the use of an antidepressant.

Some physicians are experimenting with using stimulants and antidepressants simultaneously. They have observed that the variability in moods decreases when antidepressants are used concurrently with the stimulants.[36]

Catapres™ (clonadine) is an antihypertensive medication that is used to treat high blood pressure in adults. It reduces behavioral problems of ADHD and is most frequently used with children that are very explosive and aggressive. It can be administered orally or by a patch. It can be used to also treat the sleep problems of children with ADHD and also reduces tics. It takes several weeks to reach therapeutic levels, so be patient. It should be administered by a person who has special knowledge about its management.

Tenex™ (guanfacine) is another antihypertensive that has been used in adults to reduce high blood pressure. It should be considered for children with very high levels of arousal that have a low frustration tolerance and that are not receiving sufficient help from the stimulant medications. This medication helps reduce high arousal, low frustration tolerance, sleep problems, and tics. Less research has been done on Tenex than Catapres. One of the side effects is the initial drowsiness that it produces. This medication should be closely monitored because of the impact on blood pressure.

When to Discontinue Medication

Many parents ask, "How long should my child stay on the medication?" The answer to this question depends on the individual's developmental level and the complexity of her life. Some individuals have brains that will continue to develop neurologically, thus improving their ability to cope. These individuals may no longer need the medication. If they miss several doses and continue to function adequately, this indicates that maturation has occurred. A longer trial without medication is advisable to further ascertain if the medication should be discontinued. Other individuals, at forty years of age, continue to struggle with simple tasks like sitting through a one-hour meeting or being patient with their children, unless they continue to take the medication. Unfortunately, adolescents with ADHD tend to stop taking the medication because they do not want to be "different," not because the medication stopped being beneficial. Some of these adolescents, as adults, reconsider taking medication as work and family life become increasingly complex and frustration intensifies.

Referral to a Child Psychiatrist

Children who have ADHD coexisting with other mental disorders present unique challenges when prescribing medication. The addition of a child psychiatrist to the treatment team for their additional expertise is helpful in medication management. A more exhaustive discussion on this topic is found in Thomas W. Phelan's book *All about Attention Deficit Disorder*.

13

Behavioral Interventions

Behavioral interventions have been shown to be effective in modifying the behavior of children with ADHD. They do not require insight on the part of the child, which is limited and is an inherent part of their disability. Behavioral interventions reduce the chances of inappropriate, emotional reactions to misbehavior, because they provide a clear focus on the child's behavior and not on the emotions that their misbehaviors elicit.

Behavioral interventions are used unknowingly by people, but not in a systematic way. Being aware and understanding the necessary behavioral principles will ensure effective results. We selected a well-known ABC model[37] to assist in teaching behavioral concepts and skills. This model simplifies and makes understandable what is causing and/or maintaining behavior. "A" stands for Antecedent events, which are the events that happen prior to the behavior of interest. "B" stands for the Behavior that is of interest to us. "C" stands for the Consequent events, which are the events that happen immediately after the behavior of interest. The A, B, and C are described separately to better facilitate an understanding of how to apply them. Altering the antecedent or consequent events changes the behavior of the child.

Some individuals will read this chapter and immediately apply the concepts. Others will understand the concepts but have difficulty applying them. Some will never be able to transfer the concepts from one situation to another and will need the mental health professional to develop each intervention with them

---

ABC Model

A=Antecedents: What is happening before the behavior
B=Behavior: Concrete and measurable
C=Consequences: What happens after the behavior

Defining Behaviors

Behaviors are addressed first because they are the key to the behavior-modification process. It might be surprising to know that defining a behavior might present problems. The criteria for defining the behavior of interest are that it must be measurable and concrete. The behavior must be measurable and quantifiable to determine if the intervention (e.g., modifying antecedents and consequences) was successful. For example, being "out of control" or being "bad" is not behavior that is measurable or concrete. However, breaking down "out of control" into specific behaviors, such as hitting people, throwing objects, or kicking animals—those are now measurable and concrete behaviors. For instance, after a successful intervention, a child may go from thirty kicks to ten kicks in a sixty-minute period. It was easy to ascertain the level of success with the intervention, because the number of "hits" was measurable. In order to remain consistent and reduce complexity, it is necessary to focus on only one or two behaviors at a time. Trying to modify multiple behaviors at the same time sets the adults and the child up for failure.

Defining Antecedents

An antecedent refers to the event or events that occur just before the behavior of interest. Antecedent event(s) can decrease, increase, or have no impact on the behavior. Direct observation by the adult is the best method of identifying antecedent events. This is not as simple as it sounds. For instance, the behavior of interest might occur out of sight or the only witnesses are the child with ADHD, a sibling, or a peer, who all have been unreliable historians in the past. It is also possible that siblings or peers benefit by giving misinformation that makes a scapegoat of the child with ADHD. Children with ADHD are also likely to provide misinformation. It might require some detective work to find out what the actual antecedent event(s) was and which one(s) was responsible for triggering the behavior of interest. Unless reliable results come from the detective work, it is better to *not* implement a behavioral intervention using suspicions or guesses. There will be plenty of opportunities to actively intervene with behaviors that are directly observed. Even when the adult observes the behavior of interest, a causal connection between the antecedent events and the behavior is difficult to make. Often times, the behavior is so attention-getting, we lose focus on the order that the antecedents occurred or completely miss them.

If there were multiple antecedent events and there is an inability to identify the one occurring immediately before the behavior, then there are two suggested ways to proceed. First, look for any logical connections. For example, the child with ADHD is hit by a sibling and he turns around and kicks the dog. The logical connection is that both are aggressive behaviors. Second, initiate a process of systematically eliminating one antecedent event at a time to determine the causal event. The process of systematic elimination starts with choosing one antecedent event and modifying it, then observing whether the behavior of interest changes. For example, the son kicked the dog (behavior of interest); prior to this, his brother took away his toy (antecedent); his father walked in the room yelling (antecedent); and his mother just asked him to clean his room for the hundredth time (antecedent). The first intervention to determine the causal antecedent could be to stop the father's yelling behavior, then observe if kicking the dog decreases in frequency. Over a period of several days, if the kicking behavior does not decrease, proceed to modify the next antecedent event. If in the process of systematic elimination, the kicking behavior still continues, then intervene with consequent principles, which are elaborated next.

Defining Consequences

Consequent events are those that happen immediately following the behavior of interest. They can decrease, increase, or have no impact on the behavior. For younger children (under eight), observe the events happening in the first twenty seconds after the behavior of interest has occurred. The observation period for older children should be longer. Identification of causal consequent events, like antecedents, can be difficult. Direct observation by the adult is the best method of identifying consequent events. Identification is nearly impossible when adults do not directly observe the behavior of interest. Adults should develop behavioral interventions only after observing the behavior of interest.

The same strategy utilized for identification of antecedents is helpful in identifying the consequent events. If there were multiple consequent events and identification of the one event which occurred immediately after the behavior is impossible, then there are two suggested ways to proceed. First, look for any logical connections. Second, initiate a process of systematically eliminating one consequent event at a time to determine the causal connection. The process of systematic elimination starts with choosing one consequent event, modifying it, then observing whether the behavior of interest changes. For example, the boy pulls the hair of a girl seated next to him, she screams, and the teacher reacts immediately, smiling, and says, "Don't do that." The three consequent events after the hair pulling were the girl's scream, the teacher's intervention saying "Don't do that," and the teacher smiling directly at the boy. The girl's screaming was the consequent event that occurred right after the hair pulling. The first behavioral intervention was to reward the girl for not screaming after a hair pulling incident. The hair-pulling incidents continued. Research suggests saying, "Don't do that" increases problem behavior; therefore, the teacher was asked to stop using the expression. However, the hair-pulling behavior continued. A decrease in hair-pulling episodes resulted with the elimination of the teacher's smile. Smiling was identified as the causal consequent event. The teacher did not recognize her smiling as a consequent event and only became aware of it when a trained observer came into her classroom. Consequent events that are frequently overlooked are changes in body language, e.g., tone or voice volume, smiles, eye contact, clenched fists, or aggressive posture. Sometimes using an outside observer is an effective strategy to help identify causal consequent or antecedent events.

Punishments and Incentives

There are two types of consequent events: punishments and incentives. Punishment is the most common consequence used with children diagnosed with ADHD. The use of punishment generally results from the adult's frustration and anger towards the child. If punishment is unsuccessful in changing the behavior, the adult often responds by increasing the frequency and severity of the punishment. The escalation of punishment leads to high levels of physical and emotional abuse in children with ADHD.

The use of incentives as a consequence is typically underused. Adults who are angry at their child seldom consider using an incentive as a consequence. When the concept of incentives and effective punishment are introduced, the dialogue between a parent and a mental health professional sounds something like this:

MHP: How have you been dealing with his behavior?

Dad: We take away all his toys and spank him.

MHP: Does that work?

Dad: It doesn't work—well, maybe it works for two minutes.

MHP: How about trying something different by using incentives?

Dad: It doesn't seem morally correct to give incentives to a kid who is acting like a brat all the time.

MHP: How is the punishment working?

Dad: It isn't working.

MHP: Do you want to try something new?

Dad: Yes.

MHP: How about introducing incentives?

Dad: Incentives … it just doesn't seem right. When my mom or dad said to do something, we just did it or else. (Dad smiles; he is getting the idea that trying incentives is going to be necessary, and he's also starting to understand his own anger.)

MHP: Your child is going to earn the incentives, not just be given them. I can also show you how to use punishment more effectively. Would you be willing to try it for a week to see how it works?

Dad: Well, maybe for a week.
MHP: I'll show you how well it works.

One week later, the parents report some success and some failures. They are, however, encouraged enough to continue increasing the use of incentives as a consequence. Almost uniformly, the parent's level of guilt over treating their child with punishment is reduced when they use incentives more frequently. The child's anger and misbehavior is also reduced. The ultimate goal is to establish a ratio of ten incentives for every one punishment.

Punishment

Punishment can be an effective method of reducing problem behavior when used appropriately. The use of punishment to correct undesirable behavior in challenging children, however, is problematic. While the average child experiences significant amounts of anxiety when anticipating punishment, children with ADHD experience lower levels of anxiety. This reduces the effectiveness of punishment for a child with ADHD. Thus, it is necessary to use punishment judiciously.

When punishment is the main method used to modify behavior of children with ADHD, it produces an uncooperative, oppositional, and discouraged child. A vicious cycle ensues as the adult's anger escalates—so does the child's misbehavior. In order to reverse the negative behavior pattern, the overuse of punishment must stop. The regular use of incentive, without punishment, will produce a cooperative child. Once the negative behavior pattern is reversed and the child has had experience in earning incentives, then infrequent punishment can be reintroduced.

The effective use of punishment requires instructing the child about the expected appropriate behavior. Punishment alone has limited value. For example, a child who is punished for touching a glass figurine receives no information about what he can touch. Punishment with instruction of appropriate behavior allows the child to learn what is appropriate. A child who is told that he cannot touch a glass figurine because it is fragile, but that he can touch a wooden vase, learns what is appropriate.

Effective Types of Punishment

Time-outs

A good rule of thumb for a typical child is one or two minutes for each year of age. Children with ADHD, however, require shorter time periods, depending on ADHD severity. In the Common and Enduring Problems chapter, specific details about using time-outs effectively are elaborated. Instructions on how to avoid mis-applications of this type of punishment are outlined.

Ignoring

Ignoring or not giving the child any attention after a display of negative behavior is an effective technique to reduce or stop the negative behavior. By ignoring the problem behavior, you remove the incentive. For example, a mother may respond to her child's tantrums in the grocery store with scolding and hitting. The child has gained attention through the scolding and hitting, which actually strengthens the tantrum behavior. However, if it is ignored and thereby not reinforced, it will eventually weaken and occur with less intensity and less frequency. If the child has developed a pattern of escalating to dangerous behavior when ignored, then using the technique is inappropriate. Ignoring is more effective when followed by immediate positive attention after appropriate behavior occurs.

Face aversion

Face aversion is a more dramatic form of ignoring. Attention is withdrawn by rapidly turning your face away from the child's eye contact, demonstrating a non-response to the problem behavior. Responding as if your buttons have not been pushed takes away their incentive. This will reduce the behavior if the child has learned a positive method of getting attention.

Taking money away that is earned by the child

The reason or rule for removal of a specific amount of money from the child must be clearly stated in advance of the problematic behavior. The loss of money is effective if the child has worked for it.

Taking away a child's favorite toy

If the child is required to earn the use of a favorite toy, then taking it away after a problem behavior has occurred is effective. The age of the child should determine how long the toy should be removed.

Taking away privileges

Punishing the child by taking away privileges can modify behavior if used infrequently. Change, however, will only occur if the principles of its use are understood. Privilege removal should only be for short periods of time, and the time period should relate to the child's age and the severity of the ADHD. The privilege-removal time period should be shorter for younger children and those with more severe ADHD. A monitoring system needs to be developed that provides information about the child's compliance.

Completing unpleasant tasks

Punishing the child by having them complete a task that is unpleasant for them can modify behavior if the punishment is easily enforceable and followed by an incentive. Providing an incentive after the punishment task has been completed reduces power struggles and motivates the child to comply.

Ineffective Types of Punishment

Frequent spankings or hitting
"That didn't hurt" is a common response heard from children with ADHD after being hit or spanked. Within a few moments, they are back hitting their sister. Besides being ineffective, frequent spanking produces other negative consequences, such as increased aggression and defiance. The adult administering the physical punishment is often out of control emotionally and may injure the child.

Excessive removal of privileges
Many adults who have been trying to manage a child with ADHD have used an approach that focuses on taking away privileges. As the child fails to comply, more and more privileges are removed. When this occurs, the discouraged child spirals downward into more and more problem behavior.

Shouting and yelling
It is easy to habitually yell and shout to get the child's attention. If this approach is used, the child learns is to ignore the requests until the volume hits six million decibels.

Making negative statements to the child
Saying negative things to a child with ADHD is almost universal. It does not increase the compliance of the child. It often lowers self-confidence and the feelings of worthiness. Negative statements can be direct or implied. A direct statement would be: "You stupid kid." An example of an implied negative statement is: "Why can't you do it right?" (Implied meaning—"you stupid kid"). Adults often do not recognize their implied negative statements, and they tend to use them frequently.

Grounding
Grounding is a punishment usually reserved for teenagers. The type and scope of the grounding is usually determined by the adult's level of distress and not pre-planned. Grounding a hard-to-live-with teenager is a punishment for the parent, and too often, the weary parent gives in and removes the grounding. The parenting is inconsistent and the child has been rewarded for the acting-out behavior.

Incentives

Webster's Dictionary defines "incentive" as follows: *"Something that incites into action. It spurs into action, encourages action, and even provokes action."* "Provoking and inciting" already feel like regular visitors for those involved with children who have ADHD. Focusing on the part of the definition involving encouragement seems more appropriate.

There are two major motivational issues for children with ADHD: first, finding incentives that are powerful enough to get them started on difficult tasks; and second, finding incentives that will continue to motivate them to maintain their effort. Children with ADHD need to have incentives changed more often, because the incentives lose their power to motivate. Creative thinking is required to find effective incentives. For example, a teacher challenged a non-compliant student with a creative incentive. If the student completed five social-science problems within thirty minutes, then the teacher would do anything that the student wanted for five minutes if it did not harm anyone or anything. The student, grinning from ear to ear, said, "Hop on one leg for five minutes." The teacher said, "I will do that," and upon striking the bargain, the student immediately began the problems and finished them within thirty minutes. The teacher got exercise and the student had success. The student was allowed five minutes of "control" versus letting him control the entire school day.

We often use incentives as though we are experts without realizing it. For example, when a baby is learning to use sound as a method of communication, we provide many incentives. We smile, repeat the sound back to them, and say "good talking" with only a short time delay between the baby's sound and the giving of an incentive. The rate of giving incentives is high when the child first begins to make sounds, and then the rate slows. We change the incentives given to the child for making sounds as they develop more complicated patterns of communication. They get a bite of food when they say anything that resembles please and then are given a bite only if they say it more clearly.

Guidelines and Principles for Effective Use of Incentives

Although we use incentives every day, the following guidelines and principles will allow us to understand and use them more effectively. Assisting children with ADHD requires an understanding of the proven principles for the use of incentives when implementing behavioral interventions.

Delay and Spacing

Children with ADHD best learn something new when the incentive is given immediately and frequently following the "desired behavior." However, to maintain the new and desired behavior over time, incentives need to be systematically spaced and delayed—incentives given part of the time instead of every time. When a child first learns to speak, a naturally occurring example of delaying and spacing incentives occurs. The first word is followed immediately with cheers and excitement from parents. Over time, as the child learns more words, fewer incentives occur. Gradual spacing and delaying improves the ability of the child to sustain effort and wait. Children with ADHD have a hard time waiting and sustaining effort; therefore, delaying and spacing incentives must be done in a systematic fashion. Appropriate behavioral expectations of the child's ability to tolerate spacing and delaying of incentives are necessary. As a general rule of thumb, it might be advisable to think of their ability to wait for rewards as similar to children half their chronological age.

Approximations

A new behavior will not be perfect when first attempted. Incentives are provided for approximations of the desired behavior, and then gradually the child must perform at a higher level to get the desired incentive.

Incompatibility

Use incentives to establish a behavior that is incompatible with a problem behavior. For example, if incentives are provided for cooperation, then arguing decreases automatically.

Novelty

Incentives that are new to the child usually produce more changes in behavior. The power of each incentive wears out faster for children with ADHD, and thus, the incentives must be changed frequently.

Finding incentives

The preferred methods of finding incentives are to ask or observe the child's behavior. Observe what the child frequently chooses to do with their free time, and this can be used as an incentive. For example, a fifteen-minute time at the computer can be earned for every five math problems accurately completed.

Do not give away incentives

Many potential incentives are given to the child rather than allowing them to earn the incentive. Give them money, toys, and time on video or electronic games in earned increments rather than as free gifts.

Cafeteria List
Allowing a child to choose from a pool or "cafeteria list" of potential incentives is especially effective with older children. Using the cafeteria list reduces resistance and adds novelty, as the child is empowered to make choices.

Effective Types of Incentives
A list of potential incentives that is readily available for teachers and parents will be helpful for several reasons. First, it is difficult to find an incentive when under a lot of pressure and in need of immediate help. Second, children burn out on a particular incentive and so another is quickly needed. Third, the list reminds the teacher and parents that many incentives are inexpensive and readily available.

Verbal Incentives

1. Enthusiastically describe what the child is doing. "You're pushing the vacuum!"
2. Make a positive evaluative statement "I notice that you are talking politely!"
3. Combine 1 and 2 "You did the job so well, and I am proud of you!"
4. Share your feelings. "I enjoy playing together so much when you play fair!"

Physical Incentives

Hug or a pat on the head/shoulders	Teaching pets tricks
Eye contact, smiles	Helping build objects
Water skiing	Money (Excellent with older children)
Food	Use of electronic game (in minutes)
Cutting the lawn	Play time with favorite toys (in minutes)
Use of computer (in minutes)	Building tree house (one hour at a time)
Use of bicycle (in minutes)	Helping a handicapped student
Use of tools (in minutes)	Tokens (redeemed for other incentives)
Use of telephone (in minutes)	Use of pager or cell phone (in hours)
Use of television (in minutes)	Coming in early to help teacher
Playing ball with parents	Taking out school equipment at recess
Lessons (sports, music)	Cleaning cages of animals at school
Campouts	Building campfire
Listening to recordings	Tickets to games
Caring for plants in classroom	Use of motorcycle (in minutes)
Riding horse	Playing with animals
Going to college class with parent	Helping teacher with special projects
Staying at grandparents house	Drawing time
Having friends stay overnight	Time in a private spot
Walking in the woods with parent	Receiving peer attention for on-task time

This is a sample list of incentives; keep refining and adding to the list with individualized creative ideas. One of our favorite creative uses of incentives was when a parent gave a motorcycle, piece by piece, to his teenage son when he attended school. Another favorite is when a teacher allowed a child to earn the privilege of sitting by her best friend for twenty minutes.

How to Give Instructions

The foundation of any intervention begins with giving instructions—a skill, that many people have not yet developed. Instructions are antecedent events that precede the behavior of interest. Antecedents are simple-to-learn, effective behavioral interventions, which get results! Instructions, skillfully given, increase the probability of compliance. Consequently, adults feel competent and confident when their instructions are followed. Children with ADHD feel less frustrated and have increased confidence when they successfully complete requests. Specific guidelines are provided to increase compliance when giving instructions to children with ADHD.

A primary guideline to remember is to limit the number of instructions given to the child with ADHD appropriate to their severity level. If the child has a severe form of ADHD, one instruction at a time is the appropriate expectation. If the child has a mild or a moderate form of ADHD, then two instructions are the appropriate expectation. Give instructions for things that are important, and let a lot of other things go that might normally be said to a child. For example, a parent may say when they come in the door at night, "Please hang up your coat," and then give another list of instructions: "Put your shoes in the closet; go sit at the table; and start your homework." The child has just been given four instructions in a matter of minutes. He probably will not remember more than the first two, and the adult will not be able to be consistent with follow-through. To get results, give the child one or two instructions which are the most important and leave the others until later.

First, make sure the child is fully attentive before giving any instructions. Accomplish this by touching them and making direct eye contact while giving the instruction.

Second, give instructions in a firm, calm tone. The voice volume should be slightly louder than a normal speaking voice. Avoid having a voice tone that projects anger, impatience, intimidation, nervousness, or pleading. Use an objective observer to help identify any unintended verbal or non-verbal messages being sent. Pick an observer who can provide feedback in a non-judgmental way.

Third, because children with ADHD have short attention spans, instructions must be simple, clear, and concise, with only one or two steps. The child needs to know exactly what is expected without having to remember too many steps. Examples of instructions commonly used are: "Pick up your bedroom," or a schoolteacher might say, "Clean up your desk." Both instructions for children with ADHD are too ambiguous; instructions need to be specified in clear and concrete terms. Instead of saying, "Clean up your room," say, "Please go to your bedroom and put all of your shoes on the closet floor." At school, say, "Take all the objects from the top of your desk and put them inside your desk." These instructions are clear, concise, and without multiple steps.

When a child is given challenging or multiple-step instructions, cueing can be done to help them sustain focus. The number of times they are cued can gradually be reduced. Cueing by asking questions which prompt them to remember the instruction increases their independence (e.g., "What do you do with the things on top of your desk?").

Fourth, after giving a short, clear, and concise instruction, have the child repeat them to determine if they heard and what they heard. If the child repeats back instructions, it ensures they were heard accurately.

Fifth, if the child repeats the instructions but is not complying, then restate the instructions, adding consequences for compliance and noncompliance with time limits. For example, "Put your backpack in your room and then hang up your coat in the closet. I will set the timer for five minutes. If you get this done, then we will play basketball for ten minutes. If you do not get this done before the time is up, then you will not be given the usual after-school snack." Give the child a time limit that is appropriate for his or her "adjusted age," and take into consideration the ability and skills level to increase compliance. Use a timing device that is visible to the child (see the resources section on the ideal timer for small children) makes time concrete. After the child starts to comply, give a verbal incentive such as, "Thanks for getting your backpack up to your room." When they have finished their tasks, immediately give the stated incentive for compliance (e.g., playing ten minutes of basketball). However, if the child did not comply, it is important to quickly and non-emotionally follow through with the stated consequence for noncompliance (e.g., not giving their usual after-school snack).

The child should not be able to continue to avoid complying with the initial instructions. Consequently, after the consequence for noncompliance (no snack) has had the opportunity to be effective, then repeat the initial instruction. Hopefully the consequence provided motivation for the child to now comply. If there is no change after the second attempt to get compliance, then determine by testing if the child lacks the ability to complete the task. Separating ability and incentive issues requires frequent review and is an ongoing process. If there is no compliance after modification of consequences, then determine by testing if the child lacks ability. A lack of ability or skill requires a change in the expectations and instructions accordingly. For example, the child did not complete their math assignment because they did not know how to multiply. Therefore, the expectation was inappropriate and needs to be modified.

The guidelines for giving instructions are straightforward, what could go wrong? Strong emotions like frustration and anger result in derailed good intentions. At those times, it is hard to believe what comes out of your mouth. These purely emotional responses can lead to stating inappropriate consequences or "empty threats". Inappropriate consequences are those that are not logically connected to the problem behavior e.g., child breaks your favorite vase and is told they can't eat dinner tonight. Empty threats are those consequences which cannot possibly be completed e.g., you are grounded forever from recess. Instructions with either of these consequent statements decrease compliance.

The most ineffective and overused instruction given to children with ADHD is saying, "Don't do that" or an implied form of the expression, e.g., "Stop that:" "I told you not to do that;" or "Quit that." It is understandable that these phrases can become habitual responses. Ironically, the child usually responds by doing exactly what they were told not to do.

Guidelines for Giving Instructions to Challenging Children

1. Touch the child (usually on the shoulder) before starting the instruction, and make eye contact until the instructions are complete.

2. Give instructions in a firm, calm tone.

3. Make instructions short, concise, and with only one or two steps. Use cueing as necessary.

4. Have the child repeat back the instructions, e.g., "Now what did I just say?"

5. If the child does not comply with the first request, then repeat the instructions, adding consequences for being compliant or noncompliant with stated time limits. Use a timing device that is visible to the child.

   Compliance—give verbal incentives, e.g., "Great job" when the child begins to comply, and upon completion of the task(s), give the earned incentive.

   Noncompliance—immediately give the consequence, and later, repeat the initial instructions. If noncompliance continues, re-examine the incentives used or evaluate skill and ability.

6. Avoid making *empty threats*.

7. Avoid choosing *inappropriate consequences*.

8. Avoid using *"Don't do that."*

Training Team Members to Apply Behavioral Interventions

The principles of the ABC model may be overwhelming, and almost everyone has some difficulty understanding and correctly applying them. To augment learning and application of these concepts, a DVD training film is available and listed in the Appendix. Also, the MHP repeatedly demonstrates a behavioral principle to advance the team member's understanding of its correct application. Additionally, the MHP verifies a team member's ability to correctly apply the behavioral principles. The MHP verifies by observing him or her directly in the office or via videotape. When using a videotape, set up the camera on a tripod, letting it run, and eventually, others will forget its presence. The videotape is reviewed by the MHP with the team member present. Critiquing the videotape together is a powerful learning experience. The initial attempts of a team member to demonstrate behavioral principles may be anxiety provoking; the MHP needs to verbally reinforce his or her effort. It is also important that team members understand it requires repeated attempts to master the skill. This understanding will reduce feelings of frustration and discouragement. Over time, self-confidence grows, and he or she will develop the ability to self-critique interventions.

14

Structural Interventions

Structural intervention is the process of systematically and consistently modifying a child's environment to make it simpler. Structuring a child's environment addresses the specific symptoms inherent with ADHD, such as: difficulty maintaining focus, distractibility, working-memory deficits, and restlessness. Modifying the child's surrounding environment—at school, home, and in social situations—is a proactive approach that can reduce and/or avoid problem behaviors. The simpler the surrounding environment is, the less complex it is for the child to navigate, and the easier it is for the child to successfully function. Expecting a child with ADHD to behave appropriately when placed in a stimulating and unstructured environment sets him up for failure. Initially, there may be reluctance to structurally modify the environment for *one* family member or student. However, this type of intervention, when thoughtfully implemented, is highly effective and will greatly impact the child's overall success.

Modification of the Physical and Psychosocial Environment

Carefully evaluate the child's physical and psychosocial environment without the child present prior to making any modifications. It takes practice to evaluate the environment and determine how the child is impacted by the physical layout of the space, by the activity, and by the rules and expectations. Modification, including implementing clear physical boundaries, concrete time limits, setting clear rules, systematic expectations with consequences, and fewer distracting stimuli, reduces the complexity of the environment and increases structure, thereby improving behavior.

Physical boundaries
The challenging child has great difficulty recognizing appropriate boundaries and often ignores verbal instructions. Physical modifications to the child's environment can counteract high levels of impulsivity, intense curiosity, and a high activity level. For example, a challenging child continues to open a cupboard that has unsafe products in it even after he has been repeatedly reprimanded for this behavior. Physically modifying the child's environment by putting a lock on the

cupboard door is a form of structural intervention that will provide additional structure and increase safety. Physical boundaries can include playpens, strollers, half-doors, and cubicles, and can provide the increased structure and safety as well as the decreased distractibility and violation of personal space, that can be so challenging for a child with ADHD.

Time

A child with ADHD has great difficulty with effective time management. This inability to keep track of time results in incomplete work or activities. Physical modifications—visible, child-friendly clocks/timers—help make time concrete and keep the child focused and on task. Utilizing consistent schedules—doing things in the same way, time, and place—adds predictability and simplifies their environment. Preparing the child in advance, with transition statements *before* changing activities is key. Likewise, prioritizing activities and doing difficult or challenging activities when a child is well rested is critical.

Rules

Children with ADHD have difficulty remembering and following "spoken" rules because of their disabilities. Consequently, by implementing fewer rules, stating them clearly in behavioral terms, and occasionally restating them increases compliance. For example, explaining to a child that during this activity they should remain seated, raise their hand, and wait for the teacher to call on them. Using transition statements regarding rule changes for a new activity *before* changing to the new activity prepares them for the change. Reducing the number of individuals that the child interacts with automatically reduces the number of rules necessary. Also, having the child participate in non-competitive activities reduces the complexity of rules. Children with ADHD also have great difficulty identifying "unspoken" social rules and appropriately responding. Their lack of insight regarding these social rules requires the adult to repeatedly make unspoken rules spoken. For example, "John when you placed your hand on Sally, she moved away—her action shows she did not want to be touched."

Sensory Stimulation

Children with ADHD are easily distracted by auditory, tactile, and visual stimuli. Reducing the sensory stimuli that interfere with expected task completion or compliant behavior is an effective intervention.

Auditory—Lower the room noise levels (e.g., use ear phones, reduce background noise television/music)

Tactile—Decrease the proximity of objects and people (e.g., move desk, sit between mom/dad at kitchen table)
Visual—Decrease visual distractions (e.g., face child away from windows/open doors, black out shades in bedroom)

See Chapter Fifteen—Common and Enduring Problems and Chapter Eighteen—Case Studies, for further information/examples regarding structural interventions and how to implement them in specific situations. Once you understand the general principles of structural interventions, then the intervention you employ is limited only by your creativity.

15

Common and Enduring Problems

Some behavioral problems occur almost universally for children who have ADHD. Furthermore, various situational problems routinely occur for children who have ADHD, because well-intentioned people intervene like they would for a typical child. We explain effective interventions for some of the most common, frustrating behavioral problems and situations confronting parents, siblings, teachers, physicians, and mental health professionals. First, we describe the general circumstances (dynamics) that either maintain or create the problems. Second, various creative interventions are described using combinations of the ABC behavioral model, structural interventions, and medical interventions elaborated in previous chapters. Medical interventions are almost always helpful when children have a moderate to severe form of ADHD and help make other types of interventions more effective.

Understanding the principles and guidelines contained in the earlier chapters is necessary when developing individual interventions. The multi-faceted interventions are meant to generate ideas for treatment with the realization that individual factors, such as severity of disorder and age, will require adjustments. It should also be understood that continual modification of any intervention is necessary as the child and situations change. If some of our intervention ideas are attempted without success, try using the Troubleshooting Checklist, which highlights important basic principles.

Parent Challenges

Reducing Problem Behavior in Stores and Restaurants
Stores and restaurants provide complex social situations where there are usually high levels of visual and auditory stimulation. Parents are focusing on completing their tasks, and children are required to wait to get their wants fulfilled. These environments are especially difficult for children with ADHD because they require many skills and abilities that may be lacking because of their disability. Consequently, children misbehave more frequently, causing parents to become frustrated, angry, and overwhelmed. Parents sometimes react in a negative emotional manner by making threats to the child such as: "If you don't stop it right

now, I'm going to slap your bottom." Another parental response is to avoid taking them to a store or restaurant. Neither of these options teach the child socially appropriate behavior.

Suggested interventions: Taking a child with ADHD to a restaurant or store requires a proactive plan of structural and behavioral interventions. Planning ahead to change the structure of the situation will reduce stimulation and complexity and is remarkably helpful. When possible, take only the child with ADHD, so they do not have to compete for attention. Take the child when he is rested and a lower number of people are present. Make the outings short and focused on what the parent wants to accomplish. Go to restaurants where service is prompt. Consider a seating arrangement which allows physical containment, such as the inside seat of a booth, and limit his visual and auditory stimulation. Quickly remove any problematic objects, such as the salt and pepper shaker, off the top of the table. Promptly give the child a desirable quiet activity, like playing a travel-size board game similar to *Guess Who?*®

Before going into the store or restaurant, explain the behavioral expectations and the positive and negative consequences. For example: "Johnny, Mommy is only going to get bread, milk, and eggs. If you stay seated in the cart without complaining, then you get one small bag of Skittles® at the end of the shopping; however, if you complain or attempt to get out of the cart, then you will receive no treat." It may be necessary to periodically cue the child by asking them to restate the rules. If the behavioral expectations are egregiously violated, then the child is immediately and calmly removed from the store or restaurant and placed in the car for a five-minute time-out. At the end of a successful time-out, the child is asked if they would like to try again to comply with same behavioral expectations.

Helping Them Obtain and Maintain Friendships

Children with ADHD are often outgoing, friendly, and can rapidly attract playmates. It can be difficult for them to keep friends because of their impulsivity, limited ability to empathize, and poor sportsmanship. Playtime often becomes a time of frustration for the child with ADHD, parents, and playmate(s). Parents often hear statements such as, "Nobody likes me;" "My friends are always mean to me;" and "They do not want to play with me anymore." These statements understandably produce feelings of sadness for the child.

Suggested interventions: Parents must learn to be proactive in assisting their child to select and retain friendships. If parents just leave friendship selection up to their child, they will probably select children similar to themselves. The difficulty with this is that they do not provide good role models for each other and exacerbate each other's problem behaviors. When possible, invite well-socialized children to play with your child. They also have more success playing with younger children, who are more their "emotional age," and older children, who better tolerate some of their problem behavior.

If the child is of school-age, ask their teacher who is well-socialized and positively interacts with the child. Structure playtime with non-competitive, action-oriented activities. Invite one friend over at a time to reduce complexity and stimulation. Limit the play period so that the child's fatigue level does not decrease frustration tolerance. It is important that the invited child has fun and will want to return. The parent providing favorite treats and fun activities gives them increased incentive to return for future play dates. Also, provide positive feedback to the child's parents, e.g., "Thank you for sharing your son; he is fun and is really helpful in teaching my child good manners."

Junior-high age is a more critical time to monitor friendships. Because of their increased independence and freedom, they have greater opportunity to make poor decisions. Children with antisocial or rebellious tendencies more readily accept the child with ADHD. They can encourage each other to engage in impulsive behavior, leading to disastrous results. Get the child involved in activities that encourage contact with children who are good role models, e.g., swim team, marching band, horseback riding, golf, or mountain biking, to influence healthier friendships.

Decreasing Arguing Behavior

Parents and siblings frequently express anger and frustration toward the child with ADHD for starting and maintaining arguments. This negative dynamic can be damaging to everyone involved. The question is often asked, "Why does he argue all the time?" Understanding what the child receives as a consequence or payoff for the arguing is the first step to reducing the frequency. Most often, the child receives attention as a consequence for arguing, and although it is negative attention, it can be a powerful incentive. Another consequence or payoff for the child is being able to delay or avoid aversive tasks. The most powerful consequence that maintains arguing is the adults giving into the child's argument part of the time. A child will argue every night to stay up past his bedtime, and when the parents are emotionally exhausted, they give in to the child's demands. This sends a powerful message to the child that arguing pays off.

Suggested interventions: It is important to understand how the arguing produces a payoff for the child. If receiving attention is the payoff, then reducing the negative attention will lower the frequency of arguing. The child argues about doing a simple evening chore, and the parents ignore the child by not responding either verbally or nonverbally until the arguing stops. Sometimes parents think that they are not responding to the child because they don't verbalize, but they may be looking mean, sighing, or rolling their eyes, which are nonverbal responses that may be an incentive to the child. When the child stops arguing after they are verbally and nonverbally ignored, the parent gives them immediate positive attention with ten minutes of basketball and/or the parent saying, "I love it when you do your chores." Sometimes, after a child is ignored, they will escalate their arguing because past experience has taught them the parents will eventually give in. If there is an escalation in their arguing behavior that the parent cannot tolerate, putting a behavioral incentive program in place to reduce arguing may be necessary. For example, a child with moderate ADHD is arguing with the parent an average of thirty times a day. During the first week of intervention, the child can earn verbal praise and fifteen minutes on the Game Boy® each day if the number of arguing attempts are reduced by 30 percent. Gradually, a greater time delay would be added before the incentive is given, and a reduction in the number of arguing attempts would be required to obtain the incentive. Verbal incentives are often effective for children with the mild form of ADHD, but for children with moderate or severe forms, more concrete incentives along with verbal incentives must be used.

If the child is arguing to avoid or delay a task, then find out what makes the task aversive. This understanding leads to more effective interventions. The most common reasons for avoiding or delaying are: the task is boring or unpleasant, it requires a longer attention span than the child possesses, and the task requires skill or knowledge that the child does not possess. If the task is repetitious and non-action orientated, the child will perceive it as boring. Parents will need to provide potent incentives to offset the boring nature of the task. If there is not an appropriate expectation concerning the child's attention span, the task will need to be modified. To determine an appropriate expectation regarding attention span, start by expecting responses similar to a child half their chronological age (see section on appropriate behavioral expectations in Chapter Eleven). The success, or lack of it, after the modification determines the appropriateness of your expectations. If the child continues to avoid after the addition of potent incentives and an adjustment for attention span, then it is likely that they do not have the prerequisite skills or knowledge. If lack of skills or knowledge is the problem, then teaching the requisite skills and knowledge is crucial. The Evaluation Summary Form contains significant information to help formulate appropriate expectations.

Some children are extremely effective at getting people to argue with them, which creates a dynamic that impedes adults' attempts to stop the arguing. The children are effective because they are able to emotionally hook the individual who is trying to ignore their arguing behavior. The emotional hooks are statements or actions that make the other person feel guilty, angry, or not respected. An example is the child saying something like, "You want me to go to bed so you can spend time with my brother," or "You like him better than me!" If the child's comments lead to an argument, the person has been hooked and reeled in. Learn to depersonalize the child's comments and recognize the child's skill. Don't be surprised if it is difficult to ignore arguing behavior from the child because in our culture, it is appropriate to defend beliefs and opinions by arguing.

If behavioral and structural interventions do not produce the desired changes, then evaluate medication usage. If the child has moderate or severe forms of ADHD, then medication can be helpful in modifying this destructive behavior because it will increase the ability to stay on task and to be less impulsive.

Effective Time-Outs for Children Under Ten

The theories behind the popular strategy of time-outs are that the child reflects on the misbehavior during the time-out or the child feels punished and as a result wants to modify the misbehavior. Using time-outs for correcting misbehavior is typically incorrectly administered and over-used with children having ADHD. Time-outs with children having ADHD are problematic because they have a difficult time with introspection and remaining quiet for long periods. Furthermore, punishments lose their novelty, power, and potency when over-used. Over-use of time-outs is common as parental emotions intensify in an attempt to quickly regain a sense of control. Also, the negative attention given to the child by the parent's strong emotions tend to make the time-out ineffective.

Time-out procedures are straightforward, but implementing them correctly with children having ADHD is challenging. Many complications arise when parents attempt to implement the time-out. Parents frequently have difficulty getting the child into a time-out, to not act-out during the time-out, and to remain in time-out. Power struggles between the parent and the child often erupt as the child's misbehavior escalates during the time-out process. They frequently respond to the child's escalation by threatening longer time-outs or other punishments. The initial reason for the time-out is lost during the power struggle. The child and parents are left with increased frustration and anger towards each other.

Suggested Interventions: Time-out is a punishment that can be effective in changing the behavior of children with ADHD when appropriate expectations and specific modifications are made. They are only effective if the child is being removed from a place or situation that he or she finds desirable. Time-outs also need to be reserved for serious misbehavior, e.g., hitting or throwing dangerous objects. Parents need to make proactive plans about when and how time-outs will be used. The parent ought to communicate these plans to the child prior to implementing them. The instruction includes the time-out location, the length of time, and for what misbehavior the time-out is administered. This proactive approach reduces emotional reactivity and overuse.

When choosing a time-out location at home or in public places, many factors are considered. The time-out location needs to limit the child's visual, physical, and auditory stimulation—a boring place. The location could be an enclosed staircase or the child facing into a corner in a quiet room. It must be a place the parent can easily monitor. Placing a small rug versus using a "time-out chair" in the location reduces the child's ability to receive negative attention by banging, tipping, or throwing the chair. Using the child's bedroom is seldom appropriate, but there are some circumstances when it may be necessary. For example, a three-year-old with a severe form of ADHD may refuse to stay in a specified location. Placing her in her bedroom for time-out reduces the negative attention she receives. It is important that the bedroom is organized in such a way as to reduce potential injury problems and that a half-door is used for easier monitoring. When in public places, use the backseat of your vehicle as the time-out location. To avoid giving negative attention to the child, the parent stands next to the car, where their peripheral vision can observe the child. This allows the child to feel safe, as they can still see the parent, and people passing by will know the child is being monitored.

Requesting the child to wait, be quiet, and be socially isolated are all difficult tasks for them, thus modifications in time-out procedures to minimize escalation of misbehavior and power struggles is necessary. Consider the child's "adjusted age" and the severity of the disorder in deciding the length of the time-out. The general rule is one to two minutes for every year of age. Placing a timer visible to the child gives immediate feedback on how much longer he or she has to wait.

Parents immediately initiate the time-out procedures when the designated misbehavior occurs. They obtain direct eye contact and then calmly and firmly state, "You just earned a time-out with that misbehavior—go to the time-out spot now" (state the specific behavior). Parents can count to themselves slowly to five, allowing the child a small timeframe to begin complying. If the child has not begun to move toward the time-out location by the count of five, then the parent leads the child, dealing with any physical resistance calmly. As the parent leads the child, if there is significant resistance, the parent should use face aversion and avoid verbal interchange, which minimizes negative attention. After placing the child on the time-out rug, remind him that the amount of time can be shortened by half if he is quiet during the time-out. (Remember that using positive incentives with a punishment makes it more effective.) If the child misbehaves, *ignore* it and wait until there is a few-second quiet period before ending the time-out. The time-out ought to end with the child exhibiting desirable time-out behavior in order to not reward misbehavior. Verbally praise them for the two seconds of quiet by saying, "I loved your quiet time at the end." The time-out is not extended by the parent for misbehavior in an attempt to decrease misbehavior. Threatening the child with additional punishment because of misbehavior in time-out is counterproductive (e.g., "If you don't sit quietly, you'll get another time-out.") If after several attempts at time-outs, the child becomes increasingly resistive and negative behaviors escalate, stop using time-outs and change strategies to incentive-based interventions.

Avoiding Accidental Self-Injury and Poisoning

Children with ADHD appear in emergency rooms more frequently, and their behavior presents more serious safety concerns than peers without ADHD. They have more injuries because of their high level of physical activity and impulsivity. Cuts, bruises, and broken bones result from their sense of adventure and inability to think about the consequences of their physical activity. Experiencing pain does not seem to lower their risk-taking behavior. This same adventuresome nature leads them to taste many available liquids in kitchen cabinets and in the garage. Ingesting some of these liquids can be life-threatening.[38]

Suggested interventions: Proactive interventions are necessary because of the potential for serious injury. Extra precaution needs to be taken in their physical environment to lower injury rates. Anticipate and modify any areas in the environment where falling from high places could occur. Open windows, ladders, balconies, lofts, or staircases are areas where self-injury occurs. A simple modification of a second-story window is to install permanent screens or safety locks. Encourage them to wear helmets and other protective gear when bicycle-riding or similar activities. Also, avoid letting them play in high-traffic areas. Carefully monitor their activity near or at construction sites.

Keeping dangerous chemicals and medicines in locked locations is a simple and inexpensive remedy. Continue to lock dangerous chemicals up even as the child gets older, but educate them about what chemicals are dangerous to ingest.

If the child has moderate to severe ADHD, medication can reduce activity level and impulsiveness, which typically reduces accidental self-injury and poisoning.

Gun Safety

Accidental shooting of themselves or others occurs at a higher-than-normal rate. These accidental shootings are a result of a complex set of dynamics: impulsive, curious, and attention-seeking behaviors combined with the availability and allure of firearms.[39] Accidental shootings occur in homes and on hunting trips.

Parents usually try and educate their children about guns and warn them about the dangers. They assume that education and warnings are sufficient, so the guns are not adequately secured. Furthermore, when their child is playing in other homes, parents forget or are embarrassed to ask if there are guns and if they are secured.

Suggested interventions: Parents need to secure all guns in their house with either trigger locks or locked cabinets. Ammunition should also be placed in a locked cabinet. Keep the locking keys secure from the child and out of sight.

If the child's family is one that enjoys hunting and the use of firearms, additional interventions may be necessary. Parents will have to determine if hunting is an appropriate activity for their child, depending on the severity of their disorder. Hunting trips can be modified to make them safer. Decrease the social complexity by having only one adult partner, and hunt in locations where few other people are present. Give specific safety instructions—how to carry the gun and when it is appropriate to shoot—with incentives for compliance. Walking a short distance behind the child also provides additional safety. Practice the safety rules without ammunition before going hunting. Another modification of hunting trips can be using archery rather than guns. Fatal injury is much less likely, and the skill of quiet, slow, and careful movement is emphasized.

Understanding Suicidal Statements

Children with ADHD frequently make comments like, "I might as well be dead," or "If I died, no one would care." Regular negative experiences in social interactions and academics help trigger these comments. These statements understandably create fear and dismay for parents. No parent wants to hear these distressing words from their child, and they are often confused about how to react constructively.

Suggested interventions: The most complex task is to determine whether the statements are attention-getting, task-avoiding, frustration statements, or a sincere suicidal statement. Observing the events immediately preceding the statement and the consequences immediately following the statement will reveal the underlying reason they made the statement. If a child is asked to complete a chore while playing a computer game and makes a suicidal-type comment, then it probably is not a sincere suicidal statement. Likewise, if the child is regularly not required to complete the chore after such a statement is made, it, too, was probably not a sincere suicidal statement. When suicidal statements are rewarded by avoiding odious tasks, the frequency of the statements will increase. If the statement is an attempt to avoid tasks or to get attention, then using an ignoring technique is probably most effective. If they are experiencing many failure experiences, the more appropriate intervention to say is, "Today must have been a difficult day;" then set up a structure to help them start having more successes without giving them a lot of attention about the statement.

When the parents (and team) suspect the ongoing suicidal statements are not made to avoid tasks or to only obtain attention, but are genuine statements of hopelessness, different interventions are necessary. Ignoring is not an appropriate response. The child should be more closely supervised if depression is suspected. Focusing on interventions that reduce the child's distress rather than on what they are saying reduces the likelihood of suicidal statements later becoming attention-getting. Listening to the child's comments can help the team identify the major sources of distress. Once the sources of distress are identified, then effective interventions can be planned. For example, the parents may view poor grades as the source of distress; however, the child's comments identify "no friends" as the major source of depression, and the intervention needs to focus on the child's feelings. In addition to behavioral interventions, antidepressant medication may be helpful or necessary. When evaluating the effectiveness of the interventions, use observations made by team members along with the child's reports. Remember, self-observation is difficult for children with ADHD.

Tempering Temper Tantrums

Screaming, throwing themselves to the ground, and breaking things are some common tantrum behaviors and are seen more frequently with children having ADHD. Lower frustration tolerance, difficulty with transitions, and delaying gratification all increase the likelihood of temper tantrums. The frustrated parents frequently—and unknowingly—respond in ways that maintain or increase the tantrum behaviors. In an attempt to stop the child's upsetting and embarrassing behavior, the parents give in to the child's demands. This type of response rewards the child's tantrum behaviors and increases their frequency. If parents attempt to be firm about their limits and later give in when the child escalates their tantrum behaviors, then the child learns to escalate tantrum behavior.

Sometimes the parent's urgent desire to stop the tantrum behaviors results in threatening the child with severe punishments. These severe punishments are usually the ones parents instantly regret making because the result punishes them or turns into empty threats. For example, the parent says, "If you do not stop, you won't be going fishing with Grandpa this afternoon." This threat forces the parent to lose a much-anticipated free afternoon and the child having quality time with Grandpa. This punishment also creates a resentful parent and an upset child. If the parent chooses not to carry out the threat, the child's tantrum behavior is rewarded and the parent loses credibility. This results in the child learning to ignore his parents' threats.

Suggested interventions: It is helpful to review the circumstances surrounding previous temper tantrums to identify patterns of behavior. Insights gained allows for the development of appropriate proactive interventions which reduce tantrums. These insights also help parents intervene more effectively once a tantrum has begun.

Problematic parental responses can initiate and/or maintain the child's tantrums. Reducing some problematic parental responses occurs when parents depersonalize by remembering their child's disabilities. If the parent also remembers the appropriate behavioral expectations for their child's "adjusted age," then embarrassment and frustration are less likely to determine the parental response. When the parent is able to depersonalize and has appropriate behavioral expectations, then she is more able to stop in the midst of the child's temper tantrum and ask herself, "What are the circumstances triggering this outburst?" The answer(s) provide the key to implementing the most appropriate intervention. Some of the common triggers for tantrums and interventions for children with ADHD are described.

Inappropriate expectations: Evaluate if the difficulty level of the task is too high, if incentives are ineffective or too few, and if the delay between beginning the task and receiving an incentive is too long. Consider dividing the task into smaller units and giving more frequent and desirable incentives for successful completion.

Hungry and/or tired: Determine if the child is hungry and/or tired, as the ability to manage frustration decreases under those conditions. If the child is hungry or tired, stop the activity, take care of the child's needs, and reduce expectations about compliance. Keeping the child on a regular schedule for sleeping and eating is a proactive approach that reduces tantrums.

Transitions between tasks or activities: Requesting a child to change tasks or activities frequently triggers temper tantrums. Review whether the child was transitioned too quickly or ineffectively. Ignore the tantrum with face aversion until the child is quiet, then state, "Let's try making a change so you can manage yourself better. I am putting five minutes on the timer and then we will change activities. If you quietly make the change, then you will earn five minutes on your Game Boy® (or any desirable incentive)." Cueing the child frequently about specific time limits and about the opportunity to earn desirable incentives for non-tantrum behavior is a proactive approach.

Unclear instructions: Were your instructions short, clear, and concise? Review guidelines for giving instructions. Ignore tantrum behavior and attempt to restate more effective instructions.

Delayed gratification: A tantrum is likely when the child demands immediate gratification (e.g., parental attention, a turn, or a toy) and it does not rapidly occur. A proactive approach is teaching them to delay gratification by consistently stating and enforcing a rule (e.g., saying, "You will be ignored until asking in a quiet voice 'Mother, may I talk with you?'" and then the mother responds positively.) After success with the request format, then the mother starts using a timer to help the child learn to wait for longer periods of time. The longer waiting time is encouraged by using an incentive for successful waiting. A simple hug and verbal praise may be sufficient incentives for many children.

If the child has already begun a tantrum, ignore her until she has a moment of quiet and then respond. The desired outcome is to get the child to associate getting attention with non-tantrum behavior.

Overstimulating environment: Sometimes parents inadvertently place the child in an overly stimulating environment and the child begins to have a temper tantrum. The parent can non-emotionally remove the child from the situation until the tantrum subsides. The parent determines if the environment can be modified to reduce stimulation for the child.

Medication is very helpful in reducing temper tantrums for children with moderate to severe forms of ADHD. If interventions are not proving successful, try videotaping parental interactions with child. The team reviewing the tape helps reveal any problematic dynamics.

Reducing Stealing and Shoplifting

The impulsive nature of children, coupled with their slow incorporation of social rules and their problem with thinking about consequences, lead to higher levels of stealing both inside the home and outside the home setting. Family members feel frustrated and angry, and levels of trust decline. Stealing outside the home leads to embarrassment and anger. Parents usually deal with the problem behavior by lectures and some form of punishment. These parental interventions are usually not very effective because lectures don't arouse the usual guilt the parents expect to occur, and the punishment doesn't work because the parents are not aware of how to use it effectively. The child's stealing is often maintained by them getting to use or eat what they steal for a period of time.

Suggested interventions: The easiest intervention to make in the home is to secure valued items in the home with locks. When the child is taken outside the home to a location where stealing is likely, it is easier to monitor them without other siblings present. A punishment approach can be used effectively if what is stolen must be replaced by them at twice the value of the item stolen and they must earn the money to make the payback. If a program of earning and saving money is already in place in the home, then using their savings to pay for the stolen item at twice its value can rapidly reduce stealing.

If stealing is a regular problem, then setting up an incentive program for not stealing can be put into place. For example, if a five-year-old child does not steal during each twenty-four-hour period, then a nickel is put in a clear-sided bank so the child can see the progress he is making to earn an object that he desires. The system must be set up so that earning the object does not require extended periods of time. The ability of the child to wait will need to be taken into consideration.

How to Handle Lying
When it is detected that a child with ADHD is lying, a common response of parents is to start with what is often called the inquisition approach. The parent is determined to get the child to tell the truth, and a power struggle develops that does not produce the desired result—the child admitting their dishonesty and apologizing. The lying often occurs when the child is found breaking a family rule and they lie to avoid the punishment that has been promised.

Suggested interventions: If the parent can remember that almost all children lie at times to avoid punishment or disapproval, then it helps them depersonalize and not be so hurt by the child's lying. Like many of the problems that have been discussed, medication can help reduce the impulsive tendencies of the child with ADHD and needs to be considered as an option.

Changing the structure of how we deal with lying can reduce the problems. If the parent has clear information that the child is lying, then do not ask them, "Are you lying?" because the most frequent result of this approach is to have the child lie again. A constructive approach is to tell the child, "Because you have been dishonest, the negative consequence will follow." Be careful to not fall into the argument "trap." Use the techniques outlined in the Decreasing Arguing Behavior section. The next and most important behavioral intervention is to set up an incentive program for telling the truth.

Avoid Using Negative Phrases—"Don't Do That"
Parents frustrated with misbehavior and overwhelmed with feelings of failure find themselves searching for words to say that might change behavior. They often

resort to the time-worn phrase, "Don't do that." The declaration "Don't do that" is heard so often by children with ADHD that it must sound like a recording. This phrase is often used with an angry tone of voice and follow-up comments like, "How many times do I have to tell you?" "Why do I have to repeat myself?" "Why can't you listen like your sister?" The message the child receives is that she is stupid and inadequate! The frequent sending of this message lowers self-confidence along with all the child's other failures.

Suggested interventions: Children with ADHD behaviorally respond more effectively to positively stated instructions than negatively stated instructions. Research shows that negatively stated instructions actually increase the likelihood of the misbehavior. Parents are often unaware of how frequently they use phrases like "Don't do that." Counting the frequency of these phrases provides a concrete measure for the parents and helps educate and motivate them. The parents become aware of their overuse of the phrase and its detrimental impact and are relieved to know there is a better way. To obtain the count, have a spouse or friend observe the parent for two days and record each occurrence. The count is usually so high that the parents are startled, guilt-ridden, and motivated to change.

The parents are taught a more effective way to impact their child's behavior. Reduce the phrase "Don't do that," and replace it with positive and clear instructions of what to do. For example, if a child takes a rubber band and pulls it into the shooting position toward his little sister, the urge to say, "Don't shoot your little sister!" is almost automatic. If the parental automatic response is to say "don't," the likelihood of it happening increases dramatically. Instead of telling the child "don't," give the following instruction: "See if you can hit my shoe." This instruction may sound counterintuitive; however, it allows action, gives direction that avoids harm, and decreases negative attention. As another example, when moving down the grocery aisle, the child reaches out to touch items on the shelf. Again, there is the urge to say, "Don't touch them—they will fall and break." A positive instruction would be: "Please hold this cereal box for me, so I can have more room in my basket." If the child complies, then a verbal incentive needs to be immediately given. Children who have moderate to severe ADHD may need a concrete incentive in addition to the verbal incentive.

The parents need significant encouragement from the team when trying to make this difficult change. Parents may find that it is easy to slip back into the habit, so periodic observations need to be repeated.

Getting Them Ready for Bed and to Sleep
Bedtime is the most complicated part of the day for many families. Everyone is tired and tempers are frayed. Maintaining a consistent routine with structure is

difficult. Parents might have to contend with a child that doesn't want to go to bed for fear they will miss out on something. The bedroom may have too many stimulating objects, or there may be noise from other parts of the house that keep them awake. At bedtime, the child may be fatigued and their medication might be less effective, which leads to increased arguing. It is a recipe for disaster and a time when more emotional bruises and physical shiners occur.

Suggested interventions: Parents need support and help when developing and implementing interventions, not judgment. Interventions addressing medical, structural, and behavioral concerns will reduce bedtime "battles."

Evaluating the impact of medication on sleep patterns is an appropriate place to begin. Some children experience insomnia as a side effect of their stimulant medication. This side effect usually goes away after two weeks. If after two weeks, the child is still experiencing insomnia, it is necessary to determine whether medication or a lack of medication is interfering with sleep.

Prior to making modifications to dosage and/or schedule of the child's medication, consult the child's physician. The physician may suggest either stopping the last dosage of the day or reducing the dosage for several days in order to determine whether the medication is causing the sleep disturbance. It is imperative that only one change in treatment intervention occur at a time in order to draw an accurate causal conclusion. For example, during that period when the physician is investigating whether the medication is causing the sleep disturbance, it is important that no other treatment intervention change. If the insomnia decreases after the medication change, then it is highly probable that the medication is the problem.

An additional intervention is changing the physical structure of the home to limit stimulation at bedtime. Start by examining the child's bedroom, looking for sources of stimulation. Objects too stimulating for the child should be placed in a playroom—not the bedroom. They should sleep in a darkened room with the door closed. Closing their bedroom door when they are very young helps them adjust to this method of reducing stimulation. Also evaluate the noise level within the home. If a sibling likes to listen to loud music, have her use headphones. Use dark window coverings to reduce the amount of morning light that enters the room.

Another structural change may need to be done for young or extremely hyperactive children to keep them safe and in the room. Use this only when all other interventions have been tried. Cut the door in half and put a lock on the lower portion so the child cannot escape and get outside the house while others are sleeping. This change in the physical structure can help the parents get some needed rest, because some small children are so hyperactive that just keeping them in the bedroom could exhaust a marathon runner. Remove objects from the bedroom that the child could use to climb over the lower half of the door. Use a baby monitor to keep tabs on the child; this avoids giving them attention by constantly peering into the room. They may scream for extended periods of time when this restriction is initially placed on them. Take this into consideration and warn those within earshot of your plan. The team should help develop this intervention to avoid its misuse or others misunderstanding. Keep records of its use to help verify its limited use.

Behavioral interventions use a combination of consistency, incentives, and punishments. Intervening with an early bedtime helps avoid problem behaviors due to fatigue and also gives the parents and siblings a rest. In addition, a consistent bedtime routine is important because it makes the child's world simple and predictable. The routine should have basically the same steps and order each night. During the routine, the key is to transition the child from one bedtime preparation activity to the next. Children with moderate or severe ADHD require many transition steps. For example, after dinner, state, "In fifteen minutes, it is time for your bath; if you start your bath on time, then you get to play with five of your favorite bath toys." At three minutes till bath time, repeat, "It's three minutes until bath time." Five minutes before bath time is over, state, "In five minutes, the bath is over, and next, we brush your teeth." Incentives are the most powerful motivator for compliance or cooperation and need to be clearly stated at the time of the request. The child should want to earn the incentives if they have been properly chosen. However, when the child perceives a task as especially difficult, then requests are best given using "If ..., then ...," statements, which specify both the incentive and punishment. For example, say, "If you get in bed without complaining, then I will read a story to you for five minutes." Use a timer that is visible to the child to reduce arguing about reading-time ending, and say, "If you complain about going to bed, then there will be no story tonight."

After getting the child to bed, then the next challenge is keeping them in bed. Use an "If ..., then ..." statement to let them know the consequences of their behaviors. For example, say, "If you are quiet and stay in your bedroom, then you will earn a token, and if you are not quiet and leave your bedroom, then bedtime is fifteen minutes earlier tomorrow." If the child demands attention by making statements like, "I need a drink; I need to tell you something; I need to go to the bathroom," the best response is no response. Ignoring their requests will not give them the attention they are seeking. Some children will repeatedly leave their bedroom, if they are ignored. They should be escorted back to the bedroom immediately without eye contact or comment. It may take a week of consistently taking them back to the bedroom before a new pattern of behavior is established.

Sometimes parents can take turns every other night in returning the child to the bedroom so one of them does not become overly tired. If parents get overly tired, then they have a tendency to be inconsistent and give in to the demands of the child to get some "temporary" peace. The task of getting the child to bed and getting her to sleep is so difficult for some parents that they should give themselves an appropriate incentive for their Herculean effort. For example, after two days of consistent effort, they could go treat themselves to dessert and coffee. The team can provide emotional support, as well as creative ideas, if parents' efforts fail.

If parents continue to struggle without significant success, then videotaping their efforts provides valuable information for them and the team. Together, the parents and team can evaluate the tape and gain insight into problem dynamics. This evaluation allows the team to develop new and more effective interventions.

Coping With Early Risers

Many parents pray for the child with ADHD to sleep late (at least 5:00 AM) so that the rest of the family can rest. Some of these children jump out of bed very early and demand immediate attention or use this potentially unsupervised time to be mischievous. Familial fatigue is an understandable side effect of this dynamic.

Suggested Interventions: Multiple interventions are available, and choosing those that best meet the needs of the family is important. Anticipating early-morning problem behavior allows one to develop a proactive approach.

Structural interventions aim at evaluating the level of stimulation in the early morning hours. For example, reducing noise level and light level by using blackout shades may prevent early awakening. A white-noise machine or fan blocks out early-morning noises. Some children may take the opportunity to sneak out of the house while their parents are still asleep. Because of their impulsiveness, they can get involved in dangerous activities. Placing locks on the outside doors, out of their reach, can increase safety but obviously will only work for the younger child. Another approach is to use door alarms that sound when the outside door is opened. Ask your neighbors to inform you if they observe your child alone outside the house early in the morning.

The type of behavioral intervention varies with the age of the child and the severity of the disorder. It may be sufficient to provide incentives and activities in their rooms to encourage quiet play for younger children with milder forms of ADHD. The incentives and activities will need to be changed frequently. Also, the incentives must be earned prior to the morning. For example, going to bed without arguing may earn playing time on the Game Boy® the next morning. Children with moderate to severe ADHD require supervised, action-orientated activity which does not have to be earned. For example, the early arising parent takes the child for a physical activity outside the house that they both enjoy—jogging, gardening, and bicycling. Rather than trying to diminish their activity and energy level, redirect it positively.

The early-rising children with moderate or severe ADHD may require medication adjustments. For example, Clondadine may help them sleep more hours.

Getting Them Up in the Morning

Sometimes, it is difficult getting children with ADHD out of bed, especially when they are teenagers. The dynamic between child and parent often becomes adversarial. This interaction begins the day with a negative tone and increases the number of punishment threats. Sometimes parents feel so hopeless and exasperated, they leave the house with the child in bed.

Getting them up may be more difficult for two major reasons. First, they did not get to sleep early enough the night before. Second, getting up means going to school, and if school time has been filled with failure experiences, then staying in bed is a method of avoiding future failure.

Suggested interventions: Maintain a record for a week to determine which factors may be affecting the child's ability or desire to arise. Keeping the record helps begin the depersonalizing process, creating an environment conducive for interventions. Take special note of when the child goes to bed and gets to sleep. Also, observe if the child is influenced by the next day's scheduled activities—school, job, morning soccer, or fishing. While making the observations, continue your usual approach to the child.

Observations may indicate there is a lack of sleep and/or attempt at avoiding experiences that may lead to failure. In this case, multiple interventions are necessary; initially address the lack of sleep issue by utilizing the principles already described in the Getting Them Ready for Bed and to Sleep section. That section focuses mostly on using structural and behavioral interventions.

If the child appears to be avoiding having failure experiences by staying in bed, then increasing the number of positive experiences is prudent. Frustrated parents may have a difficult time increasing incentives for a child who is driving them crazy most mornings. If the parents identify that the child may feel just as frustrated and hopeless as they do, it decreases their anger. It further allows them to reevaluate their approach and attitude. Once parents start using more incentives for getting up and judiciously use punishments, they rapidly see improvement. An example of using incentives is giving the child their favorite cereal with milk, sugar, and favorite fruit topping if they make it to the breakfast table before five minutes has elapsed after being awakened. Place a timer in their bedroom and set it for five minutes to assist their compliance. If they don't make it in five minutes, they get dry cereal for breakfast. As another example, allow them to earn fifty cents for the purchase of a favorite toy. Keep the money in a place where it can be seen, and write on the container the amount they need to earn to buy the object. It is also helpful to put a picture of the toy on the container to help keep them focused. Older children can select a reasonable incentive for arising on time—driving the car. This approach gives the teenager some feeling of control and increases cooperation.

Getting Ready for School

Morning time is usually a demanding time for parents and children. Parents and children are faced with time limits; they have to eat, get dressed, and prepare for the day. Parents often describe their house as a zoo where they repeat every instruction to their child twenty times. They wonder why their child can't remember a simple morning routine and how they can lose the same thing three times in a morning.

It is difficult for parents to have appropriate expectations of their child because they underestimate the limitations an ADHD disability pose: it requires staying focused and being task-oriented. The child's working-memory problems, impulsiveness, and overreaction to high levels of stimulation all interfere with his or her ability to comply to the request "get ready for school."

Suggested interventions: Organization and simplification strategies, along with appropriate expectations for the child, are the main interventions that compensate for the disability. Make a chart listing the morning tasks in the order to be completed, e.g., shower, eat breakfast, brush teeth, get dressed, and check backpack for school materials. Children who have moderate to severe ADHD would also require a timeframe for each activity, e.g., brush teeth from 9:00 to 9:05. Using a timer would make time visible, helping keep them on schedule and task. Incentives can be earned after completion of each task, e.g., tokens. Children with mild forms of ADHD may only need an incentive after completing the entire morning list.

After the parents and child decide the morning tasks, each task can be simplified, such as laying out clothing the night before in a pre-determined location. Also, the backpack should be kept in a specific visible location and loaded the night before. Further simplify the environment by keeping the noise level down—turn off the TV and radio. Awakening the child early, before siblings, helps parents concentrate on only assisting them. Furthermore, parents can get ready for the day before their children wake up to reduce chaos and confusion. Children with severe ADHD will probably require medication in addition to using the above recommendations.

It is important to keep the tasks enjoyable. For example, a parent and child could sing a song about putting clothes on that teaches order and concepts, such as right and left. For an older child, making a game out of getting ready increases the likelihood of cooperation; a "beat-the-clock game" and earning a special incentive lightens the morning mood.

Getting Their Chores Done

The child's working memory deficit, motivational problems, and short attention span all complicate their ability to successfully complete chores. It is a continual source of frustration for parents, and they often stop requiring chores. If the parents decide to stop expecting chore completion, then the child loses the opportunity to learn responsibility and develop a work ethic.

Suggested interventions: Any child can complete a chore, regardless of the severity of their disorder, if the interventions are appropriate. Using effective interventions reduces parental frustration and allows the child to succeed.

Observe the child and identify the type of activities they seem to most enjoy. The parent and child then select a chore which is similar to their enjoyed activities. Initially, we want them to think of the chores as being fun. If the chore provides highly visible cues when it is completed, it adds to their sense of accomplishment. For the child who loves to play in water—bathtub, toilet, or sink—they may decide that washing the dishes would be the chore. Using unbreakable dishes reduces complications and fears. After one chore is chosen, decide on the parameters in order to give clear, simple instructions. For example, the parent could fill the one sink with the dirty dishes and hot, soapy water and the other sink with rinse water. The child is instructed to wipe each dish with a brush and then put it in the rinse water. Initially, it is important to focus on the completion of the chore and not on the quality (approximations). If a perfect dishwashing job is expected, the child's enthusiasm will rapidly vanish. After they successfully comply with the initial instructions, then gradually increase the level of chore difficulty. Instructions should continue to be clear and concise with a limited number of steps. Verbal praise periodically given during the activity will help keep the child focused and motivated. In addition, concrete incentives may be necessary for children with moderate to severe ADHD. One chore may be sufficient for younger and/or seriously disabled children. Children who are less disabled and mature can progressively be given more chores.

Having the child start chores at an early age with a consistent routine can help parents compensate for the child's memory deficit. Initially, a consistent routine would have the child performing the same chore the same way at the same time of day.

Making Them Safe After School Time (Latchkey Children)

For older children (nine years and older), managing their after-school time can be difficult if unstructured or unsupervised. If the child is walking home without supervision, there are many opportunities to misbehave; in fact, they may have trouble even making it home. Many serious complications can arise at home without supervision. Some parents become aware of some of the problems immediately, while others may take time to reach awareness. Older children may use this time as an opportunity to experiment with alcohol, drugs, and sex. A lack of structure and their desire for exciting experiences sets the stage for disaster. Acting on impulse without thinking of the consequences is part of their disability.

Parents are usually aware of the difficulties with their child being latchkey but cannot think of desirable and affordable options. Parents face financial responsibilities, their child's resistance to some forms of supervision, and parental burnout.

Suggested interventions: Children with ADHD can be set up for success with structure and limited unsupervised time; therefore, before leaving them alone after school, evaluate their ability to safely handle this freedom and deal with unforeseen problem situations. Parents should not be leaving children with ADHD under nine years of age home alone. When evaluating their ability to be unsupervised, look at their past behavior, not their verbal promises of future behavior, e.g., whether they make it home from school on time. If the child has had past failures at independence, the parent has to carefully weigh the child's need for independence versus safety needs. Parents can provide opportunities for children to learn responsibility by gradually increasing their independence.

The severity of the child's ADHD is also a factor when determining the appropriate amount of unsupervised time. For example, a forty-year-old adult with severe ADHD may still need a spouse's supervision, especially with finances.

If it is determined that the child should not be left alone, the parents have to set up structure with supervision. The community and parents' resources determine what supervised options are available. It is not a good idea to put another sibling—or another child—in charge of the child with ADHD, because it usually leads to serious conflict. Alternative options—after-school, church, and sports programs may benefit some of the children. Others may benefit from the more individualized attention relatives, neighbors, or friends provide. These people could provide appealing job activities. If the parent has the financial resources, they could provide money for the individual to "pay" their child for their work. Ostensibly, it works betters if the individual—not the parent—pays the money to the child, even though the parent provides the money. Whoever cares for the child needs to keep them physically active.

If there are limited resources (community or parents), the job of finding supervision requires creative initiative. For example, find a mentor with similar interests to your child. If they like cars or seem to be mechanically inclined, find a responsible adult who will teach them, or call up a trade school and inquire about mentoring.

If the parents determine the child can handle some unsupervised time at home, then appropriate parameters need to be established. Structure with incentives help set the stage for success. For instance, give the child a wristwatch and fifteen minutes to get home from school when the distance is six blocks—don't give them too much time to misbehave. After arriving home, they must check in with a parent with the home phone (caller ID keeps the child honest). The child can earn an incentive for getting home on time and calling. Be cautious about using punishment for late arrival or check-in with teenagers, because it may increase their oppositional behavior. The frequency and/or potency of the incentive are modified depending on the child's ability to delay gratification and her compliance rate. Rules must be clearly spelled out, such as: no friends allowed over when adults are not present. Structure their time with a specific routine, such as: check–in with parent, eat a snack, vacuum the living room, and listen to music or call a friend. If structure at home is not working, then consider an after-school job that would provide better structure along with a monetary incentive.

Doing Homework Without a Fight

Getting schoolwork home, completed, and returned on time is a parent's fantasy but is seldom realized without significant effort. Losing the homework, lying about the homework, and a lack of ability to stay focused plague the parent and the child's interaction. Resistance to homework completion takes many forms. For example: "I will do it later," "It is too hard," and "I don't understand" are frequently used phrases whined in the ears of the parents, who often threaten them, and a power struggle ensues. The word homework becomes synonymous with the word misery for both the child and the parent.

Some parents do not know how or feel it is unnecessary to provide supervision, incentives, or structure for homework completion. When homework issues are not appropriately addressed by parents, the child is unsuccessful, the parents frustrated, and negative feelings abound.

Suggested Interventions: Increased success at completing homework requires new and creative ways of providing additional structure and incentives because of the disabilities associated with ADHD. Parents can use the following ideas for improving homework completion:

- Set up a regular communication system with the teacher to clarify what and when homework is to be completed.
- Having the child work on their homework at the same time and in the same area each day will create consistency. The designated homework area should be quiet and free from distractions. A parent should be sitting in the area or close by and frequently check on homework progress.
- Have the child work on their homework when they are well-rested and not hungry.
- Making homework fun sets the tone. Give the child's efforts lots of encouragement. Be creative with homework; turn it into a fun game.
- Set up an incentive program to increase motivation. Remind them often about the incentive to keep motivation high. Give the incentives as soon as the work is completed. Periodically, change the incentive to keep motivation high. Over time, some may tolerate a gradual delaying of the incentive.
- Use a timer to let the child know how long they need to work. The timer should be visible to the child, as it provides immediate feedback. Ten to thirty minutes is usually a maximum work period. Give clear instructions about how much work needs to be accomplished to earn an incentive.
- Checking their backpack for homework when arriving at home and when leaving for school helps the child have success.
- Medication ought to be at adequate levels during homework time for children with moderate to severe forms of ADHD.

Parents can also review later in this section under Teacher's Challenges—Coordinating Homework Efforts—to attain additional ideas. If all of these ideas have been implemented without success, then videotape a homework session and take it to a team meeting for review.

Talking on the Phone Without Interruption

Most children have discovered that when their parents are on the phone, it presents an opportunity to either continually bug and beg for something objectionable, thinking the parent will say yes to get rid of them, or use the lack of unsupervised time to get into trouble. However, children with ADHD really know how to take it to a new level. Parents feel angry and frustrated with their child's behavior and react with a negative intervention. For example, the parent stops the conversation, yells, glares at the child or hangs up in disgust. All of these parent behaviors unfortunately provide negative attention, which is an incentive for a child with ADHD to continue, increasing the problematic behaviors. Most parents understandably feel confused, inadequate, and just want a few uninterrupted moments to talk on the phone.

Suggested interventions: A proactive intervention is necessary, because it is difficult to develop one while the child is insistent about receiving immediate attention or is involved in destructive activities. Interventions use combinations of structure modifications, incentives, and ignoring strategies. Interventions address three objectives. First, the parent learns how to set an effective boundary that allows them some uninterrupted time on the phone. Second, the child learns to give the parent uninterrupted time. Third, the child learns to engage in constructive behavior while the parent is on the phone.

An overall intervention strategy relies on the parents' understanding of how to avoid giving negative attention for undesirable behavior, e.g., bugging and begging. Instead, parents focus on giving incentives for positive or desirable behavior, while utilizing ignoring strategies for undesirable behavior. If one plans on having an extended conversation—longer than fifteen minutes—then pre-arrange for the child to receive a "freebie" of a usually earned powerful incentive, e.g., TV or electronic game time. Also organize long phone conversations at times when the child is away or asleep. When receiving a phone call that could be lengthy, tell the caller the call will be returned at a more convenient time. This allows time to plan an intervention strategy.

If the phone call is going to be of short duration, a different strategy can be used. The child should be given clear instructions before incoming and outgoing calls occur and cued when necessary. A clear instruction tells the child what is expected, for how long, and what they can earn for their cooperation. For example, say, "John, while I am on the phone today, I want you to quietly draw or color for five minutes, and then you and I will immediately play a game of your choice for five minutes."

The child's activity and the incentive earned may need frequent modifications because they lose their appeal. After starting the phone conversation, the parent avoids eye contact and states to the child, "What is the rule while I'm on the phone?" This reminds the child what she should be doing and the payoff. A visible timer helps her wait for the specified time.

If the child exhibits any attention-getting behavior, it is important to not respond until the phone call is completed. The child is told with a non-emotional voice and calm demeanor, "You did not follow the rule, so no game this time." If the child fails to comply, it may mean the time period was too long, the incentive was not motivating, or unintentional attention was given. It may take the child several times to decide that it is more beneficial to cooperate, especially if there is a long history of "successful" interruptions. It may take the parent a while to be consistent with this new approach.

Handling Embarrassing Behavior When Visitors Arrive

When visitors arrive, children with ADHD exhibit immature, attention-getting behavior because of their difficulty tolerating divided attention, the increased stimulation, and more complex social rules. Although people endure "showing-off" behavior in young children, it becomes less tolerated as they get older. The child's actions are often embarrassing and/or annoying. The parents become distressed and angry at the child, which tends to escalate the problem behavior. When the child's problem behavior escalates, the parent typically responds by either threatening punishment or offering bribes. Neither approach provides long-term effectiveness in changing the child's behavior.

Suggested interventions: A plan needs to be crafted before visitors arrive that takes into account the child's disabilities. Effective interventions combine structure changes, visitor education, ignoring strategies, and incentives. A structure change that reduces the stimulation and complexity of the social environment is to have an available individual take the child to another location for some one-on-one time. The one-on-one time reduces the child's need to compete for attention. It is helpful to have the time include action-orientated activities, e.g., playing catch.

If the visitors have a better understanding of the child's disability, then they are more likely to support the parent's interventions. Visitors who are either one time or infrequent are given limited information. For example, a mom can tell a salesman, "As you can see, John is excited about you being here; because it is difficult for him, I am going to send him to have some fun in the backyard with his older brother." However, if the individual(s) entering the home are regular visitors, then more detailed education is offered. If the child especially likes a visitor, then a plan could be established where they spend the first fifteen minutes playing together before the visitor interacts with the rest of the household.

Initially, siblings may feel jealous about this special treatment, but they soon see the benefit because the child with ADHD is less annoying throughout the visit. Overall, less time is spent arguing or fighting and everyone gets more individual attention.

Also, the visitor is taught the principles and benefits of using ignoring techniques for inappropriate or undesirable behavior. For example, if the parents are trying to teach John waiting skills, then ignoring is part of teaching that skill. When John is repeatedly pulling at your sleeve and calling your name, use face aversion until he stops and then immediately give him a positive response. Another intervention to assist a child with ADHD to wait for his or her turn during conversations is to use a "talking stick." John is given the following instruction in front of the visitors: "I will give our visitor the talking stick to hold while she talks. When it is your turn, I will give you the talking stick to hold. When your turn is over, I will take the stick from you, and each of us will get regular turns going around the circle. If you talk without the stick, you miss your next turn." (Use a special small, artistic stick to hold. Too big and it could become a weapon.) In addition to the incentive of holding the stick and getting to talk uninterrupted, give verbal praise for their successful waiting.

Structure, combined with using immediate verbal praise for the main incentive, usually is adequate to produce the desired changes. Providing verbal "kudos" to your helpful visitors is also a good idea.

Organizing Successful Birthday Parties

Parents want to have a birthday party for their child, involving people who love and care for their family. This results in the parents inviting many people to the birthday party. As the guests arrive, the excitement builds, as does the social complexity. Being able to handle the complexity of this situation is not a forte of the child with ADHD. Birthday parties that last more than one hour and include many people usually result in a social disaster for everyone.

Suggested interventions: A successful birthday party for a child with ADHD requires modifications from a more traditional party. The parents and child may need help in understanding the need for modifications. After the parents and child accept this idea, then a plan that simplifies the social environment is developed. The ADHD severity level determines the required intervention changes in structure: a limit on the number of guests, time, and activities. The party should be preplanned, with careful attention to the order of events.

A child with mild ADHD could better enjoy a party with only three other children which lasts for ninety minutes. Choose action-oriented activities appropriate for younger children, and change the activities more frequently. To decrease arguing, cheating, and feelings of frustration, avoid having activities where the children compete against each other. For example, hang four large pieces of poster board on the fence and ask the children to draw their favorite object. Help the children transition from one activity to the next by regularly reminding them about the next upcoming event. The parents verbalize by saying, "After we get done eating cake and ice cream, then John gets to open his three presents." Limiting the number of presents to be opened at the birthday party decreases disruptive stimulation. Extra presents can be placed in a closet and used as incentives for appropriate behavior. If the child is taking medication, administer it at a time that ensures maximum effectiveness during the party.

Children with moderate or severe ADHD experience more success when only one other child—preferably not another child with ADHD—is invited and the party lasts no more than an hour. The activities should be action-orientated, structured, and noncompetitive. Carefully arrange the order of activities, taking into consideration their limited ability to wait and delay gratification. It may be preferable to open the present first, eat second, and then play a game. Incentives for appropriate party behavior can be given throughout the party. Explain the order of activities at the beginning of the party and before each transition.

If the parent wants to include more family and friends, consider having multiple parties on different days to maintain a small party size.

Pleasant Family Vacations

Family burnout due to the concentrated time with a child with ADHD on vacations is a regularly occurring problem. Vacations usually alter everyone's sleeping, eating, and physical activity, which is especially distressing to a child with ADHD. The result is children fighting, parents shouting, and everyone wondering "Are we having fun yet?"

If the vacation includes long hours spent traveling in the car, there is a tendency for everyone to lose their sense of humor and sanity. The boredom, restricted physical activity, and limited space are ingredients for a vacation disaster.

Suggested interventions: Reviewing successes and failures of past vacations provides information about where new interventions are necessary. This review helps refocus the family on creatively developing modifications that take into consideration the individual disabilities of the child with ADHD, thereby allowing the entire family to experience a more positive vacation. Explore the commonalities among the success and failure experiences; then use the information in designing future vacations. One family noted that when each of the children had an electronic game to play during travel time—with volume control—that arguing and fighting decreased dramatically for about sixty minutes and then increased. After a brief discussion, the parents decided on the next vacation to add an additional intervention which was to schedule frequent stops—every forty-five minutes—to play catch with a Frisbee. The combined interventions made a four-hour trip a positive experience for the entire family. The additional physical activity addresses the child's short attention span, hyperactivity, and need for increased personal space. The electronic games decrease boredom and the amount of social interaction. The games also provide immediate and systematic rules with built-in incentives through visual feedback.

When planning a vacation, parents should address their child's disabilities, including: the need for increased individual attention, short attention span, the need for increased physical activity, and an uncomplicated social environment. Children with moderate and severe ADHD require such concentrated individual effort and attention by the family that burnout is almost always a problem. One solution is to arrange for a young adult to accompany the family on their vacation as the child's companion.

Burnout can also be reduced by limiting the length of the vacation and by the rest of the family taking a vacation without the child with ADHD. To avoid the child with ADHD feeling left out, arrange for them to stay with the grandparents, where they can receive special and individual attention, or arrange for a parent to take them on a short vacation without the other members of the family.

Academic Remediation During School Breaks

The summer vacation from school, if not handled appropriately, can make integration back into school problematic. Many are behind in academic work and skills. Some of these children lose some of the gains that were made during the academic year in staying focused on their schoolwork.

Suggested interventions: If the child is significantly behind in information and skills, some schools provide a summer school that is individually focused to assist the child. These programs can be very helpful in maintaining skills and learning new information if run properly, but are often only a few weeks in duration.

If the school is not offering appropriate assistance, then the parents can establish a program of regular schoolwork assignments for an hour every morning during the summer. An hour of work a day does not exhaust the parent or the child and helps maintain skills in addition to acquiring new academic information. Coordination with the teacher before school is dismissed for summer can provide the parent with the necessary academic material. Getting learning material in areas that are difficult for the child, but also obtaining material in areas where the child has good skills, can give the child a balance of easy and difficult tasks to accomplish. The difficult tasks should be done first so that each work session ends doing the easy work and thus on a positive note. The home schoolwork should be done at the same time every morning, at the same place and at a location free from distraction. Schedule the work at a time when the parent can give effective supervision. Giving the child regular incentives for staying focused and for not complaining should be a part of the intervention. If the parent lacks the patience to maintain this effort, then find a college student that is home for the summer who has an interest in children.

Helping the Family Survive the Summer

The many additional hours that a child is at home during school breaks usually adds to the family stress that already may be backbreaking. Proactive planning needs to occur that keeps the child involved in positive activities and the parent from becoming exhausted. If planning does not occur, then family frustration, neighborhood problems, and legal problems may rapidly escalate.

Suggested interventions: In order to keep family frustration from increasing and also to help parents facing exhaustion, plan for the child to spend some time away from home. The other alternative is to have one of the parents leave home for a week and go to an environment where they are nurtured. If it is a single parent's home, pay for someone to stay with the child and send the other children to stay with friends. Another way to avoid exhaustion is to have the child with ADHD spend a week with relatives that have good skills in dealing with children but have few other children at home. These individuals can provide individual attention coupled with action-oriented activities like learning how to ride a horse or building a birdhouse.

Other activities that can help relieve the family and at the same time help the child with ADHD are organized activities, like going swimming daily or joining the neighborhood swim team. This activity can help organize several hours a day of the child's time, and the parent can be free from monitoring the child's behavior. If the parent sits and watches the child during the lesson, they may not be escaping from the responsibility.

Develop a relationship with another parent that allows playtime at their home for half a day. Keeping friends is often difficult for children with ADHD because their self-centered and impulsive behavior. To help them maintain a relationship with a playmate, invite one other child to play with your child and feed them well so that they will want to return. Provide incentives for following play rules that have been established.

Reducing Frustration During Church

Sitting quietly through an hour of preaching is very difficult due to boredom and social complexity in the church setting. When parents' quiet threats and dirty looks do not have the desired impact, they become too embarrassed to keep the child in the church service. Typically, parents respond with anger and forcefully take the child from the service. Then they allow the child to run up and down the hallway hoping to prevent a screaming tantrum—but reinforcing the child's problem behavior. Often parents just give up and stop attending church.

Suggested interventions: The type of intervention is determined by the parents' goals. Is the major goal for the parents to be able to listen carefully to the service or to help the child learn to attend church as a family? If the parents would like to focus on the spiritual experience, placing the child in the nursery or hiring a babysitter for home are reasonable interventions. However, if the parents' goal is for the family to attend church together, then realistic expectations and multiple interventions are necessary. If a small child has little experience sitting quietly for any length of time, taking them to church and expecting them to sit quietly through a sermon for more than a few moments is unrealistic without implementing structural and behavioral interventions. Parents can play "church" at home and model the behavior expected of the child and describe the incentives they earn for compliance. Visual incentives can be used and may include snacks that will not stain the carpet or make loud noises. Parents should gradually increase the time the child spends quietly sitting, cueing the child often about the rules and the incentives for complying. Quiet activities, such as drawing or knitting, can be provided to keep the child busy. If the child can sustain quiet activity for about fifteen minutes, the child is ready to attend church.

Parents can consider a church where there is a great deal of verbal and physical activity during the sermon. It is also important to consider which church session to take the child to as well as where and by whom the child will sit. It is generally best to attend an early service and sit in a place where it is difficult to escape— against a wall. Reducing the number of people that will have physical contact with the child also reduces the social complexity. Educate adults sitting near your child to avoid interacting with the child during the service and encourage them to praise the child for sitting quietly.

If the child is in a Sunday school class with peers and has moderate to severe ADHD, it is advisable to assign an adult to provide one-on-one attention. It is desirable to choose an adult with behavior skills and who is firm, but patient. For children with severe ADHD, it may be necessary to choose only one aspect of the church experience for the child to attend. This will promote success both for the child and the attending adults. The appropriate use of medication will dramatically increase successful experiences at church.

Losing Them in Public Places

Children with ADHD wander away in public places and frequently get lost because they are easily distracted, curious, and usually less fearful. Parents express panic, frustration, and anger when their best efforts result in the child repeatedly becoming separated from them in public places. Some parents choose to leave the child at home with an adult, but that is not the only safe solution.

Suggested Interventions: The type of interventions used will depend on the age of the child, the severity of the disorder, and the type of public place being visited. There are several useful guidelines parents should consider when planning to take their child to a public place. Initially, take only the child with ADHD to the public place and only when they are well-rested. Every time, before the child enters a public place, the expectations and consequences for compliant and noncompliant behavior are explained. Also, visits to public places should be short and preferably to places that are minimally stimulating. A good choice would be a fifteen-minute visit to a grocery store during off-peak shopping hours. Before they enter the store, the child is told they will be given a lollipop for keeping his hands inside the cart as soon as the visit is over. If he grabs items from the shelf, the child will immediately be taken to the car. It is important that the parent remove the child from the store and complete the intervention without showing strong emotions. The parent will place the child in his safety seat and sit in the car with him without looking or talking for five minutes. After the five minutes, the rule is reiterated to the child and then they return to the store.

All children eventually outgrow the use of strollers and carts and will need to learn how to walk safely beside their parent. The age at which the process of teaching them begins depends on the severity of ADHD. Begin the process of teaching the child in an environment that is safe and uncomplicated. For example, walking down a sidewalk when few people or cars are present is a good place to start. The child is informed if she wants to try walking rather than be in the stroller, she must be willing to follow the parent's instructions. The parent tells the child, "If you allow me to hold onto your hand without complaining or trying to get away, then you can stay out of the stroller. If you complain or try to get away, then you immediately go back into the stroller for the rest of the outing." Parents should be very liberal with the verbal praise for their child's successful efforts. After the child consistently follows these instructions, and if the environment is relatively safe, then they are gradually given more freedom until they can walk beside the parent without physical contact.

The chosen interventions depend on the type of public place, e.g., a shopping mall versus a park. For children with severe forms of ADHD, visiting a shopping mall requires so much energy and planning that parents should carefully weigh the costs versus benefits before going. If the parent desires to take the child into a complex and stimulating environment, then taking a second adult to carefully monitor the child's actions is advisable. Otherwise, only tortured shopping occurs.

Keeping the child from wandering off requires the parents to recognize it is an ongoing problem that necessitates continual reevaluation using appropriate expectations. The appropriate use of medication can significantly reduce the wandering-off problem for children who have moderate or severe forms of ADHD.

Avoiding Mishandling of Small Animals

Some children with ADHD tend to be aggressive and rough with small animals for several reasons. The children have a decreased ability to interpret the behavior that animals exhibit to let others know how they like to be treated. Because the children disregard the animal's signals, they appear to have little empathy for the animal's discomfort. When they mishandle an animal, the immediate negative response from the animal and witnessing adults often becomes an incentive due to the attention the child receives. This attention increases the likelihood that the inappropriate behavior will be repeated. The child picks up a cat by the tail; the cat immediately struggles and lets out a screech. The parent runs from the kitchen upon hearing the cat's screeches and yells, "Don't do that; how would you like it if I picked you up by your hair?" The child smiles at the parent, which further distresses them. The child now has an effective way to gain immediate, negative attention from both animal and parent—both now distressed.

Some parents may try to protect their child and animals by avoiding encounters with animals; however, it usually doesn't work, because children with ADHD are physically active and can quickly seek out an animal. They are usually less fearful of being injured, which restrains other children from approaching unknown animals. Ironically, some parents have put a leash on their child as a way of controlling dangerous animal contact.

Suggested interventions: The goal of interventions is to teach the child how to get safe, positive attention from animals, as well as positive attention from humans. When the family has pets or is willing to obtain a pet, then the intervention will be different than if the child has limited access to animals.

If the majority of the child's contact with animals is comprised of chance meetings with unknown animals, then addressing safety issues is a priority. Teach the children to stay beside the adult, and if animals are encountered, ask the owner if it is safe to touch them. Once safety rules are established, appropriate touching can be taught. We suggest teaching appropriate touch first with a stuffed animal. The parent can demonstrate touching, including sound effects. Demonstrate sounds associated with welcomed touching and sounds associated with unwelcome touching. Have the child replicate appropriate touch with sound effects on the stuffed animal. Then the child is given verbal praise for their success. Praise may be a sufficient incentive for some children, while others may need a concrete incentive, like a potato chip.

If your family is planning on obtaining a pet, consider several factors. Select an easygoing, friendly pet. Stay away from any animals that have aggressive tendencies and could seriously injure the child. Choose an animal for the child that protects itself by retreating rather than attacking. Animals that can be rapidly taught tricks will be more enjoyable for the child and will allow them to receive positive attention for their training efforts. It is usually best to have the child with ADHD be the owner and trainer of the pet. This gives them special status, focuses responsibility, and reduces competition between siblings.

If it is a source of continual conflict between siblings, then they can each have their own pet. Hopefully, the child with ADHD will take better care of their pet if they view the pet as their responsibility. Have the child attend a pet-training class to learn the best way to care for and train their pet. If the child is too young to attend a class, then the parent can attend the class and teach their child the skills.

The child can teach the pet tricks by learning how to use incentives as a training tool. This will create opportunities for the child to demonstrate his pet's ability to do tricks and to receive positive attention. When a child trained a Bantam rooster to sit on his shoulder, visitors and family members applauded his great skill. The positive attention increased the child's self-confidence and reduced negative behaviors when visitors came to the house.

A child with ADHD will probably have periodic problems mishandling animals. The parents should regularly evaluate safety concerns for the child and pet. The best approach is to continue to provide incentives for good animal care.

Combating Their Attempts to Split and Divide Parents
Children naturally learn to split or divide their parents. If their mom says no to a request, they may quietly approach their dad to see if they can get a yes response. When the parents are split knowingly or unknowingly, the child learns how to manipulate the parental team. Because a child with ADHD requires more interventions that are complicated in nature, the problem of splitting and dividing is typically magnified. The child's behavior is more frustrating and produces stronger emotional responses, making it easier for nonsystematic parenting to occur. The inherent conflict produced by splitting uses valuable family energy as parents vent counterproductive anger toward each other. Another consequence of the parental anger is that a systematic approach to the child is not developed.

Suggested interventions: The cornerstone of intervening with a child who has ADHD is for the parents to have an agreed-upon and consistent behavioral approach, which is often undermined for several reasons. First, parents may lack communication between them. For example, they do not discuss a request made by the child. The child asks mom, "Can I go over to Shawn's house to play?" after the father has already said no. The mom should ask the child, "What did your father say?" If the child says that father says yes, then if possible, the mom should verify with the father. If it is determined that the child has lied, apply an immediate consequence. This helps teach the child not to attempt splitting parents.

Second, splitting may be a reoccurring problem due to parents having differences in child-rearing philosophies and they are unable or do not have the skills to make compromises to develop a unified approach. When the parents are unable to compromise, increased frustration, blaming, and anger are the byproducts. Visits to a therapist who understands ADHD can help them compromise and teach them new skills about parenting interventions, which reduce their blaming and conflict. For example, a therapist can suggest that if one parent corrects the child and the second parent disagrees, there should be no discussion of the disagreement in front of the child. The parents should go into a separate room to discuss the differences and decide on the approach to be used and then interact with the child in a united manner. The therapist can help the parents develop proactive approaches for any problems likely to split or divide parents. It helps to write down the agreed-upon interventions and post them in a visible location. The new skills learned by the parents dramatically increase their ability to be consistent, which results in more success for the entire family.

Successful Parenting with Multiple Households
The necessary systematic and consistent approach to child-rearing for children with ADHD is made more difficult when the child is living in two or more different households. The number of people involved complicates the communication process essential for consistency in implementing interventions. Some parents from multiple households are willing to work together because they have focused on what is best for the child, but even with this positive attitude, communication gets complicated. In other cases, there may be unresolved interpersonal conflicts among the parents which place the child in the middle. The mixed messages and confusing emotions the child is exposed to result in increased acting-out behaviors and splitting among all family members. Conflicts among the parents make the development of an intervention program similar to walking through an uncharted minefield. The uncharted minefield becomes an impediment in assisting the child as they move through their own ADHD minefield.

Suggested interventions: All of the parents need to understand the importance of developing and implementing an ongoing unified parenting plan for the child with ADHD. The treatment team needs to be involved to assist the parents because the problems they face are so complicated. Keeping all the parents updated on the problems of the child and the necessary interventions requires frequent, non-judgmental and open communication. It is inevitable that there will be periodic breakdowns in the communication. These occasional breakdowns are generally easier to resolve than protracted and regular breakdowns. Ongoing communication difficulties require an objective inquiry to determine the causes. The treatment team can help pinpoint the impediments and make recommendations for good, clear communication. If the team determines the major problem for the inadequate communication is due to frequency and/or insufficient content, then the team can help develop a more effective system. They can help the parents decide upon a regular time for communication, means of communication, and the general content of the communication. For example, the biological mother will call the biological father every Friday at 7:00 PM. They will discuss homework assignments and school updates. Each parent is responsible for passing along the information learned to the rest of their household. After the parents have had some success communicating to each other regarding school issues, then they can tackle behavioral problems. Parents can also request the school send information to both households to further facilitate communication.

In another instance, the team may determine that the parents' communication is affected by their high levels of anger and blaming behavior. Upon further investigation, they find that the misplaced anger and blaming is a result of the parents feeling like failures in modifying the child's behavior. This information requires the team to develop a plan of intervention that helps the parents to experience more success. The team will generally simplify and clarify the behavioral interventions for the parents and focus on one of the child's most annoying or destructive behaviors.

The most complicated problem which negatively affects communication arises from serious unrecognized and/or unresolved conflicts among the two households. It is almost impossible to implement a systematic intervention if the parents have hidden agendas or agendas about proving who the "good parent" is and who the "bad parent" is. Typically, this difficult situation is only improved when the parents are willing to do difficult work with a skilled therapist. The therapist openly and non-judgmentally addresses their conflicts and provides skills for resolving them. Additionally, if the therapist can demonstrate the gains possible for everyone by establishing cooperation and effective communication, then conflict will be reduced.

The child can help create or intensify conflict between households by not relaying information accurately and by pitting one household against the other. The child frequently makes negative comparisons, e.g., "Father is a lot more fun and he does not make me do chores." If the parents suspect inaccurate information being relayed, confirm it with the other household and decide on an approach that unifies the households.

Preventing Sneaking Out at Night

The problem of sneaking out at night after the parents have fallen asleep is very alarming to parents. It can start happening when the child reaches the teen years. During these late night excursions, they are more likely to be associating with other teens having authority problems. Associating with others who have problem behavior increases the probability that there will be antisocial behavior. Parents often lay awake at night wondering if their child has left the house and find little help in keeping the child safe.

Suggested interventions: A structured living arrangement can help. Have the child sleep on the same floor of the house as the parents and in a bedroom that requires them to pass the parents' bedroom. Alarms that sound if an outside door is opened can alert parents.

If punishment is the only method that parents use to try to keep the child in the house at night, a pattern can develop where the child starts staying out all night or late into the night to delay punishment. Powerful incentives to stay in the house are needed, because what happens with friends at night can be very interesting. Driving the car to school the next day if they stay in the house can be a very powerful incentive.

If the child develops a regular pattern of leaving the house late at night despite a curfew set by the parents, and incentives cannot be found that are powerful enough to obtain compliance, then creative solutions need to be found. For example, after trying many approaches with little success, a parent set up the following program. The child had been coming back to the house at 2:00 or 3:00 AM. The curfew was at 11:00 PM, and the doors would be locked at two minutes after. If late, he would need to sleep in the unheated garage, where a cot and blankets were provided. This program was initiated in the winter when temperatures were cold, but he was given sufficient bedding so that he would not be in physical danger. The parents, along with the team, discussed the possibility of the child beating on the door until the parents answered it. The parents pledged to the team that they would not answer the door or respond to the knocking. The discomfort of the garage-sleeping decreased the nights out after curfew. Both verbal and concrete incentives were given for the improved curfew compliance.

Enforcing Their Responsible Use of Motorized Vehicles

The thrill of risk-taking behavior and the exhilarating speed of motorized vehicles entice some children with ADHD into dangerous situations. Their impulsiveness, diminished fear response, and attention-seeking behavior dramatically increase the number of serious accidents or legal complications.[40]

Sometimes parents feel relieved by having the child "out of their hair" for a while because they desperately need a break. Consequently, they tend to allow unsupervised riding. It is especially tempting for families that live in rural areas or where the child's friends frequently ride. It can be very difficult for parents to say no when the child is older and argues, "You are treating me like a baby and all of my friends are doing it."

Suggested interventions: Potentially more serious consequences for children with ADHD exist compared to other children when using motorized vehicles, especially if unsupervised and unprotected. The increased availability and variability of motorized vehicles designed for use by very young children has amplified potential injury and parental concern. To decrease the danger for young children, a wise choice might be to downplay the use of motorized vehicles until they are more mature. A non-motorized experience can still help the child to harness some of their energy in a positive and safe manner. The opportunity to ride a fast vehicle can be the most positive part of their day. Look for places and vehicles where safety and speed is carefully controlled, like a supervised skateboard park.

Parents must establish clear rules about when the child can ride, which vehicle can be ridden, places to ride, and what protective gear is to be worn. Also, the parents must teach how to ride safely while still having fun. The parents and the child are best served by using the riding time as an incentive for difficult and/ or unpleasant tasks. If a child is to ride a motorized vehicle, require supervision and safety gear. Riding in areas with a minimal number of objects to hit—e.g., trees, rocks, or cars—decreases the chance of injury. Having them ride on tracks designed for dirt bikes can provide plenty of excitement.

For most sixteen-year-old adolescents with ADHD, obtaining their driver's license is their biggest dream come true and their parents worst nightmare. Parents need to set up rules before driving begins. The rules must take into account the child's emotional immaturity. There should be clear rules about when they can drive the car, who can ride in it, where it can be driven, and the consequences of disobeying the rules, tickets, and accidents. Checking the odometer periodically can help keep the child honest. If the rule is drive straight to the game and then straight home, write down the mileage before they go and when they return. Parents have been known to drive the route, noting the mileage, to avoid arguments. Punishment for breaking the rules should be immediate and severe. For a serious infraction, the driving privilege is suspended a month and they pay the cost of the increased family car insurance, if any. To reward responsible driving, give increased driving time.

For children with moderate forms of ADHD, using motorized vehicles should probably not be allowed unless they are medicated. Their ability to stay focused, obey safety rules, and plan ahead to avoid accidents is so impaired without the medication that the risks are too high. A child with moderate ADHD can drive successfully with medication and structure and still have the positive excitement of driving in his or her life.

Children with severe forms of ADHD ought to have very limited use of motorized vehicles, even when they are on medication, because their disability puts them and others at high risk. Help them find alternative activities like water skiing, mountain biking, and snowboarding that will still provide plenty of excitement and movement.

Developing Guidelines for Dating and Sexuality

Because of increased impulsivity, need for immediate gratification, and lack of planning, a child with ADHD has a greater probability of early sexual exploration. Parents may be so overwhelmed with day-to-day living with a child having ADHD that addressing sexuality is neglected or avoided. Other parents may fear or dread their child's sexual development and vocalize their concerns by stating "don'ts" followed by threats such as, "If you get a girl pregnant, don't bother coming home." The parents' increased anxiety and verbalizations may cause the child to focus more on sexuality.

A parent might feel like their nightmare has just started if they discover their eleven-year-old is already sexually active and have no idea how to prevent further problems, such as disease and pregnancy.

Parents may resort to rigid and negative controlling behavior or give up providing parental structure. It is easy to understand parents' panic at this point because of the serious consequences to the family.

Suggested interventions: Ideally, a proactive approach addressing dating and sexuality must begin early in the child's life. During the child's early years, parents can provide an environment that does not encourage and sensationalize sexuality. Downplay sexuality, but do not ignore it. To avoid making sex education taboo, thus more fascinating, make it matter of fact. Sexuality is approached this way to decrease a preoccupation with it. Monitor the media they are exposed to, which sensationalizes sexuality, and limit their contact. Use non-emotional language to develop a clear and consistent structure about how they spend their free time with the opposite sex. Establish rules about who is in the house with them when the parents are not present. Limit the time it takes to get home from school, and provide incentives for complying. Talk with them in their early years about how old they need to be before dating occurs so that they will be prepared for it to be delayed.

Once sexual behavior has begun, an additional focus needs to be on how to prevent disease and pregnancy. Parents understandably have a tendency to emotionally react and try to control their child's behavior with threats of punishments when they first learn of their child's sexual encounters. Unfortunately, emotionally determined punishment usually has the opposite intended effect. The most productive approach is to continue monitoring and structuring their free time, while increasing the frequency and power of incentives given for complying with parental rules. An example of a powerful teenage incentive may be to offer bungee or skydiving jumps for compliance. It is difficult for some parents in this emotionally loaded situation to think of a positive way to assist the child. One set of parents made a difficult decision to help their daughter obtain a birth-control shot after offering powerful incentives, using structure, and going so far as to nail her bedroom windows shut failed to reduce her sexual behavior. They realized because of her disability that she would not be able to practice safe and responsible sex. The parents had to accept that their daughter would not be able to responsibly use any other form of birth control. They also had her checked regularly for sexual diseases.

Reducing Alcohol and Other Drug Use

Children with ADHD have more difficulty managing uncomfortable feelings, such as boredom, feelings of failure, rejection, or sadness. The use of alcohol and other drugs can be attractive to them because of the rapid change of feelings they produce. Their impulsiveness, decreased ability to think about consequences, and desire for peer acceptance can make them more vulnerable to the use and abuse of drugs. Alcohol is one of the most frequently abused drugs and further increases impulsiveness leading to more behavioral problems.

Parents typically become aware of drug use because children with ADHD are not good at planning or hiding problem behavior. The parents usually respond by either trying to provide drug education and/or to threaten and punish. These responses are insufficient.

Suggested interventions: Early in the child's life, parents can be proactive by learning how to provide a structured environment that provides successes and reduces boredom, thus reducing their vulnerability to drugs. Parents will need to continually structure the child's environment to fit the child's age, development, and interests. For example, a father spent an hour each night helping his son to be an expert at archery. On Saturdays, they attended archery contests locally and then nationally. The boy was kept busy in the evening by a task he enjoyed. He received frequent verbal incentives for making improvement as well as the opportunity to earn better equipment. His father accompanied him to provide additional structure that helped exclude nights out with the boys for drinking parties.

In addition to using structural and behavioral interventions, research indicates correctly using stimulant medication for the child beginning in early grade school significantly reduces their later abuse of alcohol and other drugs.[41] This information may be contrary to what many people believe or have been told. It is thought that the use of medication may reduce drug abuse because the medication helps the child experience more success in almost all areas of their lives.

If a child with ADHD is currently using or abusing drugs, it is important for the parent to evaluate the extent of usage, type of drug, how and from whom the drugs are obtained. Parents also need to know when drug usage is occurring and with whom. The underlying dynamics prompting the child to use—boredom, lack of successes, and/or lack of acceptance from non-using peers—will determine the intervention type. In addressing these issues, it is important that the parents identify and evaluate prior intervention attempts to learn what was effective and ineffective. They must also be aware of their emotional responses to the child's drug usage, because their emotions could inadvertently increase drug usage. If the parents are shouting, screaming, and threatening, they may trigger rebellion or the desire to reduce uncomfortable feelings, increasing the child's motivation to use. For example, the parents discovered that their child's rebellion started after his best friend, who was a non-user, had moved. He had spent time with this friend for several hours after school, and a parent was always present to provide structure and enjoyable after-school activities. The new friend's family was not providing appropriate supervision, and the new friend was a user. Changing after-school free time by enrolling him in a school wrestling program provided both structure he needed and opportunities to make new non-using friends. The coach also agreed to be part of the treatment team and was taught how to use frequent verbal incentives.

Obtaining and Maintaining Employment for the Child
Some children need employment out of financial necessity, and others need employment to keep them constructively occupied. Employment also provides a constructive outlet for their energy, as most jobs available to them are action-oriented. Whatever the reason, a job prepares them for adult responsibilities and they typically have more success experiences than at school. Many of the children with ADHD are outgoing and have an easy time getting jobs as a teenager, but holding on to them is another matter. They rapidly become bored, forget the rules, and become argumentative.

Suggested interventions: A careful analysis of the parents' expectations and the child's abilities is necessary to help teenage children with ADHD to obtain and maintain successful employment. For example, if the child has not been required to earn money and taught how to manage it, money may not be an important incentive to keep them working. As parents, it may be prudent to develop the child's relationship with money by revising how children receive money in the home before sending them to work outside the home. To increase the power of money as an incentive, do not give them an allowance or money for items that are important to them; give them the opportunity to earn it.

If they are ready to seek employment, parents should help their child find a job that has structure and is not socially complex. For example, working with multiple customers in a fast-food restaurant may be overwhelming, whereas doing simple food preparation in the back may be more desirable. Children with ADHD blossom under supervisors who are organized and positive without being over-controlling and obsessive about details.

Once employment is obtained and before the first paycheck arrives, parents should talk to the child about how they will manage the money—with their assistance. Encourage them to budget and save for long-and short-term goals. If the child talks incessantly about buying a sound system for his bedroom—a long-term goal—assist him in saving the money to buy it.

To reduce the chances of impulsive spending, have the child put half of his paycheck into a savings account that requires a parent's signature to remove the money. Keep reminding him why he is saving the money. If it takes too long for him to earn the money for the sound system, he may stop making an effort. To keep the child focused and hopeful, help him select a less expensive system or provide matching money. Setting up a visible chart of his progress in earning enough money is helpful if they are cued regularly to look at the chart.

The second half of the paycheck may be spent within twenty-four hours if some parental structure is not provided. Some parents will divide this money into daily allotments to help reduce their impulsive spending on inappropriate items. As the child becomes successful at money management, structure is gradually reduced.

If the child starts complaining about the boring nature of the job, do not wait to act until they quit or are fired. Help her find a new job that will maintain her interest.

Parents will need to monitor their child's work hours to avoid serious fatigue problems resulting from excessive working. The fatigue developing from long hours of work can significantly reduce the child's ability to stay focused at work and readiness for the next day's schoolwork.

To reduce impulsivity and help sustain focus, make sure the child's medication is in effect during work time.

Sibling Challenges

Coping With "It's Not Fair"

A common complaint of siblings is that the child with ADHD gets preferential treatment. The sibling's complaining is usually motivated by wanting to get more privileges, more attention, or less work. They may also be angry with their sibling because they feel like the child with ADHD deserves more punishment and not incentives.

Suggested interventions: Educate all the siblings about the dynamics of ADHD to provide them with an understanding of ADHD and the reasons for special consideration. The siblings need to learn that special incentives help the child with ADHD complete tasks that are difficult for them. If the complaining sibling is then offered an opportunity to earn special incentives for doing tasks they find difficult, then the complaints usually go away. Some siblings, however, will choose to increase their efforts to earn incentives, and as they earn their incentives, complaining decreases.

Strategies to Decrease Privacy and Personal-Property Violations

Children with ADHD frequently invade the personal boundaries of others, especially their siblings. They have difficulty remembering rules or thinking about consequences and others' feelings. There is a lot of excitement about going into a forbidden room or using a sibling's valuable objects.

Out of desperation, the siblings may ask their parents for help, and if they do not successfully intervene, resentment becomes a major problem. Parents may have attempted interventions that have failed and have given up trying to assist the sibling.

Suggested interventions: Parents need to carefully examine any violations of privacy and property by the child with ADHD and observe the siblings' dynamics. Parents should observe for several days without intervening unless there is physical danger. After the observational period, parents should talk privately with the sibling about his feelings regarding privacy and property violations—let him vent.

The information gathered is used to develop interventions involving the parent and the sibling. Successful interventions use a combination of structural changes, incentives, and punishments to protect privacy and personal property. These interventions will also increase positive sibling interactions. Parents can arrange a family meeting to discuss the ongoing conflicts about privacy and personal-property issues. The parents use a non-blaming approach to describe the need to reduce conflict within the family. The parents might say:

> "We would like to reduce the amount of conflict and have more positive time together by making the following changes: Jess and Tom, you are going to have separate bedrooms with doors that lock from the inside. Your mother and I will have keys to your room, but we will always knock before entering. Each of you will also have a locked cabinet in your room to store your treasures. We will also have keys to those in case yours get lost. If you stay out of each other's rooms when they are unlocked, then each of you can earn an incentive that we agree upon. If we see you go into the other's room without their permission, then you will pay your sibling one dollar from money that you have earned. If we see one of you having the other's 'designated treasures,' then that person will lose the use of one of their 'designated treasures' for two days. These new changes will help us become a happier family. Are there any questions?"

The parents more frequently intervene when the siblings are young and/or when there is a severe form of ADHD. As the siblings mature, the parents and/or treatment team provide ongoing skill training on how to constructively respond to privacy and property violations. The kind of training provided depends on the siblings' interaction style. The siblings benefit from learning to use the same behavioral techniques that the parents utilize, such as incentives for desired behavior and ignoring negative attention-getting behavior. For example, the sibling could tell the brother or sister, "If you use my bicycle only with my permission today, then I will play your favorite game with you for fifteen minutes tonight."

Alleviating Anger and Resentment Toward the Challenging Sibling and Parents

The sibling typically feels angry and resentful toward the challenging sibling because of the embarrassing, annoying, and negative attention-getting behaviors. This behavior requires extra patience, energy, and attention, which usually impacts them negatively. If the child perceives that the parents are not dealing constructively with the challenging child, his or her anger is focused toward the parent.

The sibling expresses feelings in different ways, depending on his or her dominant interaction style. Most of these interaction styles create negative sibling and family dynamics. Some siblings are afraid of the child with ADHD and acquiesce; others are confrontational.

Suggested interventions: Parents need to acknowledge and validate the sibling's anger and resentment without defensiveness. If the sibling is listened to carefully and her feelings validated, then her anger and resentment starts to decrease. An empathetic and open style of communication promotes closeness and cooperation. In this cooperative environment, it becomes easier to educate the sibling about the nature of ADHD, which helps them to depersonalize the problem behaviors and allows them to be better problem-solvers. Parents sometimes intervene to reduce the sibling's feelings of resentment; at other times, they teach the sibling how to intervene. The parents more frequently intervene when the siblings are young and/or when there is a severe form of ADHD. As the siblings mature, the parents and/or treatment team provide ongoing skill training on how to constructively respond to the challenging sibling. The kind of training provided depends on the sibling's interaction style. These interaction styles are described in Chapter Eight—Family Evaluation, under Sibling Dynamics, or recorded in the Treatment Assessment Summary form. Each interaction style is best modified by tailored interventions.

1. Scapegoating/Blaming
   Maintaining dynamics: avoids undesirable tasks, desires getting even, and/or enjoys "victimization" attention
   Skill training/interventions: incentives given for reduced scapegoating behavior, separate siblings during task time, ignore "victimization" pleas to teach positive attention-getting behaviors

2. Protective/Caretaking
   Maintaining dynamics: avoids conflict, wanting parental recognition, values caretaking
   Skill training/interventions: teach discrimination between over-protection/caretaking and appropriate protection/caretaking, incentives given to sibling when encourages responsibility in child with ADHD

3. Confrontational/Combative
   Maintaining dynamics: expression of resentment and frustration feelings, inability to constructively manage anger and sadness
   Skill training/interventions: teach conflict/resolution skills, teach ignoring skills, give incentives for avoiding conflict

4. Acquiescent/Give-in

Maintaining dynamics: intimidated by verbal and physical assault, low self-worth, lack of assertiveness skills, trying to avoid conflict

Skill training/interventions: teach assertiveness skills, teach skills to deal with physical aggression, teach positive self-talk and goal-attainment strategies

5 Avoidant/Ignoring

Maintaining dynamics: feelings of frustration and hopelessness about constructive change, seeking positive attention/interactions

Skill training/interventions: teach behavioral skills that facilitate positive interactions, individualized time with parents, incentives given for engaging with family

6. Supportive/Encouraging

Maintaining dynamics: modeling by parents, understanding ADHD disabilities, depersonalization skills, self-confidence

Skill training/interventions: teach self-care, give regular incentives for efforts

Parents and the treatment team should be aware that this is extremely difficult work for the siblings. Using simple interventions, designed to give the sibling a break from coping with annoying behavior, can reduce or prevent the sibling's resentment. Resentment is also reduced when the sibling receives valued incentives for using the new skills that have been learned. It is important that the incentives are powerful enough to encourage the sibling to make a sustained effort. If the sibling with ADHD attempts to use negative attention-getting behavior and their sibling successfully uses an ignoring strategy on two or more occasions, then the parents allow that sibling to stay up for an extra thirty minutes. Siblings can also be taught to give themselves incentives. A sibling may say to themselves, "If I do not argue with my brother for two hours, my incentive will be quiet time alone in my bedroom."

Managing Interference with Friendships

When a sibling's friend comes over to play, there is usually an increase in conflict, resentment, and jealousy. The child with ADHD most frequently wants to be included and if they aren't, they sabotage the play date. Parents often make the situation worse if they intervene in the following two ways. They force the sibling and friend to play with the child, which increases the sibling's feelings of resentment. Then the sibling may choose to act on the feelings of resentment by making the child with ADHD a scapegoat. The parents may also attempt to intervene by keeping the child with ADHD away from the sibling without using appropriate structure and incentives. Then the child with ADHD often becomes resentful, jealous, and angry, which increases negative behavior. Consequently, the sibling adversarial relationship increases and the parents become ineffective referees.

Suggested interventions: Parents can develop a proactive approach that addresses sibling conflict and jealousy surrounding friendships. The age and maturity of the sibling determines his or her involvement in developing the proactive approach. The parent recognizes that this is a difficult situation for both children. The sibling needs to be able to set individual boundaries about his or her friendships, even when the child with ADHD desires to be more included. The sibling should not be forced to include the child with ADHD for the entire play date, but can be given incentives, such as cookies, for including him or her for a short time at the beginning of the play date. The activity for this time of inclusion should be carefully planned and structured. The activity should have a time limit and clear rules, such as playing a game of "horse," where parents initially supervise. If the child with ADHD starts to argue or break the rules, then she has to sit out for the remainder of the game. Following the brief participation in the play date, the child with ADHD should have a separate preplanned activity where visual contact with her sibling is not possible. The main idea is to keep the child with ADHD busy doing something enjoyable for the remainder of the play date. If for some reason, it is not feasible to include the child with ADHD during the play date, then another desirable alternative is provided. Possibly the child with ADHD can visit another home during the play date or have special time doing a project with a parent, such as playing a board game.

Everyone in the family benefits when the needs of the children are addressed in a constructive manner.

Avoiding Physical Altercations

Siblings experience several negative consequences as a result of physical confrontation with the sibling with ADHD. An older sibling may feel guilt about losing control of his anger and hurting the sibling with ADHD. A younger sibling may be fearful of being injured and avoid the sibling with ADHD. Both younger and older siblings need help avoiding fights and also dealing with their feelings of fear, guilt, resentment, and anger. If parents are not effectively intervening, then siblings often become angry with parents. Their anger can be channeled into sabotaging parental efforts to assist the child with ADHD.

Suggested interventions: The most effective, proactive interventions address structure, incentives, and teaching siblings age-appropriate skills to reduce escalation of anger and physical aggression. Parents should carefully evaluate their use of punishment when intervening during sibling conflict, because non-judicious use of punishment may increase physical aggression.

Modifying structure is the easiest and most simple intervention to reduce physical aggression. Parents should identify which situations increase frustration and physical aggression during play time. If the children fight over toys, then providing structure with rules and incentives is necessary. For example, if there is conflict over a favorite toy car, then the parent can use a timer to oversee five-minute turns with the toy. Any toys or objects that can be used as weapons, such as bats, golf clubs, and guns, should be removed prior to play time. It is also advisable to discourage play fighting, as it often results in hurtful behavior.

Another frequent source of conflict which leads to physical aggression is the invasion of personal space. This conflict can be reduced by modifying the environment to provide separate bedrooms and/or play areas. Play area can be divided by gates, playpens, or tape on the floor. After the siblings have separate play areas, then for brief periods, they might be able to play together without physical aggression. After the play area has been prepared, parents initially will need to remain in the area and provide close supervision. Direct observation allows the parent to implement the new interventions that include incentives. The more impulsive the children, the more important it is to closely supervise and clearly state the rules and incentives governing play time, such as: if they play fifteen minutes without kicking, biting, or hitting, each will immediately be read his or her favorite book. The flip of a coin or a choosing rhyme game will decide which book is read first. Once the aggressive behavior is under control, less supervision is required. *Hint:* Parents should thoughtfully select an activity or chore that allows close supervision of the children while the parent accomplishes necessary work, such as: folding laundry, clipping coupons, or dusting in the same room.

Increasing the sibling's level of knowledge about how to constructively respond can reduce the probability of fighting. The age and sophistication of the sibling determine the type of information and training provided. For example, an older sibling ought to be taught to understand the dynamics of ADHD and how to depersonalize. He can learn to identify the behavioral stages of escalating anger and which strategy to implement. Staying non-emotional, looking physically non-threatening, calmly asking "What do you want," and leaving the area are all possible interventions. A younger sibling might have difficulty understanding the dynamics of ADHD or the different stages of escalating anger; therefore, a training program that focuses on how to physically respond might be more appropriate.

The most easily taught strategy for a younger sibling is to merely walk away. Parents should be modeling the "quietly walk away" strategy. The younger sibling is taught to walk to the parent and quietly give a prearranged signal that indicates protection is needed as they are trying to avoid a physical confrontation. The sibling should receive powerful incentives when they use the skills they have been taught. Strong negative feelings will dissipate rapidly when the sibling has the skills to avoid physical fighting and is given incentives for using those skills.

Teacher Challenges

Decreasing Arguing Behavior
A chronically arguing student is an emotional button-pusher for teachers. Because of the school environment, teachers of children with ADHD are forced to develop strategies to manage this annoying behavior. School is an extremely challenging environment for children with ADHD, given that during a typical day, the teachers and staff make more than one hundred requests of them. This presents a potential of at least that many arguments per day requiring a teacher's response.

When children with ADHD argue, they may receive attention, delay or avoid beginning the task, or get the teacher to renegotiate. These are powerful incentives that maintain and increase arguing behavior for the child. Understandably, teachers can become exhausted and angry toward an argumentative child with ADHD. It is easy for the teacher to respond by arguing with the child, bribing her to comply, and/or threatening punishment. These strategies are not effective in the long run and create a negative dynamic that is damaging to everyone involved.

Suggested interventions: There are many effective interventions that a teacher can implement regarding arguing behavior; however, the goal of the intervention needs to be realistic to avoid failure and further feelings of frustration. A realistic goal is to reduce arguing behavior, not completely eliminate it.

Seven different interventions have proven effective in reducing arguing behavior. The interventions focus on how instructions are given, how and what incentives are given, how to reduce negative attention, depersonalization, action learning, appropriate expectations, and medication. It may be necessary to use several of these interventions in combination to obtain the desired results.

Arguing typically starts when a teacher makes a request of the child; therefore, how the instruction or request is given can either reduce or increase the arguing behavior. We specify how to give instructions or requests in Chapter Thirteen—Behavioral Interventions. Review the section on How to Give Instructions, and then evaluate your performance. Sometimes it is helpful to videotape your interaction with the child to obtain objectivity. There may be some habitual responses or patterns of nonproductive behavior, like an angry tone of voice or multiple-step requests that become apparent. One of the most common habitual responses is to use a form of "don't do that" statements. This increases arguing behavior. It can be a very difficult pattern to change. Increased self-monitoring, videotaping, and having an outside observer are all helpful in increasing your awareness.

Most often, the child receives attention from the teacher and/or peers for arguing, although it is generally negative attention—a powerful incentive. If receiving attention is the payoff, then reducing the negative attention lowers the frequency of arguing. Ignoring—including face aversion—is the primary strategy used to reduce giving negative attention. For example, when a child argues with a teacher about completing a task, then the teacher ignores the child by not responding either verbally or non-verbally until the arguing stops. Teachers can also instruct other students how to effectively ignore arguing behavior. Students are usually willing to assist when they understand how they can be helpful and receive incentives. Sometimes teachers and peers are ineffectual with the ignoring strategy because they still give nonverbal negative attention—looking mean, sighing, or rolling their eyes. Also, because the ignoring strategy reduces the total amount of attention the child receives, positive attention needs to be augmented by verbal or other concrete incentives. For example, when the child stops arguing after they are verbally and nonverbally ignored, the teacher gives them immediate positive attention with ten minutes of computer time or saying, "I love it when you follow my instructions." Sometimes, even when ignoring and incentives have been correctly used, a child escalates his arguing behavior because past experience taught him that the teacher would eventually renegotiate.

Some children are extremely effective at getting people to argue with them because they are able to emotionally hook the individual. The emotional hooks are statements or actions that make the other person feel guilty, angry, or not respected. An example is the child saying something like, "You like Susan better than me." If the child's comments initiate arguing, know that the bait was taken and be prepared to be reeled in. Learn to depersonalize the child's comments and recognize these as attempts to modify your behavior. See the section on Understanding and Utilizing the Principles of Depersonalization, Appropriate Behavioral Expectations, and Proactive Strategies for further explanation of how to depersonalize.

When a child's arguing behavior consistently disrupts classroom activities, it may be necessary to develop an ongoing behavioral incentive program to reduce the arguing. Reread the section Guidelines and Principles for Effective Use of Incentives. Helping the child become aware of each instance of arguing and the teacher communicating this information to them without it providing negative attention is tricky. One method is to describe ahead of time to the child where and how each episode of arguing behavior will be recorded: *without* a verbal comment, a check mark is placed on upper right-hand corner of the blackboard. The child is informed how many checkmarks he or she can receive and still earn the incentive. For example, a child with moderate ADHD is arguing with the teacher an average of thirty times a day. During the first week of intervention, the child earns verbal praise about other appropriate behaviors to offset the attention he was getting for arguing and given concrete incentives when arguing behaviors were reduced by 30 percent. A concrete incentive would be five minutes on the Game Boy® for each hour that the reduction took place. Gradually, a greater time delay would be added before the incentive is given, and a reduction in the number of arguing behaviors would be required to obtain the incentive.

Sometimes a child argues about doing a given task because they do not have the ability to successfully complete it. The task may require a longer attention span or academic skills that the child does not possess. Arguing helps delay and/or avoids the beginning or completion of the task. If the teacher observes regular episodes of arguing when certain tasks are assigned, then understanding the causes leads to more effective interventions.

If there is not an appropriate expectation concerning the child's attention span, the task will need to be modified. To determine an appropriate expectation regarding attention span, start by expecting responses similar to a child half his or her chronological age. See the section on Understanding and Utilizing the Principles of Depersonalization, Appropriate Behavioral Expectations, and Proactive Strategies. The success, or lack of it, after the modification determines the appropriateness of your expectations. If the child continues to avoid after the addition of potent incentives and an adjustment for attention span, then it is likely that they do not have the prerequisite skills or knowledge. If lack of skills or knowledge is the problem, teaching the requisite skills and knowledge is crucial.

Action learning helps decrease arguing by increasing the child's ability to stay focused with tasks they perceive as repetitious or boring. Many workbooks are available that contain action-learning strategies.

Evaluate medication, and discuss with the parents the usage and dosage as a means to reduce arguing. When a child is properly medicated, they have increased ability to stay on task, follow rules, and be less impulsive.

Difficulties with Trips to the Principal's Office
As a teacher becomes increasingly frustrated with the misbehavior of a child with ADHD and is at their wits-end about what to do, "Off to the office we go." It is an understandable reaction, and the teacher often has the hope that the trip will have some beneficial consequences—other than giving the teacher and students

a rest. It also may fit school policy for misbehavior. The student proceeds to the office, and if not accompanied, may not make a successful trip. Once at the office, the secretary sits them down to await that dreaded—for some students who don't have ADHD—few minutes with the principal. The secretary talks with him or her, which gives him or her attention. After some delay, the student is inside the principal's office. If punishment is to be effective, it must be given immediately—not thirty minutes later. The principal begins to listen to the child's version of the events and then gives a lecture about being a good citizen. The child receives some additional attention by being the object of the lecture. The assumption using this procedure is the lecture will be a punishment and the child will introspect and feel guilty about the misbehavior. Children with ADHD usually have low levels of guilt—and introspection is not one of their well-developed skills. It also may be that the child is escaping from a difficult task in the classroom. If they are avoiding a difficult task, then an escape to the principal's office can be an incentive to misbehave.

Going to the principal's office is usually not a deterrent for misbehavior unless the child is missing something in the classroom that is very appealing to them.

Suggested Interventions: The classroom is the most effective place to address the child's misbehaviors—unless their behavior presents a danger to others. Giving good instructions, utilizing action learning, providing appropriate structure, and using an effective incentive program should take the place of visits to the principal's office. If the teacher needs a rest, then a visit out of the classroom can be pre-planned in a way that does not give the child negative attention. The child can be taken out of the classroom with some schoolwork to a quiet, boring room. The accompanying adult provides minimal interaction, including little eye contact—face aversion. The adult requests them to start their schoolwork. The child is returned to their regular classroom at a specified time period (e.g., elementary children, fifteen minutes max, middle and high school children, thirty minutes max).

If behavioral and structural interventions do not produce the desired changes, then evaluate medication usage with the parents. Medication for children with moderate or severe levels of ADHD reduces the need to go to the principal's office because the child can focus better on schoolwork and is less impulsive.

Responses to Peers Saying, "It's not fair"

Peers become aware of the fact that the child with ADHD receives special incentives for complying or working on tasks. A complaint is often registered with the teacher in the form of, "It is not fair, he gets more computer time than I do." This complaint can be registered by an individual or brought up by many students in the class. The complaint—which deserves a reasonable answer—can be given to a specific student or to the entire class.

Suggested interventions: A response which usually takes care of the problem is, "It is hard for Jake to do his work in math, so he needs extra encouragement to be successful. If you do extra work that is difficult for you, incentives will be made available." Some children will take the deal, but most will say okay and never bring up the subject again. The explanation presents the philosophy that it is "fair" to meet individual needs.

Organizing Successful Field Trips

Field trips—more stimulating and less structured than the classroom—present additional challenges to children with ADHD; therefore, they will misbehave more frequently in that environment. The rules during field trips are different and the new environment is stimulating and makes it difficult for the child. Sometimes dangerous situations, like a child getting lost or falling, occur on field trips making planning important. The solution is not to deny them the opportunity to go on field trips, but to anticipate the challenges that might be faced for the individual child.

Suggested interventions: Taking into consideration the child's severity of ADHD is important when making a plan for a field trip. If the child has a moderate or severe form of ADHD, during the trip an adult should be assigned to them. The teacher will need to meet with the adult helper beforehand to develop and discuss the plan. First, the teacher can talk with the parents and request their assistance during the field trip. If the parents aren't available, recruit another adult good with challenging children. The plan will provide more structure, which helps decrease the stimulation felt by the child. There should be stated incentives and punishments for specified behavior for the entire trip, including the bus rides. The child should sit with the adult in the front of the bus. He can be given an action-orientated activity to keep him busy with incentives, such as playing checkers, for good behavior. The adult should frequently remind the child of the rules during the outing. For example, "Jake we are going to the zoo and I do not want to lose you. Hold onto my hand as we go through the zoo unless I give you permission to let go. If you hold onto my hand as I request, then you will get a piece of candy at the end of fifteen minutes. If you let go of my hand without my permission, then we will have to go back to the bus and sit quietly for ten minutes." Jake is then told that if he sits quietly for the ten minutes, then the tour of the zoo will resume. Every few minutes, the child should be reminded of the rule by the adult asking them, "What is the rule?" This holding-hand instruction is appropriate for children in the first few years of school. As they get older, the instruction could be to stay within three feet of the adult.

If providing an adult helper for a child with severe or moderate ADHD is not an option, consider taking the child the day before with an adult. The child can report back to the classroom what to look for and what was most exciting about the trip. This gives the child an important role and makes them feel included.

If the child has mild ADHD, it may only be necessary to have the child stay next to the teacher or another adult during the field trip. Again, the rules must be clearly stated and the incentives and consequences defined.

The teacher can reduce some of the confusion and stimulation in a field trip by having a rule for all of the students not to run and to stay behind the teacher at all times.

This is a time when medication can assist the child by reducing reactions to the stimulation and decreasing impulsiveness, making the trip a happy and safer adventure.

Less Lunchtime Lunacy

The typical cafeteria-style lunchroom presents many challenges that are likely to promote misbehavior for children with ADHD. The children have to wait in line, sit in close proximity to other students, confront complex social dynamics, and be subjected to higher levels of visual and auditory stimulation.

Suggested interventions: Ideally, the student should eat in a quieter, simpler environment. Therefore, modifications to the environment are indicated; for example, staggering lunchtimes so fewer students are eating in the cafeteria at one time. Another example is eliminating or significantly reducing waiting by having the child with ADHD go to the front of the line or timing her arrival when the line is short. Consider assigning the child to sit at a table at the periphery of the room with pre-selected children. Monitor whether the child needs assistance in eating appropriate levels of food. Some children with ADHD gulp their food quickly, while others are focused on talking and forget to eat. If the child forgets to eat, then set up an incentive program—but do not try to force the child to eat.

In some schools, the children eat in their classrooms. This is typically better for children with ADHD because stimulation and waiting time is decreased, and there are less complex social dynamics. It is also easier to transition from schoolwork to lunchtime.

Incentives and consequences can be added at lunchtime to encourage appropriate behavior, such as keeping their hands to themselves.

If the child is on short-acting medication, give a dose thirty minutes prior to lunchtime. The impulsivity will be significantly reduced.

Strategies for Fewer Recess Difficulties

Recess can be an especially difficult time because of complex rules and lack of structure. For example, playing a game of soccer requires picking two team captains, deciding on a system to select team members, and setting up the rules for the game. Negotiating with other individuals, delaying gratification, following established rules, and good sportsmanship are all requisite behaviors for successful playground interaction. Play rules are developed around "fairness," and children with ADHD frequently violate those rules in order to try and win. When they break the play rules, other children react negatively. Arguments and fighting are by-products of this interaction pattern.

Suggested interventions: The challenge is to find ways to provide more structure and incentives that help the child adhere to rules. If the child has a severe form of ADHD, then in order for them to be successful during recess time, they need close supervision by an adult and appropriate medication. Recess time at some schools is monitored by a few adults, and at times, adults with little training in behavior management, which complicates intervention plans. A child with a severe disability may qualify for a paid aide. If obtaining an aide is not possible, a next step can be recruiting and training volunteers. When volunteers are not available, recruiting and training an older, socially sophisticated student is an option. This student can work individually with the student with ADHD on one or two play skills at a time. A specific behavioral program is developed. If a recruited student is involved, they should be given an appropriate incentive, e.g., school credit or flex time.

Role playing in the classroom can further facilitate play skills. The students are asked to play typical conflict situations that occur on the playground and then verbalize feelings about the conflict. They are next instructed to role-play conflict resolution while verbalizing the unstated play rules and the rationale behind their use. The child with ADHD should be a part of the role-playing to keep him or her involved and active.

If a child has a mild form of ADHD, then a few structural changes and some behavioral interventions will be all that is necessary. The teacher determines what activities the child with ADHD enjoys and then can set up small teams or pick playmates prior to leaving the classroom. The teacher also has the child choose a location for his or her play prior to leaving the classroom. This proactive approach can eliminate potential problems. Upon returning to the classroom, the playmates or teammates are asked to report about play behavior. If the report is generally positive, all involved are given a pre-determined incentive. Everybody can win!

If the child has moderate forms of ADHD, again, proper medication is an intervention that should be considered in conjunction with structural and behavioral interventions. For example, the recess monitor carries with them tokens, which are given to the child when they are observed to be playing cooperatively. The child can redeem the tokens for pre-arranged incentives—cafeteria-style—immediately following the recess. If the child is observed using aggressive behavior toward another student, such as hitting or shoving, then a punishment is immediately given. Potential punishments could be having them forfeit all their earned tokens or having them stand in a time-out circle on the playground for three to ten minutes. The recess monitor sets a sturdy timer and gives it to the child. The child is instructed to return the timer upon completion. If the child leaves the circle, then the monitor resets the timer. Sending the child into the classroom as a punishment often results in the child getting individual attention, and the teacher is punished by having no free time.

Addressing Bullying Behavior

Children with ADHD exhibit impulsiveness, difficulty recognizing other's feelings, and delaying gratification, which can lead to frustration and aggressive behavior. Children with ADHD are often labeled "bullies" because their aggressive play is viewed as intentional. The educational staff generally has negative feelings toward them since it is viewed as intentional, and school policy for bullying behavior is punishment.

In school situations where there is limited structure, or during transition periods, the child with ADHD has greater difficulty controlling impulsivity and remembering social rules and is more likely to display aggressive behavior. Also, in situations where another student does not allow the child with ADHD to be in charge, then bullying behavior increases. This aggressive or bullying behavior is most often seen during recess, as it is unstructured and students are competing for "top dog" positions.

Suggested interventions: Most schools have anti-bullying programs that are primarily based on increasing a student's insight into their feelings and others'. These programs are typically not very effective for children with ADHD because they use insight and punishment. If a child with ADHD's aggressive behavior is viewed as intentional rather than resulting from their disability, more negative feeling s are directed at him or her. Intention requires forethought and insight into the other person's feelings, which are underdeveloped skills with children with ADHD. Interventions designed to address the disabilities of children with

ADHD are more successful. Proactive interventions that use a combination of behavioral modification using incentives, increased social structure, and appropriate medication are helpful.

In order to individualize and be proactive with interventions, observe when, why, and with whom the bullying behavior occurs. Observations direct your efforts with interventions. Children with ADHD will benefit from increased structure and learning socially appropriate play behavior, especially when they are frustrated. It will most likely occur when there is less structure (e.g., recess) and when the child with ADHD has to be patient in obtaining something desirable to them (e.g., being in charge). Generally, the bullying behavior occurs repeatedly with the same children. Interventions that increase social and physical structure reduce opportunities for bullying behavior—placing the child with ADHD in a small group of class members of children who are not usually targets of bullying. Define for the child what constitutes appropriate play behavior in specific, behavioral terms—taking turns, saying "good job" to others, keeping hands to self—and then providing incentives for increase use of these positive behaviors. In the first stages of implementation, provide cues often.

Stimulant medication reduces the amount of aggression because impulsivity and frustration are reduced. For a small percentage of children who are very aggressive, an additional medication called Clonadine can be effective. This medication should be administered by a child psychiatrist.

Preparing for Holiday Seasons

Because of structural changes, holiday time can present problems. Preparing them for the changes in advance can help decrease the problems. The level of arousal or excitement usually increases in all the students close to a major holiday such as Christmas. Children with ADHD do not cope well to all the extra excitement. They usually will have extra problems talking and accomplishing classroom work.

Suggested interventions: By increasing the number of quiet times and the frequency of quiet activities, the teacher can help lower the arousal level of the entire class. General quiet times can consist of five-minute periods when all students close their eyes and rest their heads on the desk. An individual quiet activity place could be made out of a cardboard refrigerator box. Cut it to about four feet tall and place a small table and chair inside. The top is open so the teacher can easily look inside, but the sides are tall enough that most of the students cannot. Give all students an opportunity to spend short time periods in this quiet place. Set it up so that it is seen as a special place that all students can earn or request and is seen in a positive way. When the child with ADHD is over-stimulated and moving constantly, the teacher can say, "John, it is your turn for some quiet time. Here is the timer and it is set for ten minutes. Practice sitting still by listening to the earphone music that is on the desk while you are inside. Come out when the ten minutes is up. Thank you." This gives the child a few moments of quiet, structured time.

If a child is on medication, there is an increased chance that a dosage will be missed because of all the excitement and changes in scheduling during a holiday season. If the child is having an especially difficult day, it would be important to check and determine if the child has received his or her medication. Gently reminding the parents of the importance of the medication will often reduce the days of missed medication.

Coordinating Homework Efforts

Teachers often get frustrated with the student and parents around the issue of homework. A teacher's frustration may lead to labeling the child as lazy and/or the parent as uncaring about their child's education. The labeling can increase the probability of adversarial relationships. Some of the most common circumstances creating homework frustration and challenges are:

- parents *perceive* inappropriate amounts of homework are given;
- the child not getting homework and/or instructional material necessary to complete the homework in backpack or to home;
- the child is not telling or lying to the parent about homework assignments;
- the child is not able to complete homework because of academic abilities, lack of structure, or limited and ineffective incentives;
- the child is not getting homework in backpack to go back to school or losing it on the way to school;
- the child is not remembering to hand in completed homework;
- the teacher is giving inappropriate levels of homework and sending home incomplete classroom work;
- or the child finds homework boring and has negative feelings about completing it.

Suggested interventions: The homework challenges surrounding a child with ADHD are multiple. Children with ADHD often have a working-memory deficit, decreased ability to stay focused on tasks, and limited listening skills, which makes remembering to take and return their work difficult. These challenges require appropriate expectations regarding homework, increasing structure, and increased use of incentives. Also, ongoing communication between parents and teacher(s) makes development and application of interventions possible. The earlier this communication starts, the better. Ideally, if a teacher has knowledge of a child with homework problems prior to the first day of school, then setting up an early consultation with parents is a proactive strategy.

The collaborative effort of the teacher and parent in assisting the child with homework greatly enhances the child's success. Ideally, there must be an open and regular dialogue between home and school. Setting up regular communication between home and school increases the chances of homework arriving home, getting completed, and being returned to school. Daily contact may be necessary when children have moderate to severe levels of ADHD. If the child has a mild level of ADHD, then contact can occur weekly rather than daily. The parent and teacher need to work out a contact system that is easy to maintain. If the teacher and parent have access to the Internet, contact can be handled easily. Telephone calls and a note system can also be used. The Appendix contains an easy-to-use homework note that provides information about the completion and accuracy.

Open dialogue between the child, parent, and teacher also helps pinpoint any reoccurring circumstances influencing homework, such as homework not arriving home or the child's resistance to completing homework. Once the specific circumstances are identified, then appropriate interventions can be discussed. When developing the interventions, have appropriate and realistic expectations, factoring in the resources at home and school, the severity of the child's disorder, and academic ability. Appropriate expectations guide the teacher in developing effective strategies which increase the chances of homework success. For example, not all parents are in a position to furnish significant help with homework. A child may live in a home where parents do not speak English or the parent has a chronic disability. The severity of the disorder also helps the teacher determine the amount of homework that is reasonable. For example, a child with a severe level of ADHD may not initially be able to complete more than ten minutes of homework a day.

Regularly sending home uncompleted classroom work for a child with moderate or severe levels of ADHD sets up an environment that is punishing to the parent. It also sets up a negative dynamic between parent and child. The teacher needs to revaluate the classroom behavioral program for the child. The sections Getting Started on Classroom Work and On-Task Time provide helpful strategies.

Interventions that increase or modify structure are easiest to implement. Increasing and modifying structure can often be accomplished with minimal effort. For instance, before the student leaves school, the teacher can ask to see if the homework is in the backpack. The next morning, the teacher can check the child's backpack to retrieve the completed homework. Children who have a moderate or severe form of ADHD may benefit from having a second set of books and a log of daily homework assignments at home. This eliminates the hassles of lost or misplaced books or assignments.

The use of incentives helps motivate the child to take, complete, and return homework. The frequency, potency, and the immediacy of the incentives depend on the severity of the child's disorder combined with the resources at home and school. For example, if the child arrives home with the appropriate homework assignment, a verbal or another motivating incentive is immediately given. When giving an incentive at home is not feasible, then the teacher can develop alternate strategies to provide motivation and structure. The child could be placed in an after-school tutorial program where homework is completed.

The teacher may be a resource for the parent on how to provide more structure and incentives regarding homework. Often, parents, when provided extra help, are able to more effectively assist their child with homework. There is a section to give parents the needed assistance to improve homework strategies.

If the child is still failing to complete the homework assignments after the home environment has been modified and an incentives program implemented, then evaluate for non-apparent skill and/or knowledge deficits. For example, the child had numerous absences and had not learned the basic information necessary to complete the current homework. Classroom curriculums tend to build on mastering each previous unit, and without remediation, failure will continue. The team can help organize tutorial efforts aimed at increasing the child's knowledge base.

If the child is taking medication, there may be less in the bloodstream during the evening, and the child will then be having more problems staying focused. Increasing the amount of the medication in the system can be accomplished in two ways. First, the child can receive a small additional dose after school, and second, they can be given a stimulant medication that is designed to work into the evening, such as Concerta.

The teacher benefits from regularly utilizing the treatment team—especially in more difficult situations—because he or she can provide a fresh perspective with creative ideas. These new ideas may allow for the development and implementation of successful homework interventions. The team also provides the teacher with the emotional support needed when dealing with frustrating and difficult problems.

Getting Them Started on Classroom Work

Children with ADHD have difficulty getting started on classroom work because of their poor organization, poor listening skills, working-memory deficits, inability to stay focused, and motivational issues. The following situation commonly occurs in a classroom: A second-grade boy with ADHD is asked to begin an assignment. Ten minutes pass and he still has not started on the assignment. Other students start to take their completed work to the teacher. He has yet to obtain a pencil or get the correct book for the assignment. The student's desk is messy and disorganized. This is a situation that is both humorous and sad. The teacher feels unable to give the boy adequate attention without sacrificing time and energy for the other students. The teacher starts to resent the extra time that the child with ADHD requires, further complicating the situation. If the teacher becomes resentful, he or she may not use appropriate interventions to help the student get started on classwork.

Suggested interventions: Multiple interventions will be necessary to address the inherent disabilities that interfere with the student's ability to initiate schoolwork. Structural interventions are a good place to start. The placement of the child's desk in the front row next to the teacher's teaching station allows swifter interventions, fewer distractions for the child, and easier observation for the teacher. To decrease the problem of a messy and overflowing desk, keep part of the student's work and work tools in an organized filing system. Getting the entire class in the habit of returning items to the appropriate file area gives increased structure. This will help the teacher monitor what the child keeps in her desk. How the initial instructions are given impacts the students' ability to listen and follow them. There are guidelines for giving instructions in an earlier section. These guidelines help the student focus and listen. Giving simple one-or two-step instructions accommodates for the deficit in working memory and decreased attention span.

It is useful to divide class assignments into smaller units, which facilitates working memory, increases motivation and attention span, and provides more opportunities to earn incentives. Providing a set of cues can help the student focus. For example, the teacher can state, "Get your workbook and pencil ready; now, at the count of three, begin your work—one, two, three." If the student with ADHD starts working, then give them immediate verbal praise. It may be necessary to use a token economy with students who have a severe level of ADHD. He would receive immediate and frequent tokens as he begins the assignment.

The team can develop strategies to reduce resentment felt by the teacher towards the student with ADHD. For example, it might be beneficial if the team encouraged the school to provide an aide and/or further behavioral-management training.

Medication is especially helpful in improving listening, focusing ability, and motivation for children with moderate to severe levels of ADHD.

Increasing Their On-Task Time

Once the teacher is able to get them started on class work, the next challenge is to keep them focused and on-task. Keeping the child with ADHD focused on uninteresting or difficult work is a challenge because it exacerbates the problems inherent in their disabilities. Unfortunately, a child with ADHD might categorize 90 percent of his or her work as uninteresting or difficult. Teachers understandably become frustrated if significant progress is not made. They express concern and frustration about the valuable teaching time lost for the children without ADHD. These negative feelings can lead to more punishment and fewer incentives given to children with ADHD. Some teachers may not understand that attending to the child when they are off-task may increase off-task behavior. Negative attention may become an incentive for staying off-task. Once again, children with ADHD prefer negative attention rather than none. Also, the extra time and effort expended on the child's off-task behavior can increase the tendency to forget him or her when they are on-task, which results in not continuing to deliver the necessary incentives (e.g., paying attention to the desired behavior).

Suggested interventions: A successful intervention starts with an understanding that on-task behavior requires regular incentives, while off-task behavior needs to be ignored. Most of us think that by pointing out a lack of progress that the student will be motivated to increase their effort, but it can be ineffective unless done correctly. It is helpful to redirect them by stating what is to be accomplished and the consequences that follow. This cueing about the task and consequences needs to be done in a firm and non-emotional manner.

If the teacher is not in the habit of providing regular incentives, they might need to retrain themselves to provide more frequent incentives. This retraining can be accomplished by implementing a system that reminds the teacher to give incentives for on-task behaviors. The teacher can wear a vibrating timer set for short intervals, such as five minutes. Each time there is a vibration, the teacher briefly observes the child. If the child is on–task, the teacher gives a verbal or non-verbal incentive. Children with moderate or severe forms of ADHD need concrete, frequent, and novel incentives. A cafeteria-style incentive list using tokens is remarkably effective. Motivation increases because a wide range of incentives are available. The rapidity and ease with which tokens can be delivered makes them effective. Children with severe levels of ADHD will usually need to be placed in classrooms with few children to distract them.

Giving clear instructions is the first step for success. The work should be divided into smaller units with a chance for an incentive to be given at the end of each segment. A usual math assignment of ten problems is broken into two units of five problems. The student takes page one—which has five problems—to the teacher after they are finished and receives verbal praise. After the second page is finished and given to the teacher, again, verbal praise is given. If the child has a timer on the desk and the teacher tells them how much time there is to complete each page, performance is better. If the child is in a regular classroom, place them in a desk close to the teacher where distractions are minimized. This seat placement also allows for easy observation and makes the delivery of incentives more convenient.

Medication is the single most helpful intervention to improve on-task time and is useful for many individuals into their adulthood when tasks similar to schoolwork are necessary. For example, an individual who was effective at individual action-oriented work is made a supervisor and now must attend long meetings. They may be unable to do so successfully without medication.

Dealing With Accuracy and Neatness of Schoolwork Issues

Most children with ADHD focus on getting a task done that is unpleasant, rather than on doing it neatly or accurately. Many of the children also have difficulty with fine-motor coordination, so that neatness is difficult for them. If the child is having many failures in getting homework accurate, not accepting the homework or telling them to do it over will most often result in lower performance.

Suggested interventions: It is better to put effort into improving accuracy and not put a lot of effort into neatness. Neatness can be improved a little without a lot of effort by using larger writing spaces and spaces that are outlined clearly or by allowing the child to do much of the written work on a computer, which automatically makes clear letters and uniform spaces. Accuracy can be improved by giving instructions like this, "Nick, how many correct words are needed to get five minutes on the computer?" This instruction tells him the incentive and has him repeat the rule for getting the incentive.

Reducing Annoying Behavior Toward Other Students

Class clowning, talk-outs, poking, and teasing are typical problem behaviors and results in the child with ADHD getting attention that is negative. Reducing the annoying behavior is important if she is to be socially accepted.

Suggested interventions: Children with ADHD will not have as much time to annoy other students if they are actively engaged in other more productive activities. Providing other students incentives for not responding to the annoying behavior can work wonders. When the teacher observes a student not responding to the negative behavior of the child with ADHD, the teacher quietly indicates to the student to go the teacher's desk a get a small treat for themselves.

How to Handle Lying, Stealing, and Cheating

One or more of these behaviors is usually a problem for children with ADHD because of their impulsivity and difficulty internalizing societal norms. These children typically experience less guilt and anxiety about breaking social norms. Children with ADHD have difficulty waiting and sustaining effort. Lying, stealing, and cheating are used by the child to rapidly and with minimal effort obtain what they desire. For example, obtaining money, toys, and higher scores on a test can all be achieved by lying, cheating, and stealing. Because the child gets the desired result part of the time, it becomes difficult to modify.

An additional complicating factor is that if these behaviors happen on a regular basis, a negative attitude develops toward the child. This negative attitude usually results in increased anger directed toward the child. This increase in anger often results in more problem behavior. It is important to reduce these socially unacceptable behaviors so the child and others can experience increased positive interactions.

Suggested interventions: Interventions will focus on modifying the emotional responses of the teacher and other students and the behavior of the child. Using the depersonalization skills outlined in this book will be of considerable help in modifying the emotional responses to the child. Once negative reactions are ameliorated, it is easier to start other interventions.

A proactive approach reduces temptation and the effort necessary to manage the child's problem behavior. Set up a structure at school that makes stealing or cheating difficult, reducing the opportunities for a child to misbehave. For example, valuables are kept in a secure place and the child with ADHD is never left alone in the classroom.

The child can earn incentives when he or she decreases the problem behaviors. This approach seems inappropriate to many adults, because they view the behavior as immoral and believe the child should be punished. These objections need to be addressed with a reminder that the child has a disability and that incentives effectively reduce problem behaviors. For example, the child who is heard lying ten times a week can earn the privilege of carrying out the soccer ball at recess if they reduce that rate to five. If they are successful, then the expectation can be increased and the rate of lying decreased further.

If powerful incentives have not decreased the problem behavior, then the effective use of punishment can produce positive results. Punishment is often overused and misused, so please review the section on punishment in Chapter Thirteen—Effective Types of Punishment. The team can assist the teacher in proactively determining when and how punishment will be administered. In a proactive approach, the punishment rules must be clearly stated to the child prior to misbehavior. The individualized program using punishment may not follow stated school policy. If there is resistance to the individualized program, the team can assist the teacher in reducing the opposition.

It is difficult to find an effective punishment because the child is not emotionally invested in many of the usual punishments. For example, they may not be affected by the principal's lecture or losing recess time. Furthermore, because they are not emotionally invested in "usual punishments," it is necessary to modify the way punishment is used to make it powerful. This is done by making the punishment immediately severe without using a gradual increase in the severity level. Also, the punishment will be more severe and effective if the student loses something he has previously earned. Losing something he has earned increases the chances of emotional investment. For example, if the student has earned tokens to buy incentives by doing schoolwork, immediately, charge him a large "fee" each time he lies, steals, or cheats.

Some children with ADHD have been stereotyped as always being liars, cheaters, and stealers. This stereotype makes them easy targets for scapegoating by other students. If these children are negatively stereotyped, then they will more likely increase their problem behavior because they have on occasion been inappropriately punished. The child feels "No one believes me if I'm honest, so why try to be honest?" To avoid this stereotyping dynamic, the child should only be punished when the teacher directly observes the child lying, cheating, or stealing. Direct observation has another benefit; it eliminates the use of inquisition techniques to find out the truth. Inquisition techniques generally increase defensiveness and may set up a situation where the child feels backed into the corner and lies to avoid consequences.

Decreasing Swearing
Children with ADHD sometimes use swearing as a method of obtaining immediate attention. The attention received, however, is often negative. Usually schools discourage profanity by using varying levels of punishment which are often not

effective with children having ADHD. For example, getting suspended may be an incentive to them.

Developing a strategy to reduce swearing will depend on the motive behind it, either self-expression or attention-getting. Sometimes their swearing is environmental if they have grown up in neighborhoods and in families where swearing is a normative behavior and a means of self expression.

Suggested Interventions: The teacher must make observations during an hour-long period at school to obtain a baseline number of swearing incidents before an intervention is set up. This baseline number is needed to help evaluate whether or not an intervention is effective. Also, it must be noted what occurs directly after the swearing incident. For example, observe whether the student receives a strong emotional reaction from others. Evaluate the emotional reaction data after the swearing to determine if it appears the student is receiving strong reactions a majority of the time. If the student receives attention for the swearing, it is likely that the swearing is being maintained by the attention. To further evaluate this conclusion, have other students ignore the child when the swearing occurs. The students and the teacher need to ignore the child's swearing for an entire school week. Face aversion is the best ignoring intervention to use during this week. The teacher and students in the classroom need to be trained in face-aversion techniques and given incentives for their effort. After an ignoring intervention has been successfully used for a school week, then take another count of the child's swearing. If the number of swearing incidents has decreased, then it can be concluded that attention is the major factor is maintaining swearing. The most effective intervention for future episodes of swearing is to use an ignoring intervention.

If it is determined that ignoring does not reduce swearing, it is probably a means of self-expression, and then another type of intervention will be required. In a team meeting, discuss with the parents the rules about profanity at school and determine if swearing is a part of the language pattern at home or in the neighborhood. When there is a pattern of swearing, enlist their efforts in reducing the swearing at home. Help them set up a fun game at home that includes incentives for all of the family members when swearing is reduced. For example, have the family keep a chart of the swearing incidents on a door in the kitchen and if the number of incidents is reduced from thirty a day to twenty a day, the whole family gets ice cream for a treat. At school, have the teacher explain what words can be used to replace swear words for the whole class and then set up incentives for reducing their use. If there is no swearing during a day, then the class gets ten minutes of any activity they choose. It is also possible to just focus on the child that is swearing frequently and tutor him in selecting more positive language. Give incentives for a reduction in the swearing rate.

Making Music or Choir Time Successful

Choir time that is not action-oriented presents a challenge for children with ADHD. They are expected to stay focused on the director, listen, follow instructions, and sing in unison. Students are usually in close proximity to each other, which increases the amount of stimulation and temptation to bother your neighbor. When the child with ADHD does something negative, he or she usually receives immediate attention from the teacher and laughter from some of the students. Laughter is a powerful incentive to keep misbehaving.

Suggested interventions: Structural changes, teaching ignoring behavior, increasing action learning, providing incentives, and medication are all useful interventions during music time. Children with a mild form of ADHD benefit from being placed in the front row at the edge of the classroom or choir. The child with ADHD should stand next to a student who can ignore their problem behavior. This student could receive a special incentive for their extra effort. It is also useful to increase personal space between students. If the child has a moderate or severe form of ADHD, then a structural change that eliminates problems is giving the child individual music lessons and/or skipping the group music activities. An individual lesson can increase the student's confidence and allows them to receive special attention for their talent. The lessons provide positive attention, which reduces the probability they will misbehave. It may be necessary and helpful to place a trained aide, who can provide cues about appropriate behavior, next to the student.

Both the teacher and other students should put into practice the behavioral intervention of ignoring. However, ignoring is most effective in modifying inappropriate behavior if both the teacher and students simultaneously put it into practice. The teacher needs to model ignoring and also provide powerful group and individual incentives for ignoring behavior used by the other students. For example, a powerful group incentive might be letting the children dance to the music they are singing, and individual incentive could be allowing a student to play a musical instrument as an accompaniment. The teacher can describe the incentive to the entire class for ignoring inappropriate behavior. The teacher ought to decide in advance to ignore all problem behaviors except those which are dangerous.

Action learning decreases problem behavior, and by giving the student with ADHD a task that is action-oriented, the child receives immediate and positive attention. For example, have him or her lead part of the choir in a special part of the song or sing a solo. Playing a musical instrument, like the drums, is action learning and can be used as a powerful incentive for appropriate behavior.

Medication is especially helpful in improving listening, focusing ability, and maintaining motivation for children with moderate to severe levels of ADHD. Medication will reduce the impulsiveness, increase the ability to focus, and increase the ability to follow directions.

Strategies for Taking Standardized Tests

The motivation problems, the impulsiveness, distractibility, and the problems with short-term memory make it difficult for them to be successful at taking standardized tests. Having previous failure experiences at taking tests may also reduce their effort in test-taking. A lack of skill and/or a lack of information may also produce failure at test-taking.

Suggested interventions: The multiple factors that produce reduced scores on standardized tests can be addressed in several ways. First, if the child has lowered skill and information, then an accelerated tutoring program needs to be initiated. Second, place a screen around the student so visual contact with other students is limited but they are easily viewed by the teacher. Have them practice taking other tests in this arrangement so that they become comfortable taking tests in this environment. Third, give the test in smaller segments and provide a short break with a treat at the end of each session. Fourth, if possible, give the test in the morning, when they tend to be less fatigued and can focus more effectively. Fifth, have them practice taking tests that are of the same structure as the standardized test. Sixth, give them additional time to take the test if there is clear evidence that they are trying to answer the questions. Seventh, make time more meaningful by putting a timer clock on their desk to remind them how much time is left to finish the test.

Medication will help them attend better during the testing period but will not give them skills and information they do not have. It is important to make sure they have had their medication on the day of the testing.

Helping Them Avoid Alcohol and Other Drug Use

As these students with ADHD move to middle school and high school, they are at an increased risk to be involved in drug abuse. Alcohol is the drug most frequently abused. Their feelings of lack of success, their inability to wait for feeling to change, and the immediate effect of drugs are all part of the dynamic that makes them susceptible to abusing drugs. Connecting socially with drug-abusing peers that readily accept them is another powerful dynamic.

Suggested interventions: The most helpful interventions start in early childhood when home and school provide the necessary support for ongoing success. This helps reduce the feelings of failure, which often are precursors to the use of drugs. In the teenage years, when peer acceptance is so important, helping them connect with non-abusing friends is important. To help them connect with more constructive friendships, provide them with opportunities to be involved in action-oriented activities that take place in an adult-supervised location. Gymnastics, racquetball, music lessons, competitive bow-and-arrow shooting, and karate all provide action, a lot of individual attention, and a positive structure. Many of the traditional team sports are difficult for them because of the complex nature of the interactions. If they are successful in these team activities, encourage them. Keep them busy with activities they enjoy so that alcohol and drugs do not have a great deal of appeal.

The appropriate use of stimulant medication, which helps children be more successful, has a tendency to help reduce the abuse of drugs later in their life.

Reducing Concern About Giving Them Preferential Treatment

Some teachers have stated their concern about giving these children special care and attention, which they often feel is at the expense of other students.

Suggested interventions: The teacher needs to know that the child has a disability, and treating the child with ADHD just like they are an average student does not provide them with an equal education. If they require extra time and effort and the teacher cannot provide such help, then additional paid staff or appropriately trained volunteers need to be sought.

Physician Challenges

Addressing Resistance to the Use of Medication

A major role of the physician on the treatment team is to prescribe medication for children having ADHD. When continued resistance to the use of medication is expressed by parents and/or teachers, physicians may become frustrated. Some frustrated physicians give in too easily, even though they know the child would benefit, because they do not have appropriate strategies to deal with the resistance. Other physicians may cope with the resistance by becoming authoritarian and then stop listening to parental and teacher concerns. These approaches are both problematic.

Suggested interventions: The physician should thoroughly and non-judgmentally address the team member's fears, concerns, and knowledge about medication for ADHD. One of the frustrating things is this can be time-consuming. Physicians should allow adequate time when scheduling appointments to alleviate any fears, concerns, and provide education about ADHD medication.

The next section outlines how and what information decreases the resistance of team members to medication usage and sets the stage for a collaborative relationship.

Increasing Medication Compliance in Older Children

Physicians should expect that, even though the child has been successfully medicated in the early years, teenagers' resistance to taking the medication is common. Physicians, along with the other team members, can proactively create a strategy that neutralizes the teenager's resistance. The teenager often states things like, "Taking the meds makes me different from my friends and makes me feel different, and I don't *!*# need it anymore." The most common intervention tried is to use insight-based statements. The physician states, "You know you do better when taking the medication." Children with ADHD have difficulty using insight as a means of making decisions. The problem is further complicated by the teenager's desire to be more independent, which is part of normal development.

Suggested interventions: The physician enlists the team to provide behavioral evidence that supports taking medication to help reduce the child's resistance. The team provides specific evidence of behavioral changes that cannot be disputed. The teenager must be made aware of how she directly benefits from taking the medication—what is in it for her! Review with the teenager the number of detentions at school while taking the medication compared to the number of detentions while not taking the medication. Review the number of groundings at home while on and off medication. Usually detentions and groundings are viewed by the teenager in negative terms and she can see that taking the medication reduces these negative consequences. Also use incentives to further reduce the resistance. The incentives used for teenagers should be highly desirable. Every day the teenager takes the medication without complaint, she can drive the car to school and back home.

The physician needs ongoing behavioral feedback from home and school prior to appointments in order to make persuasive and optimistic statements to the teenager about the medication's effectiveness.

Getting Accurate Feedback on Medication Impact

It is difficult for the physician to evaluate the effectiveness of a particular medication or the dosage without regular and objective feedback. Feedback from just the child is generally not sufficient for making decisions, because children with

ADHD are generally not good self-observers. Parents who have ADHD also have difficulty making systematic observations, which suggests the need for observations from a parent without ADHD.

Suggested interventions: The feedback given to the physician should be objective, behavioral observations from multiple sources. The physician can use behavioral questionnaires to assist in making decisions. Also, a prearranged system of regular communication between the physician's office and the relevant team members can guide the physician's decisions. Assigning a staff person in the office with the responsibility of sending and retrieving the questionnaires can reduce the workload for the physician. The staff member could communicate by phone or e-mail if that is more convenient.

Pressure to Use the Most Recently Released Medication

In today's media-saturated world, physicians are pressured to use the latest advertised medication. Parents armed with this media advertising want their child to have the newest and supposedly the best medication possible. It is reasonable for the parents to have and express this desire; however, determining what, if any, medication to use is based on many factors, not just "latest is the greatest."

Suggested interventions: The physician can constructively address the parents' requests for the newest medication by educating them about the pros and cons of available medications designed to help children with ADHD. A handout may be devised to show each medication's side effects, cost, improvement rates, and available research (minimal to extensive). Once the initial handout is developed, it can easily be updated. Armed with this information, it will become easier for the parents and the physician to agree upon which medication is appropriate.

Handling Disruptive Waiting-Room Behavior

A child with moderate or severe levels of ADHD can be a disturbing force for everyone in a crowded, stimulating waiting room. The waiting-room environment exacerbates the problem behavior of the child with ADHD.

Suggested interventions: If the physician's goal is to keep the waiting room stress-free for everyone, then scheduling an appointment early in the morning or the last appointment of the day reduces disruption in the waiting room. Another intervention is to reduce stimulation by immediately placing the child and parent in an exam room with an interesting TV/computer game available.

Mental Health Professional Challenges

Responses to "Fix Or Cure My Child"

Parents and teachers who are experiencing frustration desperately plead to a mental health professional to fix the child with ADHD. Frequently, parents and teachers will have received incorrect information that implies a fix is possible. The parent or teacher may see the MHP as incompetent if he or she does not offer a cure. An MHP may become defensive or authoritarian with a parent or teacher when this unrealistic expectation is requested. If the MHP becomes defensive or authoritarian, then the collaborative effort with parents and teachers is seriously hindered.

Another dynamic that occurs is that parents and teachers want the MHP to assume all the responsibility for changing the child's behavior. If the MHP does not carefully confront this unrealistic expectation, then the collaboration process breaks down and the MHP loses credibility. When an MHP accepts this unrealistic responsibility, "burnout" is likely to occur.

Suggested interventions: The MHP should openly and non-judgmentally address the parents' or teacher's understandable desire to have the child fixed or cured. In this environment, a collaborative team effort begins to develop. Then the MHP provides education about ADHD and the fact that there is no known quick fix or cure. Although there is no quick fix or cure, the MHP optimistically outlines proven treatment strategies. A team approach is explained so that the parents and teachers feel supported in this difficult undertaking.

Understanding Noncompliance of Team Members

The mental health professional has the role of detective when interventions are unsuccessful due to continuing noncompliance of a team member(s). The MHP reviews the attempted application of the intervention to determine the reason(s) for the lack of success. If the MHP does not address and assess the reasons that team member(s) are non-compliant, then the team may become discouraged, angry, or blaming. Also, the MHP loses credibility as the facilitator and educator of the team.

Suggested Interventions: An effective MHP emotionally invests in and focuses on helping each team member be successful at implementing the planned interventions. The MHP needs to know or ascertain the team members' abilities and any changes in life circumstances that may affect their performance. When a team member is consistently non-compliant, then the MHP needs to reassess the team member(s) intellectual ability, mental health status, their motivation, and energy level. The MHP has probably over-or underestimated the team member's ability to successfully comply and needs to make modifications according to which area(s) are problematic. For example, a parent does not have sufficient money to purchase his or her antidepressant medication and the depression has increased, thus reducing energy level. As another example: a teacher finally admitted that he was physically and emotionally exhausted from interacting with the child having ADHD. By Thursday of each week, the teacher had stopped giving the child incentives as a planned part of the intervention. The team developed a plan to give the teacher a break one day a week by the parents schooling the child at home. This motivated the teacher to comply with the intervention plan.

If the MHP has ruled out the above factors affecting compliance rates and the non-compliant team member's words do not match their behaviors, then a "hidden agenda" is likely. Evaluating for a hidden agenda requires careful and thoughtful probing by the MHP. One hidden agenda can be a teacher wanting a child to fail so they can be removed from the classroom. Another is one parent wanting the other parent to fail. There are many possible hidden agendas, but once they are openly identified, then corrective action can occur.

Addressing or Avoiding Perceived Alliances

Inevitably, there will be times when a team member(s) perceives that the MHP is allied against them with other members of the team. This dynamic, if not addressed and corrected, can result in alienation and withdrawal of effort by those members of the team. Also, if the dynamic is not corrected, the MHP's credibility is reduced.

Suggested interventions: The MHP may be directly told of a perceived alliance problem or has to surmise that a problem exists based on changes in a team member's behavior. If a team member openly admits concerns to the MHP, then it is easier to correct the situation. Usually, if the MHP demonstrates genuine interest for the member's feelings and ideas by empathetic listening, then the problem decreases in intensity.

When the MHP observes a dramatic change in team member's affect and behavior toward the MHP or other team members, careful inquiry to determine the reasons is necessary. If a team member perceives a problematic alliance and is unable to verbalize his or her feelings, then withdrawal and negativity are typical responses. The MHP can clarify the situation and obtain further information about the changes by making non-judgmental observations (e.g., "I notice you are very quiet today."). Usually, this probing response invites the member to more openly state his or her feelings. With this additional information, the MHP can devise a strategy for addressing the problem.

The MHP regularly needs to review issues of transference and counter-transference, which can make problem alliances more likely to occur. For example, an MHP grew up in a home where there was physical abuse, and as a result, over-reacted to the father spanking a child on one occasion. The MHP alienated the father and aligned himself with the mother.

16

Parents' and Educators' Self-Care

Parents and educators spend many hours a day in the trenches trying to assist challenging children. In order to maintain patience and persistence, they must continually address their own emotional and physical well-being. The ongoing adventure with these children requires that they pace themselves for the long and arduous journey. Long-term effort is different depending on the relationship with the individual child; for parents, long-term may mean a lifetime, and for educators, it may mean their entire career.

Sustaining or promoting emotional and physical well-being is addressed in the following three sections: *Self-confidence, Oomph,* and *Support.* The frequently heard distress call is HELP! HELP! It is no accident that the acronym is *SOS.* This easily remembered acronym is a reminder to evaluate well-being in these three areas.

Two common stories, representative of the difficulties encountered with close involvement with children who have ADHD, illustrate the importance of good self-care. Friday afternoon, a grandmother of a child with ADHD arrived at the office for her scheduled appointment. It was only the third time she had come for assistance. The first two visits had been primarily for diagnosis. The child was noticeably absent at this third appointment. She immediately volunteered that she had left him with her husband and needed to talk. A flood of tears ensued. After a short time, she regained her composure, only to begin crying again. The child she was caring for was her four-year-old grandson. She had obtained legal guardianship because the biological mother and father were both unable to care for him. The grandmother reported that her husband was not helpful in managing the grandson. She then described her emotional and physical fatigue. While sobbing, she asked, "Can I keep this up for another twenty years?" She knew the answer. Unless something changed, she could not maintain her energy and effort. In addition to her emotional and physical exhaustion, she was plagued by feelings of failure, anger, and guilt—guilt for feeling she wanted to get rid of him because nothing seemed to work. She felt guilty about not liking him. Anger resulted from losing an old way of life where she could sit quietly with her husband and read a delicious book.

Another story was relayed from a teacher at a conference concerning a child with ADHD. The teacher wondered if it was time to give up his career. He reported his fire and enthusiasm in the fall had waned, and by early spring, he was regularly arguing with the two children in his class that had ADHD. This was a response he knew was counterproductive and increased his frustration, anger, and guilt. His Wednesday-to-Friday fantasy was that the parents relocated to another state.

Both of these scenarios are similar to ones happening in many homes and schools. These stories represent normal feelings—frustration, guilt, hopelessness—and responses to all the hard work. When the strength, intensity, and duration of these emotional responses are reduced, it is easier to hang in for the long haul. Learning to recognize and normalize the feelings and even find some humor in the situation reduces the intensity. Individuals who work regularly with challenging children sometimes find relief when they can express "dark humor" without guilt. In one parent support group, a joke was told by a parent who helped others recognize and laugh about their negative feelings without guilt. The joke was about secretly wanting to say to their son, "Chad, do you want to go play in the street today?" as the gravel trucks went by every five minutes. The laughter was healing because each parent was able to recognize having a similar thought.

Self-Confidence

Good self-confidence allows one to manage stressful events in life more effectively. Most fundamental to self-confidence is the willingness and ability to take care of oneself. Low self-confidence can lead to unhealthy amounts of guilt, anxiety, anger, and depression. Self-confidence can be described as a way of feeling, thinking, and behaving that implies self-acceptance, trust, respect, and belief in oneself. When accepting and respecting oneself, a comfortable attitude about personal strengths and weaknesses develops.

Self-confidence is not developed overnight or as a result of any single insight, decision, or modification in your behavior. It is built gradually by working on a number of different areas or needs in one's life. Examples of some of these needs are: unconditional love, friendship, sense of belonging, creativity, fun and play, respect and validation, sense of accomplishment, spiritual awareness, physical touch, financial security, and a sense of personal freedom. Examine these areas and work on one or two of them at a time. Going through these steps creates a feeling of accomplishment and increased self-confidence. Integral to developing self-confidence is achieving a sense of accomplishment—most noticeable after success at a specific task. For example, finishing the book started, finishing the race trained for, or receiving the promotion worked for can all increase your self-confidence.

Self-confidence is also directly related to our self-talk, which are the messages we give ourselves. Self-talk is usually so automatic and subtle that it is not noticed, nor is the effect it has on moods and feelings. What we say to ourselves in response to any particular situation mainly determines our mood and feelings. For example, two adults are walking along the beach for the first time. One of them is excited and anxious to go play in the three-foot waves; the other one is fearful and intimidated. The self-talk is quite different in each case. The excited adult is saying, "This could be fun," and the fearful adult is saying, "This is dangerous and scary."

Unfortunately, many people decrease their self-confidence because they have an overly critical voice in their self-talk which is negatively judging and evaluating their behavior: "That was stupid; I always mess up." If one already has a tendency for negative self-talk, they will be more susceptible to the actual and implied criticism from others when the child with ADHD misbehaves. Others may give looks or make comments that are disparaging. Being aware of negative or critical self-talk and how others' perceptions can have a powerful influence is the first step in changing this self-defeating pattern. This process involves evaluating your self-talk and determining if your perception is distorted or irrational. Some examples of distorted or irrational thinking are: all-or-nothing thinking, "should statements," and overgeneralization. The statement "I am a *horrible* person because I yelled at my child" is an example of all-or-nothing thinking. People with all-or-nothing thinking evaluate their personal qualities and others in extreme black-and-white categories, which are unrealistic because life is rarely completely one way or another. If we try and force our experiences into absolute categories, we will be depressed or discredited. The statement "I *should* be a better parent" is an example of a "should statement." "Should statements" that are directed against yourself lead to frustration and guilt, and those directed toward other people and things lead to anger and frustration. The statement "I *always* lose my temper with Johnny, no matter how hard I try" is an example of overgeneralization. A *single* negative event is seen as a neverending pattern of defeat. For valuable information which goes beyond the scope of this book, please refer to the Appendix for an additional resource which explores how to change self-talk in greater detail (see *The Feeling Good Handbook*).

There are many potential sources of information which could lower self-confidence if allowed. It is important to be one's own judge. Competence with these children means being willing to learn and gradually get better at management of the child. Learn to self-talk about effort rather than about imperfections. If one overidentifies with being a good parent, effective teacher, or a principal with no visible problems, then the failure of the child with ADHD will become *too* important. Let this identity be only one part of your life, not all of your life! Develop other parts where success is not so difficult.

Preserve and/or Develop Self-Confidence

- Do not restrict one's self to just one role, e.g., teaching or parenting.
- Develop some of your other talents and interests.
- Do activities that will almost guarantee positive feedback: take music lessons or exercise.
- Keep reminding yourself this is a difficult job.
- Remember to set obtainable goals so you feel a sense of accomplishment.
- Learn to monitor self-talk to keep from responding in a manner that lowers your self-esteem

---

Oomph

It is *extremely* valuable to preserve and/or develop our *Oomph!* This is the energy or the "get up and go" to take on each day. If we do not have it, nothing much else follows. We need to maintain balance for personal wellness by taking care of spiritual, physical, and emotional needs. A commitment has to be made to take care of one's self first, or caring for others is difficult. Caring for our spiritual needs may not be as easy as nurturing other aspects of ourselves, but to nurture our spirit is essential.

Good physical care gives back oomph. Basic physical care involves a balanced diet, regular exercise, and adequate sleep. There are many benefits to regular exercise such as reducing muscle tension, releasing pent-up frustration, overcoming fatigue, and increasing the metabolic rate. It also stimulates the production of endorphins, which are natural substances in the body resembling morphine chemically and its effects. Some additional benefits include an increased sense of well-being, improved sleep, and reduced depression. It is helpful to keep a daily record of exercise to focus on the process of exercise instead of outcomes. Be sure to give yourself incentives to start or maintain exercising.

Emotional well-being is a key component of oomph, because if emotionally drained, the ability to cope and problem-solve effectively is dramatically decreased. Taking care of one's self emotionally requires balance and discipline. Determine what is desired from life. Is day-to-day life working? Is your life lacking intimacy, a sense of belonging, or feelings of worthiness? Asking yourself questions like these helps obtain perspective and encourages the reevaluation process. It is very easy to get so involved in the busyness of our daily lives that we lose sight of what is truly most important to us. People accomplish this through various ways including relaxation, meditation, or some form of quiet time away from daily activities. Our peace of mind and enjoyment of our lives determine the difference between existence and life well-lived.

Nurturing mind, body, and spirit gives the oomph needed to have a happy and successful life. Nurturing activities like warm baths, breakfast in bed, long, relaxed walks, or going to bed early will enhance feelings of well-being and efforts with a challenging child more effective.

Support

We have broken down the area of "support" in two ways to help facilitate the best possible self-care. One form of support involves utilizing competent individuals to take temporary physical care of the child to provide free time without guilt or apprehension. Another form of support is emotional support, which comes from a strong network of friends and family who listen in a nonjudgmental way. Joining a local or online ADHD support group can provide additional support. They can make the difference between coping and just surviving. This kind of support provides encouragement even after a brief contact. When surveys of human values have been done, many people rank close friends near the top.

Creativity is necessary in finding others who are willing and capable to temporarily care for the ADHD child. On the surface, this sounds like an easy task, but it's hard to retain capable child care because these children present some special challenges. There might be other factors making it difficult to even find child care, such as location, limited financial resources, or limited community resources. For example, a single mother with several other children may need several times a week to be away from a more difficult child and may have a limited income to achieve this.

Some ideas to assist in taking "time-outs:"

- In the spring, discuss with the teacher the possibility of keeping the child home for a day if the teacher needs a break.
- Parents should sometimes take siblings out on evening excursions without the child.
- Send a sibling to an extended family member's house for a few days.
- Let the sibling stay at a friend's house occasionally.
- Move different classmates close to the child with ADHD so one child does not have all the stress.
- Assign an adult volunteer to the child on field trips so the classmates and teacher do not have to be the behavior managers.
- Have the aide take the child for a walk.

We would also like to emphasize that teachers, siblings, and classmates also need time-outs from the more challenging child. Some more ideas are:

- If a college is close-by, put notices on the bulletin boards of the psychology departments letting students know they can learn some psychology by caring for a child with ADHD.
- Use extended family members. Train them on behavior techniques so you feel safe being away. Try using neighborhood kids while you are still at home so you can educate them on management skills.
- Trade baby-sitting with a neighbor.
- Send the child to relative's house for a couple of weeks during the summer.
- Well-organized summer camps are great.
- Send the child to a YWCA or YMCA program two nights a week.
- Tell your spouse it's her turn tonight.
- Go into the bedroom, lock the door, take a magazine, and read for thirty minutes.

The idea of just giving them away may at times seem like the only solution. If this idea occurs too often, then reread this chapter as needed.

17

Individualized Treatment Plans

The treatment team is organized, educated, and trained on basic interventions effective with ADHD and now is ready to develop an individualized treatment plan. The completion of the Treatment Assessment Summary Form, found in the Appendix, helps the team organize the available information on the child, home, and school. The information contained on the form helps develop realistic and appropriate expectations for team members and the child via summarizing problem areas and strengths. Changing circumstances may require ongoing modification of expectations for the child, family, or school.

Completing the Treatment Intervention Plan

On the Treatment Assessment Summary Form, the three most difficult problems at home and at school are listed. This is a starting place for the team to begin making plans for an intervention. The parents and teachers usually have strong feelings about which behaviors they want addressed first. Acknowledging their frustrations by first focusing on those behaviors increases their motivation and compliance and leads to success. Initially, one or two of these problems or concerns is behaviorally defined and selected for the initial focus of treatment.

After the team has decided on the initial focus, the MHP can help break the chosen problem behavior or concern into criteria that can be objectively measured and the desired specific outcome goals. Next, the type(s) of interventions are selected. Sometimes, before an intervention with a child can be effectively implemented, prior interventions are necessary with the parents and/or teachers. A parent may need to be treated for depression before they have sufficient energy to be consistent in implementing a behavioral intervention for their child. A teacher may need an assistant in order to focus on the behavioral intervention. Any interventions that require little effort and resources are tried before more complex interventions such as implementing a structural change. Typically, one intervention is implemented at a time; however, in some crisis situations, multiple interventions may be simultaneously implemented. When behavioral interventions are considered, the MHP must evaluate the team members' proficiency at performing the behavioral technique.

The Treatment Intervention Form, found in the Appendix, helps the treatment team organize and outline the interventions to be implemented. This form improves communication and consistency and provides a written record of interventions. The form prompts the team to describe the problem behaviorally, detail the specific intervention, and to evaluate the intervention. The following sample of a completed Treatment Intervention Form illustrates its use and demonstrates the dynamic nature of any intervention plan. The form also describes incentives used to keep team members motivated.

TREATMENT INTERVENTION PLAN (SAMPLE)

Date of implementation: 2-7-2004

Problem or concern (specific measurable behaviors): Arguing with peers/school and family/home. Baseline was taken during first and fourth school hour. The average number of arguing episodes was twenty for the two-hour period. Baseline of arguing with parents and siblings was established by observing arguing episodes during mealtimes. The average number of arguing episodes at mealtimes was thirty per day.

Past Interventions Attempted: Chuckie is moved to the front of the classroom, reducing arguing episodes by 20 percent.

Intervention(s) at school: 1. Class members were taught how to ignore arguing behavior by using face aversion. Each student was given an incentive each time they successfully used ignoring with Chuckie. The incentive was a trip to the gumball machine. 2. Chuckie was given a choice of an incentive from a "cafeteria list" at the end of each day if he reduced his arguing episodes by 20 percent from the baseline average. After Chuckie has had two consecutive weeks of meeting the 20 percent goal, then the goal is raised to 40 percent and raised again after another two consecutive weeks of success until arguing is no longer a problem behavior. At the end of the two-week intervention, the parent sent a letter to the teacher thanking her for her help.

Intervention(s) at home: 1.Parents and siblings were taught how to ignore arguing behavior by using face aversion. 2. Each time a sibling ignores Chuckie's arguing behavior, they are immediately given 15 minutes of a pre-selected favorite activity. 3. Chuckie is given an incentive from a "cafeteria list" each day if he decreases arguing by 20 percent from the baseline average. After Chuckie has had two consecutive weeks of meeting the 20 percent goal, then the goal is raised to 40 percent and raised again after another two consecutive weeks of success until arguing is no longer a problem behavior. Parents give themselves a Friday night date if Chuckie makes a 20 percent reduction in arguing episodes four out of the five weekdays (excluding Saturday and Sunday).

Desired outcome goals with the intervention:

Short-term goals: 1. Increase the number of times peers, siblings, and parents ignore arguing behavior. 2. Decrease the number of times Chuckie attempts to start arguments.

Long-term goals: 1. Decrease arguing, which will increase the number of times peers and family members initiate positive interactions with Chuckie. Peers and family members will learn the technique of ignoring irritating behavior.

Evaluation after two weeks of intervention using objective measures (circle one):

1. *Decreased problem behavior*
2. No change in problem behavior
3. Increased problem behavior

Modifications of the initial intervention to increase progress: The teacher observed that two peers continued to argue with Chuckie. The incentive was changed to fifteen minutes of computer time for the two peers, given immediately after ignoring.

Evaluation of modifications: The two peers successfully ignored the problem behavior; the new incentive was effective.

Status of problem or concern (circle):

Resolved (Date): 4-28-2004

Ongoing:

Increasing in severity: Chuckie's father left home for work on 4-1-2004, and during that week, his arguing temporarily increased.

Another Treatment Intervention Form describing a new problem or concern is developed with the expectation that the previously addressed problem will periodically need attention.

Checklist for Ineffective Interventions

It is not unusual for intervention plans to need modifications; sometimes, it will be apparent where changes are necessary. However, there are times when identifying why the intervention was not effective is difficult to ascertain. The checklist provides a systematic way to review potential problem areas.

1. Did you use a behavioral intervention that would fit a child much younger in chronological age (e.g., their "adjusted age")?
2. Was the length between the desired behavior and the incentive too long? The younger the child, the more impulsive the child; therefore, the less delay they can tolerate.
3. Has the incentive been used too frequently? With some incentives, frequent use erodes the novelty of the item and thus effectiveness.
4. Is the incentive offered to the child motivating enough to get a difficult task accomplished?
5. Is the incentive concrete enough (can they physically touch it)?
6. Is the child being cued often to help him remember what the "rule" is to get him the incentive?
7. Has the child been exposed to enough positive experiences to establish you as an ongoing source of positive interactions?
8. Evaluate for the use of alcohol and drugs.
9. Evaluate the frequency of negative attention by school staff and family.
10. Have you forgotten to provide ongoing incentives when the child is meeting expectations?
11. Is the child extra tired? If so, reduce expectations.
12. Are siblings and classmates triggering problem behavior (e.g., scapegoating)?
13. Occasionally, we all wake up grouchy and irritable, and so do children with ADHD. Don't be alarmed and change your strategy for one bad day.
14. Videotape the intervention to help identify reasons for ineffectiveness.

18

Case Studies

Three cases studies present a review of the evaluation and treatment principles described in the book. The case studies are composites of interactions with many different clients seen over an extended period of time. The names used are fictional.

The case studies follow the child into early adulthood; therefore, not every single intervention is illustrated. We intentionally portray more successful interventions to encourage creativity. Therefore, the case studies overrepresent success in treatment. There would be many ineffective interventions attempted over the child's life span.

Case Study I

A mom went to a psychologist because of feelings of depression and inadequacy about her inability to manage her eight-year-old son's behavior. She was a single mom, and Randolph was her only child. The mom provided him with a great deal of individual attention, but lately they were spending most of their time together arguing. She was highly motivated to assist him but did not know what would be helpful. The mom had limited financial resources and a minimal support system. Randolph had no contact with his biological father. The mom reported that his biological father was a high-school dropout at age fifteen. He had difficulty maintaining employment and had never paid child support. The mom divorced him when Randolph was three years old. He had since been married and divorced three times. The mother had chosen not to date after her divorce and concentrated on raising her son. Therefore, with just mother and son, their home environment was less complex than most homes.

After the initial interview with the mom, the psychologist suggested a formal evaluation of her son. The psychologist suspected the child might have ADHD, based on the mother's description of him and the history of his biological father. The mom was given the ADHD questionnaires, included in the Appendix, to fill out and the appropriate educational ones to distribute to her son's teacher.

The psychologist performed a psychological evaluation with the child and obtained more history and background information from the mother. The psychologist learned that only recently a dramatic change in Randolph's behavior occurred after he entered second grade. He said he hated school and started argu-ing with his mom about doing schoolwork. The arguing then spread to most other requests she made. The mom became increasingly depressed about her inability to assist him. Randolph's second-grade teacher offered little feedback except negative information. The mom was confused, as the teachers in kindergarten and first grade were especially effective in helping him be successful. They gave her positive information and techniques for assisting him at home, which helped her feel like a successful parent.

The questionnaires from home and school indicated there was a noticeable discrepancy between mom's severity ratings on the questionnaires and the current second-grade teacher's. Due to these discrepancies, it was decided to contact his first-grade teacher and ask her to fill out ADHD questionnaires about his first-grade performance. The first-grade teacher's questionnaire responses indicated significant problems, but much less severe than the second-grade teacher's. His first-grade teacher also indicated that he had a high level of creativity and artistic ability. She further stated in the Educators' Positive Information Questionnaire that he liked the positive attention received while making presentations to the class.

The psychologist suggested that because such a dramatic change had occurred after entering second grade and because of the discrepancies of perception on the questionnaires, an observation period at school might be helpful as a part of the evaluation process. Randolph's lowered achievement at school was also puzzling, because the psychological evaluation indicated an average intelligence and good reading skills. In an attempt to sort out what was triggering the increase in his problems, the mom arranged for the psychologist to visit Randolph's classroom.

The second-grade class which he attended had twenty-four students with one aide for assistance. Observations and interactions with the teacher about Randolph's behavior were discouraging. In the three-hour observation period, she made thirty negative remarks to students and three positive statements. Randolph received no positive statements. Action learning was not a part of her teaching style. The teacher stated that all children in the classroom should be treated the same and was inflexible about changing. Her approach was supported by the principal.

Randolph was completing classwork in math 50 percent of the time and had a completion rate of 60 percent in other subjects. Randolph was behind his peers in math skills, but not in language skills. Returning home assignments was occur-ring about 30 percent of the time. He consistently denied having homework to his mom.

Students in the class had started to call him names and avoid him. He had been referred to the principal on three occasions in the past month for fighting on the playground. The principal used an incremental punishment system. After the first incident, Randolph received a lecture from the principal. He received a suspension of recess time for one week after the second incident. After the third incident, he was given a two-day suspension from school.

After all the evaluation information had been collected from multiple sources, he was diagnosed with ADHD (inattentive, hyperactive, and impulsive type), moderate in severity. It was also decided that the current practices at his school were exacerbating his problems. The information gathered revealed that realistic expectations were not present in his school placement. The information from the evaluation also made it clear what had been effective and what had been ineffective interventions.

The mom was diagnosed with mild depression based on her self-report and overall score received on the adult form of the Beck Depression Inventory. Her feelings of depression stemmed from her challenges with Randolph, being socially isolated, and feeling unsupported by the school system. Treating the depression was a primary undertaking before she could do a behavioral intervention program with Randolph. Her physician placed her on an antidepressant, and she joined a CHADD support group. The antidepressant allowed her to be less reactive to his problem behaviors. The support group helped decrease her feelings of isolation, guilt, and inadequacy.

The mom learned about her son's disorder and the treatment options available from the psychologist. She began to feel hopeful and encouraged about a multidisciplinary team approach. The team, initially consisting of the mother and psychologist, made a decision based on the evaluation data to move Randolph to another school and teacher. There were several other grade schools in the area that were highly recommended for their approach to atypical children. The new school chosen had a teacher and principal open to new methods of dealing with children. They were willing to develop an individualized program and be part of a team.

Together, the team discussed and decided to have Randolph see his physician to be evaluated for medication. Copies of the questionnaires were sent to his physician. The physician and mom made the decision to try medication based on several reasons:

1. Randolph had a moderate level of ADHD that was having a negative impact on his academic work. Even with an excellent teacher, a moderate level of ADHD continued to present significant challenges in his

academic achievement. The expectations with each grade level would increase, which would tax his ability to stay focused on more difficult material for longer periods of time. Medication would provide additional assistance to increase his ability to stay focused.

2. The medication would increase his ability to have more positive social interactions and increase his ability to make friendships.

3. Mom was having difficulty being consistent, and part of her depression was triggered by feelings of failure as a parent. His medication would help her be more successful in parenting.

The physician placed him on a stimulant medication and provided information to the mother and the teacher about the medication. The mother had limited finances and so the least expensive one was chosen. Questionnaires were given to the teacher and mother to evaluate his behavior after one month on the medication. However, his ability to attend and be less impulsive improved within a few days. Randolph reported to his mom that the kids were teasing him less after a week of taking the medication. The follow-up questionnaires confirmed a consistent pattern of improvement for Randolph academically and socially.

The psychologist, mom, and teacher met to discuss the behavioral-intervention part of the treatment plan. The psychologist gave some instruction about behavioral principles using the ABC model. The mom and teacher wanted to address arguing and schoolwork completion. The psychologist thought these were reasonable problem areas to address first because of Randolph's previous success in kindergarten and first grade. Also, the mom's depression was decreasing, which allowed her to be more consistent.

In order to evaluate the effectiveness of a behavioral plan, the current level of arguing and schoolwork completion needed to be ascertained before an intervention was implemented. The teacher was already collecting the information about completion rates every week, but the frequency of arguing had not been noted. The mom and teacher used a simple technique of making a tally sheet of arguing episodes during a two-hour period each day for a week. The teacher observed from 1-3:00 PM and the mother between 5-7:00 PM. These time periods were chosen because they were the most difficult times of the day for the child. The average number of times of arguing at school was six, and at home, it was thirteen times for the two-hour period.

An intervention using the ABC model was developed to increase schoolwork-completion rates and decrease arguing rates. The plan to increase schoolwork completion rates (behavior) had several steps. He was moved from the back of the classroom to a seat directly in front of the teacher (structure). The teacher modified the instructions that she gave to Randolph. She made direct eye contact and gave shorter, clearer, two-step instructions about assignments (antecedents). The teacher used verbal praise as the incentive, and initially, it was given frequently and immediately. For example, Randolph was given only three problems in math at a time instead of all twelve the class received (modification of structure). The teacher checked them immediately and gave him verbal praise (consequence) if correct. He was then given three more until all of the twelve were completed. Randolph's completion rate increased from 50 percent to 90 percent after one week of intervention. Similar interventions were set up for other school assignments. Gradually, the verbal praise was less frequent and immediate.

The intervention to decrease arguing (behavior) was developed for school and at home. At school, Randolph was told that if he could decrease his arguing by two times a day during the two-hour period (appropriate expectation) that he would immediately get fifteen minutes of extra time on the computer. At home, he would immediately get fifteen minutes of playtime with his mom playing his favorite game. The following week, he was told that to get his incentive, (consequence) he would need to decrease his arguing by another two times during each observation period. Gradually, it was necessary for him to argue no more than two times during the time to get his incentive. After his arguing had been decreased to not more than two a time period, ignoring was used as an additional consequence. It was necessary to periodically use ignoring, (consequence) because he would attempt to reuse arguing as a method of avoiding unpleasant tasks.

After the success with decreasing arguing and increasing schoolwork-completion rates, then the team made the decision to address homework. The homework needed to be brought home, completed, and returned to school. This intervention would require close coordination and communication between mother and teacher. The Homework Round-Up—in the Appendix—was used, where the mom could initial to confirm that she saw the homework for that day. The teacher would initial the returned form when she received the completed homework. Later, they decided to send the information via the Internet. The homework was designed to take only thirty minutes to complete if he stayed on task (appropriate expectation). If more than thirty minutes is expected of a child with a moderate level of ADHD, resistance and failure may occur. The work was always to be done at the kitchen table, where the mother could observe the progress (structure). The environment was quiet, and all extra objects were taken from the table. After the work was returned each day, taking the ball out at recess was his incentive. The incentive for returning the homework would gradually be delayed. For example, it would be necessary for him to return the work three days in a row before receiving the incentive.

The mom and teacher became effective at implementing the ABC model and changing the structure of the environment to help him be successful as new problems arose. They learned it was necessary to change the incentives at regular intervals to keep Randolph working and not arguing. Medication continued to be beneficial and if it was inadvertently missed, everyone noticed a negative difference in behavior. The overall treatment resulted in Randolph and his mom feeling more successful. The teacher felt so positive about implementing the behavioral techniques that she started to use similar strategies on two other challenging children.

The treatment team was able to be proactive and maintain continuity of the treatment plan from year to year. While Randolph was in the primary grades, the team met in the spring to select an appropriate teacher for him for the following year. The team met with the selected teacher to discuss what strategies had been most successful. The parent contacted the new teacher and tried to develop a positive working relationship by offering to support the teacher and her efforts with Randolph. This positive interaction started the new school year off right.

During each summer, Randolph was given schoolwork provided by his last teacher. An hour's worth of schoolwork kept him in the rhythm of school and helped remediate any academic deficits. This occurred five days a week. The mother provided an appropriate incentive program for completed work. He also participated on a swim team during much of the summer. The swimming coach was a very positive person that gave clear instructions. The plan was to keep him engaged in positive activities with little unstructured time on his hands.

The psychologist, mom, and sometimes other team members met about once a month for his grade-school years. The mom and other team members needed regular doses of encouragement. Also, new problems arose that needed to be discussed and a strategy decided on. The mother gradually got better at being able to identify the new problem and develop a solution.

Middle and high school present a more complicated environment. The team met to discuss the complex issues such as placement with multiple teachers, a less structured environment, peer pressure, and autonomy. Teachers and subjects were selected, as much as possible, that worked well with children having ADHD. The team and Randolph discussed the available elective classes, and he selected his most preferred ones. It was decided to put difficult subjects in the morning, because he had a harder time staying focused in the afternoon. Weekly communication by phone or e-mail between his mom and his teachers allowed her to stay informed of his progress. To provide structure during lunchtime, Randolph assisted a wheelchair-confined student to the cafeteria and back to class. He received positive attention from teachers and peers for this special effort. The decrease in structure was also addressed by having the teacher cue Randolph at the end of class. The teacher would make eye contact with him and say what materials were needed for the next class period. This is also the time when many children are pushing for more autonomy, and peer relationships become more important. The autonomy that Randolph could handle successfully was similar to that of a child half his chronological age. Autonomy had to be given at a slower rate than his peers. For example, he was given a maximum of twenty-five minutes of phone time each day. Randolph was not allowed to keep a phone in his room because of the monitoring difficulty. It was required that he not spend more than thirty-five minutes getting home from school. When Randolph complied, he was given forty minutes per day for the next week. He was encouraged to be involved with the school's drama club. Randolph was able to use his creative skills to build the sets for the productions and received positive attention for his creative efforts. His enjoyment of being in front of people and being the center of attention soon led to his having acting positions in the drama club and being accepted by many of his peers. In high school, extra structure was provided by an action-oriented job for two hours daily after school. He did well because his boss was positive and structured.

Typically, children having ADHD start resisting their ADHD medication in their early teens. Randolph was no exception. It was agreed that Randolph could stop taking his medication for one month. However, he agreed in return to start taking it again if his success rate in school and home decreased. He was given a month trial without the medication, and evaluations were taken just before and after the one month. The data clearly indicated that he was starting to have more difficulty at home and school. When the information was shown to him, he was still resistive about taking the medication. A successful incentive program was set up to encourage him to take the medication.

Adolescents with ADHD tend to have more problems than the typical teenager with sexuality and drug usage. The mother started early talking to him about when it would be appropriate for him to start dating. The mom decided that at sixteen, he could date in structured situations. She also discussed that sexual relations are between married couples. To avoid drug use, she kept him engaged in positive and structured activities with non-drug-using people.

He graduated from high school and found a physically active job as an apprentice to a plumber. This boss had a bad temper, and the two got into conflict almost immediately. Randolph walked off the job. The mom's friend from her CHADD support group offered to help Randolph find another plumber's apprentice job. He had insight into which type of personality would work best with Randolph.

The new boss was levelheaded and explained job expectations clearly. Randolph stayed in the plumbing business.

Randolph was married a few years later to an older woman. One year later, his wife brought him into the office of the psychologist and complained that he was not thoughtful about her feelings. The psychologist discussed with her the characteristics of ADHD and explained how to be more direct to get her needs met. The psychologist also suggested to Randolph that he take a twenty-minute run before arriving home. The running helped reduce his tension, and he was able to enter the home in a more positive and loving mood. The marriage improved with these interventions. Once a year, the couple returned to see the psychologist for a "tune-up."

Randolph had a career and family and felt successful about his life. Imagine what his story might have been like without an ongoing, positive, and creative intervention plan.

Case Study II

John's parents brought him to see a psychologist when he was three years old, after the family doctor determined there were no physical reasons to explain his behavior. They were desperate to find answers to their questions and obtain help for their son. The parents stated their son behaved unlike any other child they had known. They described spending all their time and energy trying to keep up with him and keep him safe. John behaved in ways that endangered him and others. He had broken several bones from falling and had been to the emergency room several times for cuts that needed suturing. The parents stated he had no fear and did not seem to learn from his accidents. Once, he tipped a twenty-gallon fish tank on himself and was lucky to not have received serious injury. The parents described another incident when John found the keys to the car and started it. He put the car in gear and drove into a tree. John would hit or throw objects at others, which could cause severe injury. His behavior had become so difficult to manage that his parents started keeping him away from other people. John did not follow their instructions, and the parents had little control over his behaviors. He could focus on most tasks for only a few seconds before moving on to the next activity. John had excellent motor and language skills. However, at times, he looked uncoordinated because of his falling and running into objects—this was due to him not attending to obstacles in his path.

During the first interview with the psychologist, John demonstrated his uncooperative behaviors in the office. In the first few minutes, he had energetically opened all the office drawers and climbed on top of the desk. John then quickly moved to the large plant in the corner and tipped it over while he was inspecting it. When it looked like John was going to fling the plant around, his father tried to hold him on his lap to control his behavior. He started screaming until his father gave up and released him. The psychologist offered John a fun-looking toy to play with if he would come and stand in front of him. He was not interested and remained uncooperative. The psychologist unsuccessfully tried a few more behavioral techniques with incentives. He observed the parent's futile attempts to manage his behavior. It was clear that another appointment without the child would be necessary to obtain more background and family history.

An evaluation of a young child with such hyperactivity and impulsiveness usually needs to focus on observational data rather than formal testing. Formal testing under these circumstances produces unreliable results. It was decided to delay formal testing until there was more control over his behavior. There was no family history of ADHD. However, John clearly exhibited in every environment the characteristics of ADHD in a severe form. Although it is unusual to diagnosis a child this young with ADHD, it was confirmed several years later with formal testing. Due to the severity of his disorder, early effective treatment was vital to prevent the development of more serious problems, such as juvenile crime and/or substance abuse.

The psychologist discussed with the parents that due to the severity of John's disorder, it was important to establish and maintain appropriate behavioral expectations in developing a treatment plan. Thinking outside the usual treatment approaches and being especially creative was a priority. Progress would be made in small increments. Treatment should utilize his strengths in an effort to offset negative attention. A proactive plan for the self-care of all those in regular contact with John was mandatory.

The parents and psychologist were the initial team, and they decided to include a pediatrician who specialized in ADHD. It is unusual to give a three-year-old child medication to treat this disorder. However, John's behavior was severely impairing his life and his family's, so it was decided to place him on stimulant medication. The physician saw him frequently to monitor the impact of the medication. It was determined that the medication was helpful to some extent and would be continued.

The team discussed the home environment and the family dynamics. The mother had a smaller child to care for besides John. If the mom did not physically watch the baby, John might hurt him, and if she focused on the baby, he might place himself in dangerous situations. Once, while Mom was changing a diaper on the baby, John left the house and climbed onto the roof. Needless to say, the mother started to have serious depression problems and was finding it difficult to contain her anger toward John. The father worked ten to twelve hours each day. He helped when he was at home, but he was also finding it difficult to contain his anger toward John.

The first interventions focused on keeping John physically safe, especially when his mom was attending to the younger sibling or needed personal time. The team decided to make a safe room where John could be contained for short periods. They chose his bedroom. All potentially dangerous objects were removed from the room and only safe toys remained (e.g., plastic building blocks). The door was changed into a half door; the bottom half could be locked and the top half kept open to allow visual contact. John responded well to the change after a brief initial upset. The mom felt relieved because she knew both children would be safe for those brief periods. The doors to the outside of the house had interior locks installed at the top of the door so adults only could remove. Numerous other changes were made in the car and home to increase safety. The team reassured the parents that these extreme modifications were necessary. The reassurance helped reduce their guilt feelings. After the safety interventions were made, the team focused on the parents' feelings of anger and depression. The team decided the mom needed to practice better self-care to decrease her anger and depression and would require time away from the children. The mom decided to work outside the home two days a week. The money she earned would be used to hire an individual to care for the children. The woman she hired was patient and amenable to being trained in behavioral management. The mother's depression lifted almost immediately and her ability to be constructive with John increased. The father's feelings of anger were decreased after he received further education about ADHD and developed realistic expectations for John. The father decided he could be more helpful and involved. He came up with a creative idea for using John's energy and coordination. The father helped him build a small playhouse. They worked on it each night for over a month. John painted it with his father's supervision and proudly showed to everyone in the neighborhood. The building activity was effective in reducing aggression, increasing his self-confidence, and strengthening his relationship with his father. The additional benefit with all the physical activity was fatigue, resulting in him sleeping better at night.

Progress was being made in safety issues until one day, the hired caretaker accidentally neglected to lock the back door. John escaped and climbed up to the roof of the house. A neighbor witnessed this and called Child Protective Services (CPS), reporting the child was being endangered. A CPS worker interviewed the mother and told her that she was being derelict in her parental responsibilities by using a caretaker other than herself. The mother was devastated, and her feelings of depression and hopelessness returned. The mom called the team together, and the CPS worker was invited to the meeting. The team shared with the CPS worker John's history of serious problems and described the interventions that had been initiated. They also outlined the progress that had been achieved. After the CPS worker received more information, she approved of using an outside care-taker. The CPS worker agreed to help find other resources that could be used to give the family relief on the weekends.

With the home life more stable, the team could now focus on early school intervention. The local special-education team was invited to a team meeting. After an intense and informative meeting, it was decided that John should be involved in an early developmental program at school. They would work with him for four hours a day to establish some control over his behavior. The psychologist gave the teacher special behavioral training before John began school. An aide assisted the teacher for two hours each day.

The psychologist demonstrated the first behavioral intervention for the teacher. The goal of the first intervention was to obtain compliance to a simple request. The request was to have the child move into a two-foot square that was marked on the floor with masking tape in an empty room (appropriate structure). The teacher was situated against the door during this intervention so John could not escape from the room. She was requested to make no eye contact or verbaliza-tions. It was anticipated that John would not initially comply with the request. Consequently, he would receive incentives—a raisin and verbal praise—for gradu-ally moving one step closer to the square within fifteen seconds after the request was given (appropriate behavioral expectations). The psychologist made eye con-tact (John would not allow physical contact) and then firmly stated with his finger pointing at the square "stand in the square." After fifteen seconds—if John had not moved closer to the square—then the psychologist avoided eye contact and verbal comments for two minutes before repeating the request. Giving instructions in this specific manner helped John focus only on the request. It took the psycholo-gist two hours to get him to rapidly move into the square area when requested. When John finally complied within fifteen seconds, he was allowed to play with his favorite toy for one minute as an additional incentive. After the psychologist was successful with the first behavioral intervention, he invited the mom and the aide to watch through a one-way mirror. The psychologist's goals were to demon-strate appropriate behavioral expectations and behavioral principles and to instill hopefulness that John's behavior could be changed. The mother's eyes filled with tears when she viewed John's compliance. The mom and teacher were trained, and it took one week before they were successful in getting him to move rapidly into the square. A second request was added after John was responding regularly to the first request. He was asked to stand in the square and then to go sit on a small chair next to a desk. The desk was located in the corner of the room so he had to move a longer distance to increase the difficulty. John now received his raisin and verbal praise only after compliance with both requests. He was successful after only two attempts. The goal for the next day was to comply with the first requests and then request increased sitting time at the desk. John would receive a slice of orange if he sat at the desk until a timer sounded. The slice of orange was a known desirable incentive. The sitting time necessary to receive the incentive started at one minute and was gradually increased to five minutes (appropriate expectation). John had three successful compliances staying in the chair for five minutes. Next, the teacher showed him pictures of animals and asked him to name them during the five minutes at the desk. The goal was to have John follow multiple requests that followed school-like activity. After each five-minute work session, he was given five minutes to dance to enjoyable music. John could not cope with more than three five-minute work sessions in a row. Gradually, dancing with an adult was introduced to further develop cooperative behavior. Verbal praise, physical movement, and music were the incentives used. Progressively working on academic skills was the main focus during the next eighteen months. Increasingly more complicated and time-consuming tasks were added, with verbal praise the primary incentive. Other creative incentives were also used. John could sit at his desk working on a task for fifteen minutes with only three or four verbal incentives at the end of nine months of intervention.

The team made plans for John to enter a small kindergarten class that had six students. His previous aide was assigned to work with him. It was expected that John would have great difficulties with the more complex environment, despite all the efforts and the progress that had occurred. Particularly, aggression was a problem in social interactions with his peers. He at times would hit, throw objects, and kick others, including small children, when he was frustrated. An immediate intervention was necessary due to him endangering other children. The most appropriate intervention was to place him on a medication called Clonidine. This medication is helpful for children having ADHD with serious aggression problems. Finding the correct dosage took some trial and error. His aggression still occurred, but at a reduced rate. John's aggressive outbursts were further reduced by giving him transitional cues between activities. For example, five minutes before they were to stop coloring, the teacher would say, "Look at the clock. When the long hand gets to the five, then we will start on math." She would give a final reminder at one minute. The rest of the school year, the teacher worked on socialization skills, reducing aggression, and increasing on-task behavior. The teacher was able to make significant progress throughout the school year continuing to use verbal praise as the major incentive.

The team selected the teacher for first grade in the spring. They selected a teacher who was effective in dealing with children that had ADHD. The team requested a full-time aide to assist John. However, the school administration approved an aide to assist John and another boy with behavior problems. They chose an aide with considerable experience with children. The team gave her additional training in behavioral-management techniques. The aide worked with the boys at an isolated table that prevented direct eye contact with the rest of the class. She used the same class materials and modified the instructions to adapt to the boy's skill level.

By the end of the first grade, John had not been able to sustain a peer friendship. His inability to maintain friendships was primarily due to his uncooperative behavior when playing games. He always wanted to win, cheated, and insisted on playing by his rules. The team decided to address this concern. A program was developed to teach him cooperative play. Recess was the time chosen to implement a behavioral program. The aide began the program with the simple task of just throwing a ball back and forth, giving verbal praise for cooperation. If John did not correctly return the ball (e.g., kicked it) to the aide, then she would hold onto the ball and use face aversion. She would state, using a calm, firm voice, "Let me know when you are ready to play again." Face aversion and ignoring were the only consequences used. Three days later, after John could consistently and cooperatively play ball with the aide, a student was added. Robert, an intelligent and patient student, was chosen to be his playmate. It was explained to Robert how to give positive incentives to John for playing cooperatively. Robert was given extra computer time for his assistance. Robert and John started with the simple task of throwing the ball back and forth. After five minutes of successful play, the aide added another change. John was told he could change the rule of how to throw the ball, but he had to continue with the same change for five consecutive throws. He chose to bounce it to Robert. On the sixth throw, Robert was allowed to change the rule, and he chose to kick it for five consecutive throws. Gradually, the play was increased in complexity to develop cooperative skills. This intervention was only partially successful, because his ability to play cooperatively with peers occurred infrequently without adult supervision. However, John felt positive about his experience and looked forward to "playtime" at school.

The team discussed how to keep John from regressing academically and behaviorally during summer vacation. It was decided that continuing a school-like experience would help decrease the regression. The school did not have the resources to hire a teacher during the summer. The mom asked individuals at her church to see if anyone was able and willing to tutor her son. An older woman who was a retired teacher volunteered. The volunteer was given school materials, furnished by the school, and behavioral training by the mother. She taught him four days a week for two hours a day. The summer-schooling kept his academic skills improving and maintained his ability to sit and attend. The individual attention that John received resulted in positive academic gains. The volunteer continued this relationship through his elementary school years.

Due to John's severe level of ADHD, it remained necessary throughout his elementary-school years to have an aide directly assist him in the classroom. The team discussed his middle-school placement, and the only viable option was a special-education class consisting of six children with one teacher and an aide. John continued to make slow, gradual progress academically and socially.

John entered high school, and conflict with other children and teachers increased. It had been reported that he had begun to hang around with boys that were frequently in trouble at school and with the law. It was thought that if he stayed in school full-time, he would have a good chance of ending up in jail. The team met to discuss how to best help John with the negative environment that was developing around him. It was decided to first try increasing his medications. The increase in medications produced mild positive changes. The team determined that they could not successfully intervene to modify the negative environment. Therefore, the best intervention would be to remove John from the negative environment. Further traditional schooling would result in a disaster for John. The team chose an alternative school placement with an apprenticeship house-building program, based on what had been successful for him in the past—building a playhouse with his father. The contractor was chosen because he was empathetic with John's problems. He had a disabled son and understood behavioral interventions. The contractor placed him with a patient foreman who gave clear instructions and frequently gave praise. The contractor paid John four dollars an hour, which was contributed by the parents without John's knowledge. After John became a productive worker, then the contractor paid his wages. John impulsively spent his first entire paycheck in one evening. The team and John decided how to set up a system to help him with money management. They choose to deposit 40 percent of his paycheck directly into a savings account. The remainder of the money was equally divided and placed into four envelopes. John received one envelope each week. In order to withdraw any money from his savings, John needed his parents to co-sign. As a part of the apprenticeship program, John took two classes a day at the alternative school. He learned additional skills that directly applied to his work. John was happy with his apprenticeship program and developed positive relationships with adults. His self-confidence increased dramatically, and he avoided contact with negative peers.

In John's adult years, he remained working in the contracting and building trades. He earned a good living and stayed out of jail. John continued to struggle with peer relationships and was unable to develop close peer relationships until he was in his forties. This success story was made possible by a committed and knowledgeable team consisting of parents, professionals, and John.

Case Study III

One month after Raydeen started the first grade, the teacher suggested to her parents that an evaluation might be helpful. She had talked with Raydeen's kindergarten teacher, who described similar concerns: difficulty with peers, not following instructions, unable to focus except for short periods. The teacher described her as full of energy and having difficulty staying seated. Raydeen performed better in the classroom with structured action-oriented activities. During recess, she was bossy and dominating with the other girls. The boys avoided playing with her.

Because they were concerned about her problems at home and at school, the parents agreed to visit their family physician about Raydeen. The family physician took a brief history and performed a physical exam. Raydeen was physically healthy. The physician referred them to child psychologist.

During the initial visit with the psychologist, the parents gave the following background information. Raydeen was the third daughter in a family of six children. The mother and father noticed that she seemed more difficult from the time she was brought home from the hospital. Raydeen had more stomach upset and was harder to console than other siblings. She seemed to be in constant motion and was seldom observed sitting still. Raydeen had difficulty getting and staying asleep as a baby and continued to struggle with sleep problems. She disturbed the other children that slept in the same bedroom. In an attempt to remedy this problem, they placed Raydeen in their bed. Their solution only caused them to lose sleep. They also observed that she was more difficult to manage as she got older. Raydeen reacted strongly to frustrations and had temper tantrums more frequently than their other children. The parents stated that she had been lost many times while they were in stores, and she never got scared. They would find her looking over items in the store, and she seemed unconcerned that her parents were not within sight. Raydeen was easier to handle when she was not around other children. If Raydeen was not getting attention, then she would act out in ways that guaranteed attention. They expressed their avoidance of taking her to grocery stores, restaurants, and birthday parties, because it was too embarrassing. Even family meals at home were a disaster. She would throw food at other family members. The older children resented her attention-getting behaviors and had started to tease her. They seemed to enjoy her strong emotional responses. The parents noticed when Raydeen was gone, it was more peaceful and enjoyable. They expressed guilt about liking her absent from the home.

The family was already functioning under high stress levels. The mother reported a rather high level of stress because of financial problems and the ailing health of her parents. She felt responsible for helping care for them. The mother did not work outside the home and tended to be isolated. The father worked twelve hour days but was helpful when he was at home. He was able to be more empathetic with Raydeen because he had similar problems. His mother nick-named him "Speed" because of his high energy level. His mom kept him busy and out of trouble.

The psychologist observed that the mother was patient with Raydeen in his office. She expressed willingness to be taught new ways of helping her. The mom realized that lectures and time-outs were not working. She used time-outs frequently and inappropriately. For example, Raydeen took time-outs in her bedroom surrounded by her favorite toys. The psychologist noted that the father had more success than the mother in managing Raydeen's behavior. He was more successful because he engaged her in action-oriented games. The father reported being distressed about all the teasing Raydeen received at home, but he had not found an effective way of stopping it. Neither parent reported using incentives to modify her behavior. However, the psychologist observed the father praising her.

The psychologist suspected Raydeen might have a mild form of ADHD and suggested further evaluation. He sent ADHD evaluation forms home with the parents. The mother volunteered to deliver the educational questionnaires to the kindergarten and first-grade teachers. The parents and teachers gave similar answers on the ADHD questionnaires, and their answers indicated a mild form of ADHD. The psychologist decided to do additional testing to help substantiate a diagnosis of ADHD. She was given the computerized test of attention, and the results indicated problems with attention. IQ test results indicated that Raydeen had normal intelligence but had a mild deficit in working memory. She was impulsive and quickly tired of any repetitious task. School testing results placed her in the normal range of reading ability for her grade. Her hearing and eyesight were evaluated at the school and no problems were identified. Based on the information collected, Raydeen was diagnosed as having a mild form of ADHD, inattentive, hyperactive, and impulsive type.

The parents were relieved because they had a better understanding of Raydeen and were encouraged about building a treatment plan. The treatment team would consist of the father, mother, teacher, and the psychologist. The teacher and parents wanted to know more about ADHD and the impact it had on Raydeen before they developed a treatment plan. The parents had been told by friends and family members that they just needed to get stricter with their discipline; however, when the parents tried to be stricter, Raydeen acted out even more. The mother asked about using medications. She was skeptical about using behavioral interventions and really wanted a trial of medications first. The mother thought medication would be an easier and faster fix. The psychologist decided to demonstrate in the office how to use the ABC Model. Raydeen was able to stay focused on a difficult task for twenty minutes when the psychologist used clear and concrete instructions combined with frequent incentives. The parents and the teacher were amazed and encouraged with the results. The mother was able to see that medication was not necessary. The demonstration produced a sense of hopefulness on the part of both the parents and the teacher.

The psychologist then had the mother try the same intervention. The results were not positive, and the mother felt defeated. The psychologist was able to explain that was his six-thousandth time doing that type of intervention and this was her first. He reassured her that she would catch on. Her performance was gently critiqued, and after the fifth attempt, she looked like a pro. Everyone cheered and praised the mother. Raydeen smiled and gave her mother a kiss. Tears appeared on the mother's cheeks. She was ready for ABC!

The father excitedly asked to try an intervention. The task was to get Raydeen to pick up all the toys in the office and put them in specific locations. He quickly broke the task down into smaller steps by making it into a game. First, he asked her to put all of the human figures in the psychologist's hands. The father said if she got it done in thirty seconds, she would get a piece of candy. He counted the seconds aloud. Second, he asked her to throw all of the stuffed animals into an empty wastebasket. He cheered with each successful throw. She enjoyed this so much that a time limit was unnecessary. The father had listened and watched carefully during the prior interventions and was able to apply the information. He received cheers—little did he know that Raydeen had been paying attention, too. Using the same behavioral techniques, Raydeen tried to modify her father's behavior the next day. The father liked her positive approach to changing his behavior rather than using negative behaviors.

The parents and teachers now felt comfortable after practicing the techniques of the ABC model and were ready to choose three problems to address. The team's next meeting was at the school because of the teacher's tight schedule. Reducing the incidents of teasing by siblings and reducing the mother's stress level would be the focus at home. The teacher would work on getting Raydeen to stay focused for longer periods of time on her math schoolwork, which lasted for thirty minutes each day.

The mother stated that her stress level would be greatly reduced if she had more help with the care of her parents. A suggestion was made to ask her brother and her parents' church friends to be of more assistance. The brother readily accepted more responsibility, and a group of seniors organized regular visits to her parents' home. This support helped reduce her stress and helped her have more energy to assist Raydeen. Periodically, it was necessary to remind her brother that his continued help was important.

The mother implemented an intervention developed by the team to reduce the teasing of Raydeen by the older two siblings. If the two siblings did not tease her for the entire hour before her bedtime, then they each would receive fifteen minutes of individual time with their mother after their usual bedtime. The length of time without teasing was gradually increased for the siblings to earn the incentive. They earned the incentive the first night, and their overall teasing at other times decreased dramatically. A family dynamic was changed with this intervention. The parents realized how neglected the siblings had been feeling with so much time focused on Raydeen. The older siblings were less angry with Raydeen because of the special attention and felt closer to their mother. Since the teasing decreased, Raydeen reduced her complaining and whining. The positive changes continued until the mother became ill and was unable to provide the incentive. When her health returned, the incentive program was resumed and the teasing again decreased. It was necessary periodically to change the incentive for the older siblings.

The team decided that increasing Raydeen's time on-task during math period would be approached in several ways. Following recess and prior to math, the teacher led the class in a quieting exercise. The exercise helped them transition from a physical, noisy activity to quiet and focused activity. The quieting exercise appears in the Appendix. To minimize visual distractions during math time, she was moved to a desk in the front of the classroom. If Raydeen was looking at her work or writing when the teacher observed her, then she received verbal praise. To help the teacher be consistent with her observations, a vibrating timer was used. The timer was set for five-minute intervals. Five-minute intervals were determined to be a realistic expectation because of prior experience with her. When the timer the vibrated, she would observe Raydeen, and if she was on-task, she was given a verbal incentive.

The time she spent on-task increased significantly, which was noted by observation and the completion of math assignments. Gradually, the teacher increased the time between verbal incentives and then developed a behavioral system for all of Raydeen's work.

The teacher switched to a token economy. Raydeen would receive a signal from the teacher when she earned a point. Raydeen was responsible for keeping track of the points earned. When she received ten points for staying on–task, she could trade her points for an item in the "treasure box." Raydeen was told before-hand that if she cheated with her recordkeeping, she would lose all ten points. The severe consequence resulted in her only cheating once. The interventions were successful in helping Raydeen focus on her schoolwork.

When several other children complained about Raydeen receiving special attention, they were given the option of doing work that was difficult for them to earn special incentives. Most students stopped complaining and chose not to do more difficult work.

After Raydeen's ability to stay on-task improved, decreasing her bossy behavior during playtime was addressed by the team. Finding a solution was difficult because of the minimal supervision available on the playgrounds. Consequently, two responsible playmates were recruited and rewarded for their help in modifying her bossy behavior. If Raydeen reduced her bossy behavior during recess by 20 percent, she would get ten minutes on a computerized learning game following recess. Bossy behavior was defined as making statements like the following: "You don't know the rules," "I'm the captain," or "If you don't play right, I'm not going to play." The playmates were taught to count the number of times Raydeen was bossy. They took turns being the one who recorded the bossy incidents. After a few days, the student helpers came up with additional bossy phrases. The student helpers were given counters that were attached to their clothing. Without Raydeen's awareness, the average daily number of bossy responses was taken for a week before the intervention began to obtain an average number so that a 20 percent reduction could be calculated. When other students asked them what they were doing, they were instructed to say, "We are doing a research project for the teacher." After the initial week, Raydeen learned about the intervention. She was taught examples of bossy and non-bossy responses. If Raydeen verbally attacked the student helpers, she would not be allowed to play during the next recess period. The first day, she lost her recess time due to verbal attacks. She went crying to the teacher and dramatically said, "Nobody likes me; I might as well kill myself." The teacher was alarmed and gave Raydeen her undivided attention for the rest of the day.

The teacher contacted the team to discuss the incident. The psychologist concluded that this was not a suicide threat, but an attention-getting statement. He explained that suicide is extremely rare for first-graders and that her general mood had been positive for weeks, which is inconsistent with suicidal feelings. Furthermore, he informed the team that it is typical for children with ADHD to make suicidal statements when they face negative consequences. Giving attention to suicidal statements in this type of situation tends to increase the number of suicidal statements.

The best way to handle this is to non-emotionally repeat the negative consequence and why it was administered. Using a phrase like, "I am sorry you're feeling sad; remember, you can get what you want by following the rules" decreases suicidal statements. Fifteen minutes after the statement has been made, look for opportunities to make positive statements about appropriate behavior. This approach reinforces positive attention-getting behaviors. The parents and teacher were relieved to have a clear strategy in dealing with this type of suicidal statement. Raydeen was later able to earn her incentive without much difficulty. The most positive result was that other students liked to play with her more.

Raydeen finished first grade with friends and academic success. The team continued to select a teacher for Raydeen through the grade-school years and to work with the teacher in understanding ADHD and behavioral interventions. In middle and high school, she was encouraged to be involved in many physical activities after school, such as basketball and soccer. The most effective incentives for good grades in high school were use of the car and kayaking with her father. Careful monitoring, provided by her teachers and parents, allowed her to successfully complete high school. She worked at a part-time job in a restaurant for a year after graduation and then entered college. Raydeen chose to become a special-education teacher. She was energetic in her teaching role and also became the girls' basketball team coach.

In her twenties, Raydeen got married to another teacher. Six months into the marriage, her husband complained about her insensitivity to his expressed feelings. He was also frustrated with her behavior after sexual intercourse. He wanted to be close and have a quiet interaction. Raydeen became super-energized and was ready to run a marathon. They could not negotiate a compromise that addressed both of their needs, and the issue interfered with their marriage. They decided to visit a professional. The professional helped them understand each other's differences and work on strategies allowing both their needs to be met. For example, they went to bed at 8:30 and made love and then cuddled for ten minutes; then she quietly moved from the bedroom. She used her energy to complete several tasks that were not bothersome to her sleeping husband.

After several visits to the psychologist, the two of them were able to negotiate on their own other problem areas arising from their different energy levels. For instance, they enjoyed going to movies on Friday nights and typically chose seats in the middle of the theater. Several times during the movie, Raydeen would crawl over him and others to get to the lobby to walk for a few minutes. This behavior greatly annoyed her husband. The solution agreed upon was to sit in the back row with her in the aisle seat. She could move to the lobby without disturbing anyone else and take care of her need to expend energy. They each learned to appreciate and understand their differences. As she learned to understand the impact of ADHD and to use her talents, more success filled her life.

19

Alternative Treatments

Over the years, many alternative treatments have been promoted as cures or effective treatments for ADHD. Today, this trend continues, and a few of the current alternative treatments are described and the available research outlined.

Natural or Nutritional Supplements

There are many natural or nutritional approaches to curing or helping children with ADHD. These approaches focus on the child's diet and/or adding supplements to address the symptoms of ADHD. There have been several books written on the subject with powerful testimonials about the efficacy of this approach. While there is clear evidence that the diet of many children is inadequate and in some cases dangerous to the child (obesity/diabetes), adequate research connecting nutrition and the successful treatment of ADHD does not exist.[42]

Vision Therapy

Clear vision and appropriate visual tracking are important for schoolwork that focuses so much on visual skills. There are optometrists who are currently of the opinion that ADHD behavior can be corrected by using visual devices that correct a complicated array of visual problems. One of the devices used is teaching the child to follow a set of lights arranged on a pair of glass-like frames. Reliable research that is supportive of this approach is not available.

Sensory-Integration Therapy

Some therapists believe children described as having ADHD should be described as having a sensory-integration dysfunction. The therapy is designed to increase the brain's ability to integrate or organize sensory information. This increased integration is purported to reduce problem behaviors. Available research at this time is inadequate to validate or invalidate this approach.

Brain-Wave Training

Brain-wave training is a biofeedback technique that uses a computerized system to help teach the child to produce specific brain-wave patterns. The child with ADHD is asked to increase brain-wave patterns similar to those found in the brain when an individual is asked be attentive. The theory behind this approach is that a child with ADHD can be trained to modify brain waves, making permanent brain changes that eliminate ADHD problems. Some of the early research results on using brain-wave biofeedback have been encouraging, but the therapist is doing much more to the child than just the brain-wave training. They are combining it with many other approaches, such as supportive psychotherapy and increased personal attention. It is difficult at this time to know what is producing the positive result because of multiple therapies the child is receiving. This is an area that will probably be more carefully evaluated by experienced independent researchers.

20

Ready, Set, Go!

Congratulations for your persistent effort! You read the entire book! You earned an incentive—did you give it to yourself? Now, begin; start the exciting process of implementing what has been learned about your specific role and the role of others in the child's life. You—the reader—have learned the following:

- ❖ an understanding of ADHD—what ADHD is and what it is not;
- ❖ how to evaluate information and research pertaining to ADHD;
- ❖ how to make an appropriate evaluation and accurate diagnosis;
- ❖ how to select treatment team members and how to coordinate their efforts;
- ❖ different types of proven treatments and how they work together;
- ❖ how to approach common and enduring problems with practical solutions;
- ❖ how to make and apply individualized treatment plans;
- ❖ a longitudinal perspective through case studies, which demonstrate applied treatments;
- ❖ and the importance of self-care strategies for team members.

The complicated nature of assisting challenging children will require reviewing treatment principles and strategies as specific problems arise. Treat this book as a resource manual. We repeat: keep trying, and do not be discouraged if all your attempts do not parallel the ideal strategies presented in the book. This is important life work; celebrate each success. A child can be saved!

Notes

About the Authors

Dr. Robert W. Atwood has thirty-five years' experience as a clinical psychologist in private practice specializing in treating disabilities (e.g., ADHD), a university psychology professor, and consultant to hospitals, schools, and other treatment centers. Dr. Atwood has received awards for excellence in teaching and providing services to schools and children.

Catherine Pugsley Getty and Ruth Wohlwend-Lloyd have MS degrees in clinical psychology and worked in private practice with Dr. Atwood.

Appendix

Questionnaires and Assessment Forms

Structured Interview

Child's Name_____Date_____

Gender: M____ or F____ Age_____ School Grade _____School name _____

Name of person(s) present at interview_____

Referred by whom_____

Name of biological mother_____

Address_____

Phone(H)_____(W)_____(C)_____

Name of biological father_____

Address_____

Phone(H)_____(W)_____(C)_____

Please list other caregivers to child (e.g., stepparent, baby-sitter, grandparent)

Name_____Relationship_____

Address_____

Phone(H)_____(W)_____(C)_____

Name_____Relationship_____

Address_____

Phone(H)_____(W)_____(C)_____

Name_____Relationship_____

Addres_____

Phone(H)_____(W)_____(C)_____

Name_____Relationship_____

Address_____

Phone(H)_____(W)_____(C)_____

Ask the parents to describe which of the interaction styles each sibling most frequently uses when dealing with the child being evaluated. Give them a definition of each of the following styles that are listed below.

1. Scapegoating/Blaming	4. Acquiescent/Give-in
2. Protective/Caretaking	5. Supportive/Encouraging
3. Confrontational/Combative	6. Avoidant/Ignoring

Name of sibling	*Relationship	*Interactive style	*% of time
1.			
2.			
3.			
4.			
5.			
6.			

How does the parent view their own parenting skills?

Circle the word that best describes the parenting style used with the child.

Parent's name	Parenting style		
1.	Authoritarian	Authoritative	Laissez-faire
2.	Authoritarian	Authoritative	Laissez-faire
3.	Authoritarian	Authoritative	Laissez-faire
4.	Authoritarian	Authoritative	Laissez-faire

History
1. When were the problems first observed?
2. What are the problems that cause the most concern?
3. What other members of the immediate and extended family have similar problems? Ask specific questions about biological father.
4. Have the problems been present for more than six months?
5. What stressful events have occurred in the child's life in the past two years?
6. Is the child's IQ over 60?
7. Has there been a recent change in the people who are providing care for the child?
8. Who spends the most time with the child as a parent?
9. What approaches have been used to address the child's problems (behavioral, medical, other)?
10. What were the precipitating events that motivated the contact with this office?
11. Who is the person most likely to get cooperation from the child?
12. Is there any prior physician evaluation information?

Office Observations
1. Does the child violate personal boundaries in a manner inappropriate for his age?

2. When the child is ignored for five minutes, what is the consequent behavior?
3. What percent of the time did the child respond positively to adult requests?
4. When the child failed to comply with requests, what was the adult response?
5. When given play materials, what was the length of time with one activity?
6. How frequently does the child change physical position?
7. How many aggressive acts were observed, and what was the aggressive behavior?
8. What were the most common methods the adults used to deal with the child's behavior?
9. Did the adults present use similar approaches when dealing with the child?
10. Count the number of negative and positive comments the child received during the interview.

Notes and other observations

Parents' Common/Enduring Challenging Situations Questionnaire (Child Ages 3 To 7)

Instructions: Does your child comply with **instructions**, **requests**, or **rules** in the following situations? Determine if the child's behavior is a challenge in the following situations (e.g., "yes" or "no") and then rate the degree of severity (from 1 to 7) only if you circled "yes." If your child is not a problem in the given situation, please circle "no" and go on to the next behavior on the form.

Situations:

	Yes/No (Circle one)		If Yes, How Severe? Mild (Circle one) Severe
	Yes	No	1 2 3 4 5 6 7
1. Taking turns/sharing toys	Yes	No	1 2 3 4 5 6 7
2. Playing with siblings	Yes	No	1 2 3 4 5 6 7
3. Playing with older children	Yes	No	1 2 3 4 5 6 7
4. Playing with multiple children	Yes	No	1 2 3 4 5 6 7
5. Playing with peers	Yes	No	1 2 3 4 5 6 7
6. Transition to new activities	Yes	No	1 2 3 4 5 6 7
7. Completing chores	Yes	No	1 2 3 4 5 6 7
8. At mealtimes	Yes	No	1 2 3 4 5 6 7
9. Riding in the car	Yes	No	1 2 3 4 5 6 7
10. Completing homework	Yes	No	1 2 3 4 5 6 7
11. Getting dressed/undressed	Yes	No	1 2 3 4 5 6 7
12. Bath time	Yes	No	1 2 3 4 5 6 7
13. During bedtime routine	Yes	No	1 2 3 4 5 6 7
14. With a baby-sitter	Yes	No	1 2 3 4 5 6 7
15. When you are on the telephone	Yes	No	1 2 3 4 5 6 7
16. When visitors are in your home	Yes	No	1 2 3 4 5 6 7
17. When sibling's friends visit	Yes	No	1 2 3 4 5 6 7
18. Watching television/video games	Yes	No	1 2 3 4 5 6 7
19. In stores, restaurants, church, etc.	Yes	No	1 2 3 4 5 6 7
20. At parties	Yes	No	1 2 3 4 5 6 7
21. When visiting others' homes	Yes	No	1 2 3 4 5 6 7
22. Mistreatment of pets	Yes	No	1 2 3 4 5 6 7
23. Compliance with time-outs	Yes	No	1 2 3 4 5 6 7

24. While on vacations   Yes   No   1 2 3 4 5 6 7
25. Gets lost in public places   Yes   No   1 2 3 4 5 6 7

Child's name_____Age_____Date_____
Behaviors rated with medication YES or NO Med/Dosage_____
Name and relationship of person completing this form_____

Parents' Common/Enduring Challenging Situations Questionnaire (Child Ages 8 To 18)

Instructions: Does your adolescent comply with **instructions**, **requests**, or **rules** in the following situations? Determine if the adolescent's behavior is a challenge in the following situations (e.g., "yes" or "no") and then rate the degree of severity (from 1 to 7) only if you circled "yes." If your adolescent is not a problem in the given situation, please circle "no" and go on to the next behavior on the form.

Situations:

	YES/NO (Circle one)	IF YES, HOW SEVERE? Mild (Circle one) Severe
	Yes No	1 2 3 4 5 6 7
1. Compliance with grounding	Yes No	1 2 3 4 5 6 7
2. Use of vehicles	Yes No	1 2 3 4 5 6 7
3. While with authority figures	Yes No	1 2 3 4 5 6 7
4. Playing with animals	Yes No	1 2 3 4 5 6 7
5. In the company of several peers	Yes No	1 2 3 4 5 6 7
6. In stores, restaurants, and malls	Yes No	1 2 3 4 5 6 7
7. When asked to complete homework	Yes No	1 2 3 4 5 6 7
8. Dating	Yes No	1 2 3 4 5 6 7
9. At church	Yes No	1 2 3 4 5 6 7
10. When asked to return home	Yes No	1 2 3 4 5 6 7
11. When parent is on the telephone	Yes No	1 2 3 4 5 6 7
12. When others compete for attention	Yes No	1 2 3 4 5 6 7
13. Unsupervised time with siblings	Yes No	1 2 3 4 5 6 7
14. While on vacations	Yes No	1 2 3 4 5 6 7
15. At bedtime	Yes No	1 2 3 4 5 6 7
16. Getting up for school	Yes No	1 2 3 4 5 6 7
17. When asked to complete chores	Yes No	1 2 3 4 5 6 7
18. When sibling's friends visit	Yes No	1 2 3 4 5 6 7
19. Drug use	Yes No	1 2 3 4 5 6 7
20. Physical fighting	Yes No	1 2 3 4 5 6 7
21. Coming home from school	Yes No	1 2 3 4 5 6 7
22. Home alone	Yes No	1 2 3 4 5 6 7
23. Unsupervised free time	Yes No	1 2 3 4 5 6 7

24. Guest at another's home	Yes No	1 2 3 4 5 6 7
25. Time-outs	Yes No	1 2 3 4 5 6 7
26. Party celebrations	Yes No	1 2 3 4 5 6 7
27. Sneaking out at night	Yes No	1 2 3 4 5 6 7

Child's name_____Age_____Date_____

Behaviors rated with medication YES or NO Med/Dosage_____

Name and relationship of person completing this form_____

Parents' Questionnaire

Circle the number that you feel most nearly describes the degree of the child's problem.

	No problem	Mild problem	Moderate problem	Severe problem
	1——2	3——4	5	6——7

1. Carries "chip" on shoulder	1	2	3	4	5	6	7
2. Does not stay seated during meals	1	2	3	4	5	6	7
3. Feels others are against them	1	2	3	4	5	6	7
4. Swears, lies, and cheats	1	2	3	4	5	6	7
5. Dramatic mood swings	1	2	3	4	5	6	7
6. Unable to keep friendships	1	2	3	4	5	6	7
7. Poor choice of friends	1	2	3	4	5	6	7
8. Physical health complaints	1	2	3	4	5	6	7
9. Irritates siblings	1	2	3	4	5	6	7
10. Daydreams	1	2	3	4	5	6	7
11. Loses personal property	1	2	3	4	5	6	7
12. Resists doing chores	1	2	3	4	5	6	7
13. Resists doing homework	1	2	3	4	5	6	7
14. Accidental self-injury	1	2	3	4	5	6	7
15. Argumentative	1	2	3	4	5	6	7
16. Explosive temper	1	2	3	4	5	6	7
17. Poor impulse control	1	2	3	4	5	6	7
18. Appears immature	1	2	3	4	5	6	7
19. Difficulty adjusting to change	1	2	3	4	5	6	7
20. Picks on smaller children	1	2	3	4	5	6	7
21. Punishment seems ineffective	1	2	3	4	5	6	7
22. Desires to be center of attention	1	2	3	4	5	6	7
23. Difficulty remembering instructions	1	2	3	4	5	6	7
24. Appears to need constant activity	1	2	3	4	5	6	7
25. More likely to be punished	1	2	3	4	5	6	7
26. Difficulty getting to sleep	1	2	3	4	5	6	7
27. Difficulty staying asleep	1	2	3	4	5	6	7
28. Problems with concentration	1	2	3	4	5	6	7
29. Expresses frustration	1	2	3	4	5	6	7
30. Expresses resentment	1	2	3	4	5	6	7
31. Bullies other children	1	2	3	4	5	6	7

32. Makes suicidal statements	1	2	3	4	5	6	7
33. Problems expressing empathy	1	2	3	4	5	6	7
34. Expresses unhappy feelings	1	2	3	4	5	6	7
35. Appears lethargic	1	2	3	4	5	6	7
36. Appears unmotivated	1	2	3	4	5	6	7
37. Stomach aches	1	2	3	4	5	6	7
38. Non-compliance to rules	1	2	3	4	5	6	7
39. Poor listening skills	1	2	3	4	5	6	7
40. Talkative	1	2	3	4	5	6	7
41. Poor organization skills	1	2	3	4	5	6	7
42. Does not anticipate consequences	1	2	3	4	5	6	7
43. Verbally intrusive	1	2	3	4	5	6	7
44. Expressing feelings of boredom	1	2	3	4	5	6	7
45. Denies mistakes or blames others	1	2	3	4	5	6	7
46. Seeks immediate rewards	1	2	3	4	5	6	7
47. Distractible	1	2	3	4	5	6	7
48. Non-compliant with rules	1	2	3	4	5	6	7
49. Seeks immediate rewards	1	2	3	4	5	6	7
50. Easily bored	1	2	3	4	5	6	7
51. Academic problems	1	2	3	4	5	6	7
52. Getting up too early	1	2	3	4	5	6	7

Child's name_____Age_____Date_____
Behaviors rated with medication YES or NO Med/Dosage_____
Name and relationship of person completing this form_____

Parents' Stress Indicator Questionnaire

Instructions: Determine whether the following life event occurred during the past year (e.g., "yes" or "no"), and then rate the degree of severity in which the event *presently* affects your life (from 1 to 7) only if you circled "yes". If an event did not occur during the past two years, please circle "no" and go on to the next life event on the form.

	YES/NO (Circle one)		IF YES, HOW SEVERE?						
			Mild	(Circle one)					Severe
	Yes	No	1	2	3	4	5	6	7
1. Physical/mental illness diagnosed	Yes	No	1	2	3	4	5	6	7
2. Breakup with significant other	Yes	No	1	2	3	4	5	6	7
3. Victim of crime	Yes	No	1	2	3	4	5	6	7
4. Started or graduated from school	Yes	No	1	2	3	4	5	6	7
5. Divorce	Yes	No	1	2	3	4	5	6	7
6. Child left home	Yes	No	1	2	3	4	5	6	7
7. Marriage	Yes	No	1	2	3	4	5	6	7
8. Loss of employment	Yes	No	1	2	3	4	5	6	7
9. Death of child	Yes	No	1	2	3	4	5	6	7
10. Marital separation	Yes	No	1	2	3	4	5	6	7
11. Birth of child	Yes	No	1	2	3	4	5	6	7
12. Suicide of relative or friend	Yes	No	1	2	3	4	5	6	7
13. Devastating natural disaster	Yes	No	1	2	3	4	5	6	7
14. Frequent family arguments	Yes	No	1	2	3	4	5	6	7
15. Job dissatisfaction	Yes	No	1	2	3	4	5	6	7
16. Lives in high crime neighborhood	Yes	No	1	2	3	4	5	6	7
17. Marital discord	Yes	No	1	2	3	4	5	6	7
18. Serious financial problems	Yes	No	1	2	3	4	5	6	7
19. Being a single parent	Yes	No	1	2	3	4	5	6	7
20. Unemployed	Yes	No	1	2	3	4	5	6	7
21. Poverty	Yes	No	1	2	3	4	5	6	7
22. Serious chronic illness in self	Yes	No	1	2	3	4	5	6	7
23. Serious illness of family members	Yes	No	1	2	3	4	5	6	7
24. Ongoing physical or sexual abuse	Yes	No	1	2	3	4	5	6	7
25. Unwanted pregnancy	Yes	No	1	2	3	4	5	6	7
26. Death of a parent	Yes	No	1	2	3	4	5	6	7
27. Arrest of self	Yes	No	1	2	3	4	5	6	7
28. Change of residence	Yes	No	1	2	3	4	5	6	7

29. Disabled child	Yes	No	1	2	3	4	5	6	7
30. Disabled spouse	Yes	No	1	2	3	4	5	6	7
31. Alcohol/drug abuse	Yes	No	1	2	3	4	5	6	7
32. Other:_____	Yes	No	1	2	3	4	5	6	7

Child's name_____Age_____Date_____

Behaviors rated with medication YES or NO Med/Dosage_____

Name and relationship of person completing this form_____

Parents' and Educators' Positive Information Questionnaire
Child or Adolescent

A. Describe the desirable characteristics of this child.

1._____

_____

2._____

_____

3._____

_____

B. Name and describe the individuals who have a positive relationship with this child.

1._____

_____

2._____

_____

3._____

_____

C. Describe activities where this child can maintain concentration for longer periods of time.

1._____

_____

2._____

_____

3._____

_____

D. Describe tasks that the child typically completes without intervention from an adult.

1._____

_____

2._____

_____

3._____

_____

E. Briefly describe situations in which the child appears confident.

1._____

_____

2._____

_____

3._____

_____

Child's name_____Age_____Date_____

Behaviors rated with medication YES or NO Med/Dosage_____

Name and relationship of person completing this form_____

Educators' Questionnaire

Circle the number that you feel most nearly describes the degree of the child's problem.

	No problem	Mild problem	Moderate problem	Severe problem
	1——2	——3	——4——5	——6——7
1. Class clowning	1——2	——3	——4——5	——6——7
2. Swearing	1——2	——3	——4——5	——6——7
3. Lying, stealing, cheating	1——2	——3	——4——5	——6——7
4. Incomplete homework	1——2	——3	——4——5	——6——7
5. Incomplete classroom work	1——2	——3	——4——5	——6——7
6. Difficulty maintaining friendships	1——2	——3	——4——5	——6——7
7. Impulsive	1——2	——3	——4——5	——6——7
8. Distractible	1——2	——3	——4——5	——6——7
9. Forgets instructions	1——2	——3	——4——5	——6——7
10. Wide mood swings	1——2	——3	——4——5	——6——7
11. Lack of empathy	1——2	——3	——4——5	——6——7
12. Irritates peers	1——2	——3	——4——5	——6——7
13. Makes disruptive sounds	1——2	——3	——4——5	——6——7
14. Unable to concentrate	1——2	——3	——4——5	——6——7
15. High levels of frustration	1——2	——3	——4——5	——6——7
16. Can't locate classroom materials	1——2	——3	——4——5	——6——7
17. Appears emotionally younger	1——2	——3	——4——5	——6——7
18. Difficulty remembering rules	1——2	——3	——4——5	——6——7
19. Demands excessive attention	1——2	——3	——4——5	——6——7
20. Difficulty sustaining effort	1——2	——3	——4——5	——6——7
21. Academic underachievement	1——2	——3	——4——5	——6——7
22. Frequent talk outs	1——2	——3	——4——5	——6——7
23. Difficulty waiting turns	1——2	——3	——4——5	——6——7
24. Difficulty organizing school work	1——2	——3	——4——5	——6——7
25. Daydreaming	1——2	——3	——4——5	——6——7
26. Explosive temper	1——2	——3	——4——5	——6——7
27. Maintaining friendships	1——2	——3	——4——5	——6——7
28. Blames others for their mistakes	1——2	——3	——4——5	——6——7
29. Argumentative	1——2	——3	——4——5	——6——7
30. Learning disabilities	1——2	——3	——4——5	——6——7
31. Bullying behavior	1——2	——3	——4——5	——6——7

32. Inattention to details   1——2——3——4——5——6——7
33. Punishment appears ineffective 1——2——3——4——5——6——7
34. Emotional response when efforts fail 1——2——3——4——5——6——7

Child's name_____Age_____Date_____
Behaviors rated with medication YES or NO Med/Dosage_____
Name and relationship of person completing this form_____

Educators' Common/Enduring Challenging Situations Questionnaire
(Child Ages 3 To 7)

Instructions: Determine if the child's behavior is challenging in the following situations (e.g., "yes" or "no"), and then rate the degree of severity (from 1 to 7) only if you circled "yes." If this child is not a problem in the given situation, please circle "no" and go on to the next situation on the form.

	YES/NO (Circle one)		IF YES, HOW SEVERE? Mild (Circle one) Severe						
	Yes	No	1	2	3	4	5	6	7

Situations:

1. Standardized testing	Yes	No	1	2	3	4	5	6	7
2. Getting started on classroom work	Yes	No	1	2	3	4	5	6	7
3. Completing classroom work	Yes	No	1	2	3	4	5	6	7
4. When unsupervised in restrooms	Yes	No	1	2	3	4	5	6	7
5. Timed activities	Yes	No	1	2	3	4	5	6	7
6. Competitive activities	Yes	No	1	2	3	4	5	6	7
7. Large group activities	Yes	No	1	2	3	4	5	6	7
8. Lining up	Yes	No	1	2	3	4	5	6	7
9. During quiet time	Yes	No	1	2	3	4	5	6	7
10. During recess	Yes	No	1	2	3	4	5	6	7
11. In lunchroom	Yes	No	1	2	3	4	5	6	7
12. In the hallways	Yes	No	1	2	3	4	5	6	7
13. On field trips	Yes	No	1	2	3	4	5	6	7
14. On the bus	Yes	No	1	2	3	4	5	6	7
15. Playground before school	Yes	No	1	2	3	4	5	6	7
16. During music time	Yes	No	1	2	3	4	5	6	7
17. Transition to new activities	Yes	No	1	2	3	4	5	6	7
18. Classroom parties	Yes	No	1	2	3	4	5	6	7

Child's name_____Age_____Date_____
Behaviors rated with medication YES or NO Med/Dosage_____
Name and relationship of person completing this form_____

Educators' Common/Enduring Challenging Situations Questionnaire
(Child Ages 8 To 18)

Instructions: Determine if the child's behavior is challenging in the following situations (e.g., "yes" or "no"), and then rate the degree of severity (from 1 to 7) only if you circled "yes." If this child is not a problem in the given situation, please circle "no" and go on to the next situation on the form.

	YES/NO (Circle one)		IF YES, HOW SEVERE? Mild (Circle one) Severe						
	Yes	No	1	2	3	4	5	6	7

Situations:

1. Standardized testing	Yes	No	1	2	3	4	5	6	7
2. Getting started on work	Yes	No	1	2	3	4	5	6	7
3. During large group activities	Yes	No	1	2	3	4	5	6	7
4. Eating lunch	Yes	No	1	2	3	4	5	6	7
5. Unsupervised restroom time	Yes	No	1	2	3	4	5	6	7
6. Transition to next class or activity	Yes	No	1	2	3	4	5	6	7
7. Competitive activities	Yes	No	1	2	3	4	5	6	7
8. During in class study time	Yes	No	1	2	3	4	5	6	7
9. Timed classroom work	Yes	No	1	2	3	4	5	6	7
10. Bus rides	Yes	No	1	2	3	4	5	6	7
11. Before and after school time	Yes	No	1	2	3	4	5	6	7
12. Peer collaboration	Yes	No	1	2	3	4	5	6	7
13. Before/after-school programs	Yes	No	1	2	3	4	5	6	7
14. While working alone	Yes	No	1	2	3	4	5	6	7
15. When teacher lectures	Yes	No	1	2	3	4	5	6	7
16. Classroom parties	Yes	No	1	2	3	4	5	6	7
17. Completion of homework	Yes	No	1	2	3	4	5	6	7
18. Music time	Yes	No	1	2	3	4	5	6	7

Child's name_____Age_____Date_____
Behaviors rated with medication YES or NO Med/Dosage_____
Name and relationship of person completing this form_____

Educators' Style Questionnaire

How many students are in your class?
How many volunteers are in your classroom?
How many aides are in your classroom? How many hours?

How many challenging students are in your classroom?
What do you consider positive classroom behaviors?

How do you reinforce positive behaviors?

How frequently do you reinforce positive behaviors?

Estimate the length of time between positive behavior and acknowledgment.

What do you consider inappropriate or negative classroom behaviors? How are these behaviors addressed?

How frequently do you address inappropriate or negative behaviors?

Estimate the length of time between inappropriate or negative behavior and acknowledgment.

What do you do to keep inappropriate behaviors from being reinforced, increased, or maintained by peers?

Specifically, how is inappropriate behavior handled in your classroom?

Does a single child's inappropriate behavior produce consequences for the entire group?

What type of inappropriate behavior is most annoying to you?

Child's name_____Age_____Date_____
Name and relationship of person completing this form_____

Educational Performance Questionnaire

Instructions: Please circle the number which best indicates the child or adolescent's level of performance in all of their subject areas. Additional space has been provided to add subjects.

Subject
Area

School Performance

Assignments Completed

Subject	10%	20%	30%	40%	50%	60%	70%	80%	90%	100%
Math	10%	20%	30%	40%	50%	60%	70%	80%	90%	100%
Social Studies	10%	20%	30%	40%	50%	60%	70%	80%	90%	100%
Language	10%	20%	30%	40%	50%	60%	70%	80%	90%	100%
Arts	10%	20%	30%	40%	50%	60%	70%	80%	90%	100%
_____	10%	20%	30%	40%	50%	60%	70%	80%	90%	100%
_____	10%	20%	30%	40%	50%	60%	70%	80%	90%	100%
_____	10%	20%	30%	40%	50%	60%	70%	80%	90%	100%
_____	10%	20%	30%	40%	50%	60%	70%	80%	90%	100%

Accuracy of Assignments

Subject	10%	20%	30%	40%	50%	60%	70%	80%	90%	100%
Math	10%	20%	30%	40%	50%	60%	70%	80%	90%	100%
Social Studies	10%	20%	30%	40%	50%	60%	70%	80%	90%	100%
Language	10%	20%	30%	40%	50%	60%	70%	80%	90%	100%
Arts	10%	20%	30%	40%	50%	60%	70%	80%	90%	100%
_____	10%	20%	30%	40%	50%	60%	70%	80%	90%	100%
_____	10%	20%	30%	40%	50%	60%	70%	80%	90%	100%
_____	10%	20%	30%	40%	50%	60%	70%	80%	90%	100%
_____	10%	20%	30%	40%	50%	60%	70%	80%	90%	100%

Child's name_____Age_____Date_____
Name and relationship of person completing this form_____

Treatment Assessment Summary

Name of Child: Date:

Team members:

ADHD Diagnosis: 1. Inattentive   1. Mild
(Circle)   2. Hyperactive   2. Moderate
                          3. Impulsive   3. Severe

List other DSM-IV-TR Diagnosis

Briefly describe the following characteristics of the child.

1. Intellectual skills/deficits

2. Social skills/deficits

3. Academic skills/deficits

List three of the most difficult problems encountered:

Home   School
1.   1.
2.   2.
3.   3.

Describe completion rates and accuracy rates of schoolwork subjects.

Learning disabilities:

Perceptual and motor difficulties:

Visual/hearing:

Other complicating medical conditions:

List the predominant interaction style of the individuals who have regular/ frequent contact with the child: scapegoating/blaming; protective/caretaking; confrontational/combative; acquiescent/give-in; supportive/encouraging; avoidant/ignoring

Family resources: (financial, intellectual, social, child-care skills, health)

School resources: (teacher skills, class size, attitude, financial)

Describe situations in which the child has the most difficulty.

Describe situations in which the child has the most success.

Treatment Intervention Plan

Child's Name: Date implemented:

Problem or concern (specific measurable behaviors):

Past interventions attempted:

Intervention(s):

Desired outcome goals with the intervention:
        Short-term goals

        Long-term goals

Evaluation of intervention progress (objective measures):

Modifications to the initial intervention to increase progress:

        Evaluation of modifications:

Status of problem or concern (circle):
        Resolved (Date)
        Ongoing
        Increasing in severity

Homework Round-Up

Student's Name:
Teacher's Name:

Assignment(s):   Date Assignment(s) Due:

Special concerns:

Parents Circle One
Percentage of homework completed: 0% 25% 50% 75% 100%

Parent concerns:

* Please return form with Assignment

Knowledge and Skill Training Via Computers

Children with ADHD benefit from using the computer and appropriate educational software for learning and remediation at home and school. The inherent advantages of the computer address the inherent disabilities of the disorder (e.g., distractibility, lack of motivation, poor working memory, and handwriting). Structural and behavioral intervention principles are easily applied by the use of computers and software programs.

Consider this information when deciding *whether* to use a computer, *which* programs, and *how* to use them.

- Every child with ADHD can benefit by using the computer because the computer screen, computer placement in a room, and earphones reduce auditory and visual distractions.
- Software programs provide consistent, predictable, fun, immediate, and non-judgmental feedback.
- Avoid overuse of the computer as a "baby-sitter," which decreases the opportunities for social interaction.
- The child does not have to compete for adult attention and compare their work with others.
- Most software encourages the strategic use of logic, planning, and eye/hand coordination.
- Typing requires less fine-motor coordination than handwriting, thus reducing frustration.
- Each child progresses at his or her own pace.
- Lost homework is reduced by e-mailing to school or home computers.
- Specialized software evaluates academic deficits and recommends appropriate remedial programs.
- Software can be chosen to match the child's interests.
- Consider having computer time when the child is tired, bored, distracted, or disruptive.

There are many software companies that specialize in educational software. Some companies sell a total evaluation/remediation package which can be purchased for an entire school district.

Quieting Exercise

The Arctic tern quieting exercise can be used in the classroom, as it teaches curriculum while teaching children to relax. The Arctic tern is a small white bird that flies from pole to pole in a migratory fashion. Provide pictures of the Arctic tern, showing its size and wings. Inform the class about its nesting habits and its long migratory flight. It is fun to show the students on a map the actual flying path of the Arctic tern from pole to pole. Give the students some opportunity to figure out how far it is from one pole to the other and what continents it involves. The class will now imagine they are the bird. Begin by having the students stand apart with enough distance to spread their wings (arms) without touching each other. Teacher instructs, "Everyone start flapping your wings really fast so we can gain altitude." The students should continue to flap their wings until most of the class is tired. The teacher says, "We have to land briefly on a log and rest to restore our energy for the remainder of the flight." The children should rest by sitting down, closing their eyes, and letting their arms hang by their side. After two minutes, continue the next leg of the journey by flapping their wings again. Keep flapping until the majority get tired, and then have them repeat the relaxed posture. Repeat the flapping and landing for rest until the class is sufficiently quieted.

This particular style of quieting can be done with stories about fish, butterflies, and many other animals. If quieting exercises are routinely used, eventually just saying, "Okay everyone, it is time for heads down" immediately starts lowering the class energy level.

Resources

Support Organizations

Children and Adults with Attention Deficit/Hyperactivity Disorder (CHADD)
National Headquarters
8181 Professional Place
Suite 201
Landover, MD 20785
Phone: (301) 306-7070
Fax: (301) 306-7090
www.chadd.org

Attention Deficit Disorder Association (ADDA)
15000 Commerce Pkwy, Suite C
Mount Laurel, NJ 08054
Phone: (856) 439-9099
www.add.org

Computer Software

www.meritsoftware.com (Interactive Teaching Software)

Learning Tools

7707 Camargo Road
Cincinnati, OH 45243
Phone: (877) 771-TIME (8463)
Fax: (513) 561-4699
www.timetimer.com

Teacher Resources

Teach-To's Lesson Plans & Essential Advice (over 100 Behavioral Lesson Plans)
www.timetoteach.com

Parent Resources

Barkley, R.A. 1997. *Understanding the Defiant Child*. New York: The Guilford Publications. (video)

Barkley, R.A. 1997. *Managing the Defiant Child*. New York: The Guilford Publications. (video)

Phelan, T.W. 2004. *3-2-1 Magic*. (DVD)

Barkley, R.A. *The ADHD Report* (edited). New York, New York: The Guilford Press. http://www.russellbarkley.org/clinical-newsletter.htm

Bibliography

Ackerman, P.T., Newton, E.O., et al. 1998. Prevalence of post traumatic stress disorder and other psychiatric diagnoses in three groups of abused children (sexual, physical and both). *Child Abuse and Neglect.* 22 (8): 759-774.

Anders, T., Sharfstein, S., Rappley, M.D., Moore, J.W., Dokken, D., Wojnowski, L. and Nissen, S.E. 2006. ADHD drugs and cardiovascular risk. *N Engl J Med.* 354(21): 2296-2298.

American Psychiatric Association. *Diagnostic and statistical manual of mental disorders(IV-TR ed.).* Washington, DC: American Psychiatric Association, 2000.

Baeyens, D., Roeyers, H.D., Haese, L., Pieters, F., Hoebeke, K., and Walle, J.U. 2006. The prevalance of ADHD in children who have enuresis: Comparison between a tertiary and non-tertiary sample. *Acta Paediatricia* 95(3): 347-352.

Bagwell, C.L, Molina, B.S, Pilham, W.E, et al. 2001. ADHD and problems in peer relations: Predictions from childhood to adolescence. *J Am Acad Child Adolescent Psychiatry* 40 (11):1285-92.

Barkley, R.A. 1997. Behavioral inhibition, sustained attention, and executive functions: Constructing a unifying theory of ADHD. *Psychol Bull*1121: 65-94.

Barkley, R.A. 2002. Psychosocial treatments for attention-deficit/hyperactivity disorder in children. *J Clinical Psychiatry* 63: 36-43.

Barkley, R.A. *Taking Charge of ADHD.* New York, New York: The Guilford Press, 2005.

Barkley, R.A., Murphy, K.R., and Kwasnik, D. 1996. Motor vehicle driving competencies and risks in teens and young adults with attention deficit hyperactivity disorder. *Pediatrics* 98(6): 1089-95.

Biederman, J., Faraone, S.V., Keenan, K., Knee, D., and Tsuang, M.F. 1990. Family-genetic and psychosocial risk factors in DSM-III attention deficit disorder. *Journal of the American Academy of Child and Adolescent Psychiatry* 29(4): 526-533.

Blackman, J. and M. Gurka. 2007. Developmental and behavioral comorbidities of asthma in children. *Journal of Developmental and Behavioral Pediatrics* 28: (2)92-99.

Briscoe-Smith, A.M., and S.P. Hinshaw. 2006. Linkage between child abuse and attention deficit hyperactivity disorder in girls: behavioral and social correlates. *Child Abuse and Neglect* 30(11): 1239-1255.

Burns, D. *The Feeling Good Handbook*. New York, New York: HarperCollins Publishing, 1999.

Castellanos, F.X., Lee, P.P., Sharp, W., Jeffries, N.O., Greenstein, D.K., Clasen, L.S., et al. 2002. Development trajectories of brain volume abnormalities in children and adolescents with attention-deficit/hyperactivity disorder. *Journal of the American Medical Association* 288:14: 1740-1748.

Consensus Development Panel. 1982. Defined diets and childhood hyperactivity. *National Institutes of Health Consensus Development Conference Summary*, Volume 4, Number 3.

Corrin, A., ADHD Raises Teens Accident Risk. *United Press International*, Sept. 11, 2006. http://www.upi.com/Consumer_Health_Daily/Reports/2006/09/11/adhd_raises_teens_accident_risk/4082/.

Coyne-Beasley, T. 2004. Unsafe gun, poison storage in homes can turn holiday visits to grandparents, other relatives, and friends deadly. *Science Daily*, Dec. 28, 2004. http://www.sciencedaily.com/releases/2004/12/041219181949.htm

Cunningham, C.E., Benness, B.B., and Siegel, L.S. 1988. Family functioning, time allocation and parental depression in families of normal and ADHD children. *J Clinical Child Psychol* 17: 169-77.

Crutizinger, C., & D. Moore. *ADD quick tips: Practical ways to manage attention deficit disorder successfully.* Carrollton, TX: Brainworks, 1988.

Denti, L. Using the ABC model to promote behavior change. Special Education Program, California State University, Monterey Bay. http://alternativeed.sjsu.edu/documents/notes/mod3_3_notes.pdf

Diller, L, H. 1996. The Run on ritalin: Attention deficit disorder and stimulant treatment in the 1990's. The Hasting Report Center, Vol 26.

DuPaul, G.J., McGoey, D.E., Eckert, T.L., et al. 2000. Preschool children with attention-deficit/hyperactivity disorder. Impairments in behavioral, social, and school functioning. *J Am Acad Child Adolesc Psychiatry* 40: 508-15.

Faraone, S.V., and J. Beiderman. 1998. Neurobiology of attention-deficit hyperactivity disorder. *Biological Psychiatry* 44: 951-958.

Faraone, S.V., Beiderman, J., Monuteaux, M.C., et al. 2001. A psychometric measure of learning disability predicts educational failure four years later in boys with ADHD. *J Atten Disord* 4: 220-30.

Frame, K., Kelly, L., and Bayley, E. 2003. Increasing perceptions of self-worth in preadolescents diagnosed with ADHD. *J Nurs Scholarsh* 35: 225-9.

Fowler, M.C. *Maybe You Know My Kid: A Parent's Guide to Identifying, Understanding, and Helping Your Child With Attention-Deficit Hyperactivity Disorder (3rd Edition).* Secaucus, New Jersey: Birch Lane Press, 1999.

Freedman, R.D., Fast, D.K., Burd, L, et al. 2000. An international perspective on Tourette's syndrome: Selected findings from 3,500 individuals in 22 countries. *Dev Med Child Neurol* 42: 436-47.

Geller, B., Williams, M., Zimmerman, B., Frazier, J., Beringer, L., and Warner, K.L. 1998. Prepuberal and early adolescent bipolarity differentiate from ADHD by manic symptoms, grandiose delusions, ultra-rapid or ultradian cycling. *Journal of Affective Disorders* 51: 81-91.

Greenhill, L., Kollins, S., Abikoff, H., Mccracken, J., Riddle, Mark., Swanson, James., Mcgough, J., Wigal, S. et al. 2006. Efficacy and safety of immediate-release methylphenidate treatment for preschoolers with Adhd. *Journal of the American Academy of Child & Adolescent Psychiatry.* 45(11):1284-1293.

Grizenko, N., Shayan, Y.R., Polotskaia, A., TerStephanian, M., and Jacob, R. 2008. Relations of maternal stress during pregnancy to symptom severity and response to treatment for children with ADHD. *J. Psychiatry Neuroscience* 33(1): 10-16.

Halverstadt, J.S. *ADD and Romance*. Dallas, Texas: Taylor Publishing, 1998.

Hoover, D.W. and R. Milich. 1994. Effects of sugar ingestion expectancies on mother-child interaction. *Journal of Abnormal Child Psychology* 22: 501-515.

Hyman, I. R. and H. W. Wise. ed. *Corporal Punishment in American Education: Readings in the History, Practice and Alternatives*, Temple University Press, 1998.

Iannelli, V., Parenting styles, 2004, http://pediatrics.about.com/od/infantparentingtips/a/04_pntg_styles.htm

Ingersol, B. and M. Goldstein. *Attention Deficit Disorder and Learning Dsabilities: Realities, Myths, and Controversial Treatments*. New York: Doubleday, 1993.

Kavale, K. and S.R. Shervette. 1983. Hyperactivity and diet treatment: A meta-analysis of the Fiengold hypothesis. *Journal of Learning Disabilities*, 16: 324-330.

Kendall, J. 1999. Siblings accounts of attention deficit hyperactivity disorder. *Family Prac* 38: 117-36.

Kotimar, A.J., Moilanen, I., Taanila, Alk et al. 2003. Maternal smoking and hyperactivity in 8-year-old children. *J. Am Acad Child and Adolescent Psychiatry*, Jul; 42(7): 826-833.

Leibson, C.L., Katusic, S.K., Barbaresi, W.J., et al. 2001. Use and costs of medical care for children and adolescents with and without attention-deficit/hyperactivity disorder. *JAMA* 931: 60-6.

Levy, F. 1991. The dopamine theory of attention deficit hyperactivity disorder(ADHD). *Australian and New Zealand Journal of Psychiatry* 25: 277-283.

Liotti, M., Pliszka, S.R., Perez, R., Kothmann, D., and Woldorff, M.J. 2005. Abnormal brain activity related to performance monitoring and error detection in children with ADHD. *Cortex* 41(3) 337-388.

MTA Cooperative Group. 1999. A 14 month randomized clinical trial of treatment strategies for attention-deficit hyperactivity disorder (ADHD). *Archives of General Psychiatry* 56: 1073-1086.

Mannuzza, S., Klein, R.G., Bessler, A., et al. 1993. Adult outcome of hyperactive boys, educational achievement, occupational rank and psychiatric status. *Arch Gen Psychiatry* 50: 565-76.

Mannuzza, S., and R.G. Klein. 2000. Long-term prognosis in attention-deficit/hyperactivity disorder. *Child Adolesc Psychiatr Clin Am* 9: 711-26.

Max, J.E., Amdt, S., and Castillo, C.S. 1998. Attention deficit hyperactivity symptomatology after a traumatic brain injury: A prospective study. *J. Am Acad Child and Adolesc Psychiatry* 37(8): 841-847.

Milich, R., Wolraich, M., and Lindgren, S. 1996. Sugar and hyperactivity: A critical review of empirical findings. *Clinical Psychology Review* 6: 493-513.

Needleman, H.L. 1988. The persistent threat of lead: Medical and sociological issues. *Current Problems Pediatrics* 18(12): 697-744.

NIMH, press release. Brain matures a few years late in ADHD, but follows normal pattern *National Institutes of Health*, retrieved February 8, 2008. http://www.nimh.nih.gov/science-news/2007/brain-matures-a-few-years-late-in-adhd-but-follows-normal-pattern.shtml.

NIMH, What causes ADHD? *National Institutes of Health*, retrieved Jan. 23 2008. http://www.nimh.nih.gov/health/publications/adhd/what-causes-adhd.shtml.

Nunley, K.F. 2002. Why punishment based systems don't work: Yet we are stuck with them. http://www.help4teachers.com/punishment.htm

Parker, H. *The ADD Hyperactivity Workbook for Schools*. Plantation, Fl: Specialty Press, 1991.

Parker, H. *Putting Yourself in Their shoes: Understanding Where Your ADHD Teen Is Coming From*. Plantation, Florida: Specialty Press, 1998.

Phelan, T.W. *All About Attention Deficit Disorder*. (2nd edition). Glen Ellyn, Illinois: Child Management Inc. 2000.

Physicians Desk Reference (58ᵗʰ edition) Montvale, NJ: Medical Economics, 2007.

Pliszka, S. 2000. Patterns of psychiatric comorbidity with attention deficit hyperactivity disorder. *Adolesc Psychiatry Clin N Amer* 9(3): 525-540.

Podolske, C.L.,and J.T. Nigg. 2001. Parent stress and coping in relation to child ADHD severity and child disruptive behavioral problems. *J Clinical Child Psychol* 30: 503-13.

Polanczyk, K.G. DeLima, M.S, Horta, B.L, Biederman, J., and Rohde, L. A. 2007. The worldwide prevalence of ADHD: A systematic review and meta-regression analysis, *Am. J. Psychiatry* 164 (6): 942-948.

Quinn, T. *Grandma's Pet Wildebeest Ate My Homework (and Other Suspect Stories)* Dunvegan Publishing, 1998.

Rushton, J.L. and J.T. Whitmire. 2001. Pediatric stimulant and selective serotonin reuptake inhibitor prescription trends. *Archives of Pediatrics & Adolescent Medicine*, 155: 560-665.

Schettler, T. 2001. Toxic threats to neurologic development of children. *Environ Health Perspective* Dec; 109 Suppl 6:813-816.

Solden, S. (2ⁿᵈ ed.) *Women With Attention Deficit Disorder.* Grass Valley, CA: Underwood Books, 2005.

Sonuga-Barke, E.J., Dailey, D., Thompson, M., et al. 2001. Parent-based therapies for preschool attention-deficit/hyperactivity. disorder: A randomized, controlled trial with community sample. *J Am Acad Child Adolesc Psychiatry* 40: 402-8.

Soo-Churl Cho, Jun-Won Hwang, Boong-Nyun Kim, Ho-Young Lee, Hyo-Won Kim, Jae-Sung Lee, Min-Sup Shin and Dong-Soo Lee. 2007. The relationship between regional cerebral blood flow and response to methylphenidate in children with attention deficit hyperactivity disorder: Comparison between non-responders and responders as a response to methylphenidate. *Journal of Psychiatric Research* 41(6):459-465.

Steele, K. D., 2001. EPA Cleanup Plan Spreads into Basin, *Spokesman Review*, Oct. 21.

Stradford, Dan, ed. Fluorescent lights, electromagnetic radiation factors in "ADHD", International Guide to the World of Alternative Mental Health, Safe Harbor *Alternative Mental Health News* #6, http://www.alternativementalhealth. com/ezine/Ezine6.htm.

Swanson, J. 1993. The effects of stimulant medication on children with attention deficit hyperactivity disorder. A review of reviews. "Education of children with attention deficit hyperactivity disorder". Washington D.C: U.S. Dept of Education.

Swanson, J.M., Floodman, P., Kennedy, J., et al. 2000. Dopamine genes and ADHD. *Neruosc Biobehav Review* 24(1): 21-25.

Swensen, A., Bianbaum, H.G., Hamadi, R.B., and Greenberg, P. 2004. Incidence and costs of accidents among attention deficit hyperactivity disorder patients, *Journal of Adolescent Health* 35(4): 346.

Terman, M., Termam, J.S., Ross, D.C. 1998. A Controlled Trial of Timed Bright Light and Negative Air Ionization for Treatment of Winter Depression. *Arch Gen Psychiatry* 55:875-882.

Watkins, C.E., Depression in Children and Adolescents, Dec. 13, 2001. http:// hscareers.com/news/articles.asp?id=4

Wender, P.H. *ADHD: Attention-Deficit Hyperactivity Disorder in Children and Adults.* Oxford University Press, 2002.

Weiss, G. and L.T. Hechtman. *Hyperactive Children Grown up (2nd edition): ADHD in Children, Adolescents, and Adults.* New York: Guilford Press, 1993.

Wilens, T.E., Biederman, J., Spencer, T.J. 2002. Attention deficit/hyperactivity disorder across the lifespan. *Annual Review of Medicine* 53: 113-131.

Wilens, T.E., Faraone, S.V., Biederman, J., Gunawardene, S. 2003. Does stimulant therapy of attention-deficit/hyperactivity disorder beget later substance abuse? A meta-analytic review of the literature. *Pediatrics* 111: 1: 179-185.

Wolraich, M., Milich, R., Stumbo, P., and Schultz, F. 1985. The effects of sucrose ingestion on the behavior of hyperactive boys. *Pediatrics* 106; 657-682.

Zametkin, A.J, Liebenauer, L.L., Fitzgerald, B.A., et al. 1993. Brain metabolism in teenagers with attention deficit hyperactivity disorder. *Arch Gen Psychiatry* May 50: 333(5).

Zentall, S.S., and S. Goldstein. *Seven Steps to Homework Success*. Plantation, FL: Specialty Press, 1999.

Endnotes

1   Swanson, *Dopamine Genes and ADHD*, 21-25.
2   Soo-Churl Cho, *The relationship between regional cerebral blood flow and response to methylphenidate*, 459-465.
3   Zametkin, *Brain metabolism in teenagers with ADHD*, 333-335.
4   Liotti, *Abnormal brain activity related to performance monitoring and error detection in children with ADHD*. 337-388.
5   Castellanos, *Development trajectories of brain volume abnormalities in children and adolescents with ADHD*, 1740-1748.
6   Max, *Attention deficit hyperactivity symtomatology after brain injury*, 841-847.
7   Levy, *The dopamine theory of ADHD*, 277-283.
8   NIMH, *Brain matures a few years late in ADHD*.
9   Schettler, *Toxic threats to neurologic development of children*, 813-816.
10 Steele, *EPA cleanup plan spreads into Basin*.
11 Schettler, *Toxic threats to neurologic development of children*, 813-816.
12 Barkley, *Taking Charge of ADHD*, 83.
13 Hyman, *Corporal punishment in American education*, 126-142.
14 Kavale, *Hyperactivity and diet treatment*, 324-330.
15 Milich, *Sugar and hyperactivity*, 493-513.
16 NIMH, *What causes ADHD?*.
17 Grizenko, *Relations of maternal stress during pregnancy to symptom severity and response to treatment*, 10-16.
18 Terman, *Controlled trial of timed bright light and negative air ionization*, 875-882.
19 Stradford, *Florescent lights, electromagnetic radiation factors in ADHD*.
20 Polanczyk, *The worldwide prevalence of ADHD*, 942-948.
21 Iannelli, *Parenting styles*.
22 Blackman, *Developmental and behavioral comorbidities* of asthma in children, 92-99.
23 Baeyens, *The prevalence of ADHD in children who have enuresis*, 347-352.
24 Ackerman, *Prevalence of post traumatic stress disorder and other psychiatric diagnoses in three groups of abused children*, 759-774.
25 Briscoe-Smith, *Linkage between child abuse and ADHD in girls*, 1239-1255.
26 Pliszka, *Patterns of psychiatric comorbidity with ADHD*, 525-540.
27 Iannelli, *Parenting styles*.
28 Swanson, *The effects of stimulant medication on children with ADHD*.

29 Barkley, *Taking Charge of ADHD*, 270-275.
30 Wilens, *Does stimulant therapy of ADHD beget later substance abuse?*, 179-185.
31 Ingersoll, *Attention Deficit Disorder and Learning Disabilities*, 73.
32 Diller, *The Run on Ritalin*.
33 Barkley, *Taking Charge of ADHD*, 276.
34 Swanson, *The effects of stimulant medication on children with ADHD*.
35 Barkley, *Taking Charge of ADHD*, 276
36 Rushton, *Pediatric stimulant and selective serotonin reuptake inhibitor prescription trends*, 560-665.
37 Denti, *Using the ABC model to promote behavior change*.
38 Swensen, *Incidence and costs of accidents among ADHD Patients*, 346.
39 Coyne-Beasley, *Unsafe gun, poison storage in homes can turn holiday visits to grandparents, other relatives, and friends deadly*.
40 Corrin, *ADHD raises teens accident risk*.
41 Wilens, *Does stimulant therapy of ADHD beget later substance abuse?* 179-185.
42 Kavale, *Hyperactivity and diet treatment*, 324-330.

Index

Printed in the United States
131263LV00005B/106-249/P

9 780595 476657